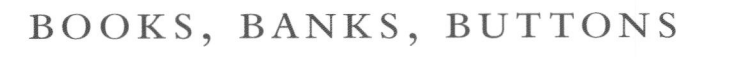

BOOKS, BANKS, BUTTONS

BOOKS vs. Banks

Chiara Frugoni

TRANSLATED BY WILLIAM M^cCUAIG

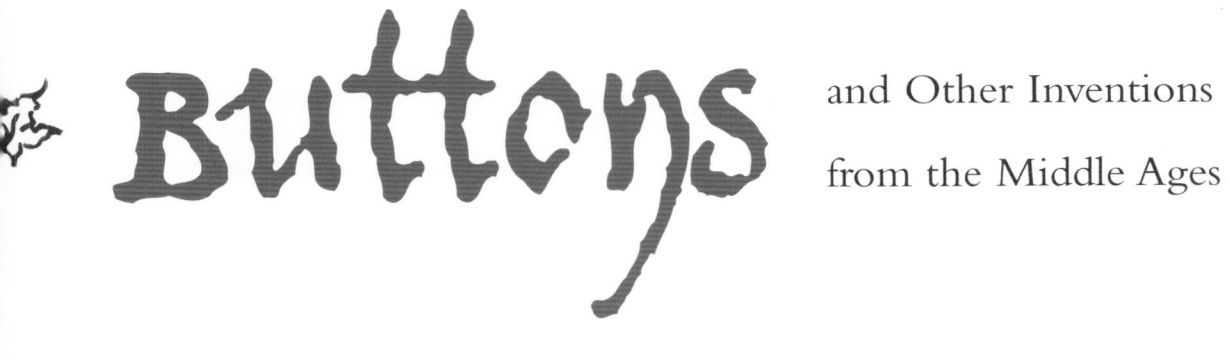 and Other Inventions

from the Middle Ages

COLUMBIA UNIVERSITY PRESS *New York*

Columbia University Press
Publishers Since 1893
New York   Chichester, West Sussex

Originally published in Italian as
Medioevo sul naso: Occhiali, bottoni e altre invenzioni medievali
© 2001 Gius. Laterza & Figli Spa

Translation copyright © 2003 Columbia University Press
All rights reserved

Library of Congress Cataloging-in-Publication Data
Frugoni, Chiara, 1940– [Medioevo sul naso. English]
Books, banks, buttons : and other inventions
from the Middle Ages / Chiara Frugoni ; translated by
William McCuaig.
p.   cm.
Originally published in Italian as: *Medioevo sul naso : occhiali,
bottoni e altre invenzioni medievali*.
Includes bibliographical references and index.
ISBN 0–231–12812–6 (cloth)
1. Technology—History. 2. Inventions—History. 3. Science,
Medieval. I. McCuaig, William, 1949–   II. Title.
T17 .F77 2003
609.4'09'02—dc21   2002025692

Printed in China
Designed by Linda Secondari

c 10 9 8 7 6 5 4 3 2 1

CONTENTS

TRANSLATOR'S NOTE

Most of the Bible quotations in the text are taken from *The Jerusalem Bible, Reader's Edition* (Garden City, NY: Doubleday, 1971), but in every case they are checked, and adapted if necessary, to make the translation accord with the meaning of the Vulgate, the Latin Bible of the Middle Ages, to which the author naturally refers.

Twice in chapter 2 and once in chapter 6, the author quotes from Dante's *Paradiso*, the third part of the *Divine Comedy*. The canto and line numbers are given in the text, and no note is added (or needed in an Italian book). At these places I have used a published English translation by Mark Musa, identifying the translator by name without adding a note, so as not to disturb the sequence of the author's notes. Hence I wish to put the full bibliographical information on record here: the quoted passages are taken from *Dante's Paradise*, translated with notes and commentary by Mark Musa (Bloomington: Indiana University Press, 1984).

In a number of other places I have also used published English translations of medieval and Renaissance authors, and this use is always indicated in the notes. In the absence of any such indication, the translation is my own, or rather mine and the author's, for the whole book was translated with her collaboration. In some cases we use a certain freedom in paraphrasing and abbreviating long passages of Latin that are given in full in the notes. She has taken the opportunity to alter, emend, and update her

text in a number of places, and I have slightly expanded and adapted it to the needs of an English-language readership in a number of others. Where I knew of and had access to an original English-language version or an English-language translation of any work cited by her in Italian or French editions, I have replaced her original reference with a corresponding reference in the notes.

PREFACE

What do we owe to the Middle Ages? Let me try to list a few things: eyeglasses, paper, watermarks, books, printing with movable type, universities, arabic numerals, the use of zero in mathematics, the date of the birth of Christ, banks, notaries, charitable lending societies, the family tree, the names of the musical notes, and the musical scale.

From the Middle Ages we get our buttons, our underwear, and our trousers; we entertain ourselves with medieval playing cards, tarot cards, and chess; carnival is a medieval festival. We began to ease our pain with anesthetics in the Middle Ages, and to fool ourselves into believing in amulets (but the bits of coral that protect children and ward off lightning also make it easy to repeat the rosary). The Middle Ages brought domesticated cats into our houses, along with glazed windows and fireplaces. They sat us around a table at mealtime (the Romans used to eat lying down) and put forks into our hands so we could eat our new favorite foods: macaroni and vermicelli and every other kind of pasta, all of it invented in the Middle Ages and made from flour that was ground by tireless new medieval machines like the windmill and the watermill. In the Middle Ages, we figured out how to use water to drive machinery, turning the gears and wheels of oil presses, sawmills, fulling mills where wool was cleaned, paper mills, and flour mills. We discovered another extraordinary motor, the horse, which was equipped with iron shoes, stirrups, and

a rigid collar that allowed the animal to draw heavy loads without choking itself to death. Human labor got easier in the Middle Ages too, with the wheelbarrow, and travel over water became safer thanks to the compass and the rudder. It was in the Middle Ages that flags bearing colorful coats of arms first fluttered over the field of battle, and gunpowder roared from the barrels of handguns and cannon. Our sense of time here on earth was formed in the Middle Ages, when clocks based on the escapement mechanism introduced hours of equal length, independent of the changing seasons; and so was our sense of time in the world to come, where a third region, purgatory, arose to free us from the hard inevitability of heaven or hell. Finally, the Middle Ages gave children Santa Claus to dream about.

This book makes no claim to enumerate all the inventions of the Middle Ages, or to trace all the expressions, proverbs, and habits born in that lost world that live on in the modern one: the wanderer who picks a handful of flowers in springtime does not rob a vast meadow of its riot of color. The bouquet I have collected here is offered as a tribute to the Middle Ages, to the countless improvements introduced then that we still benefit from today. I follow a narrative thread, relying on the beauty of images and texts from the Middle Ages, and I hope to let readers share my gratitude— and perhaps to show them a few surprises as well.

Chiara Frugoni
15 March 2001
the birthday of my brother Nini (Giovanni) 1945–1970

LIST OF ILLUSTRATIONS

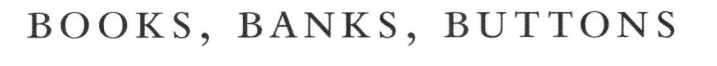

BOOKS, BANKS, BUTTONS

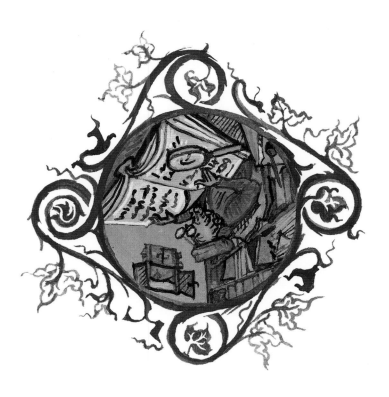

ONE Reading and Keeping the Books

The Art of Making Eyeglasses

Every morning for a few years now, the first thing I do when I wake up makes the world look just like it did to me twenty years ago, and that makes me grateful for a wonderful medieval invention: eyeglasses. Petrarch used to put them on too, but in quite a different mood. In a letter he wrote *To Posterity* (which records the events of his life down to 1351), he gives this description of himself:

> I can't boast of being handsome, but in my greener years I made a good impression. I had a fine complexion, between light and dark, ardent eyes, and a vision that was for many years very sharp. (But it failed me unexpectedly when I was over sixty, so that I was forced reluctantly to the use of spectacles.)[1]

We do not know what it was that put Petrarch off: the aesthetic problem, the difficulty of keeping a sort of pince-nez in place on his nose (as we shall see, eyeglasses had no earpieces for a long time), the inadequacy of the lenses in correcting for presbyopia, or the fact that the use of the instrument made him face up to his own advancing years.[2]

Petrarch had been born in 1304. In the following year Giordano da

Pisa delivered a sermon in Santa Maria Novella in Florence, in which he announced the marvelous new invention with great enthusiasm:

> It is not yet twenty years since they discovered the art of making eyeglasses, which let one see clearly, which is one of the finest and most necessary arts the world has, and it is such a short time since they were discovered: a new art, that never was before. And the reader added: I saw the man who first invented and made them, and spoke with him.[3]

Clearly the learned Dominican was overjoyed, along with his brother Dominicans and everyone else who depended on books, for with the new invention they were no longer forced by old age to interrupt their working lives.

Giordano's sermons have reached us through faithful collectors who wrote them down the way they heard them; in this case the devout transcriber used the phrase "And the reader added . . ." to include the first-person testimony of a *lector* (an instructor or theologian) who had spoken with the inventor of eyeglasses. Was it Giordano himself, a *lector* at Florence, who spoke the words, or one of his learned companions who was also present at the sermon?[4] This is not an entirely otiose question, for as we shall see, the point will be raised in the dispute surrounding the identity and nationality of the inventor.

It had been another Dominican, like Giordano a resident of the convent of Santa Caterina at Pisa, who had learned how to make eyeglasses. His name was Alessandro della Spina and he died in 1313; the death notice in the *Chronica antiqua* (Old Chronicle) of Santa Caterina has this to say:

> Brother Alessandro della Spina, a good and modest man, was able to reproduce any made object he saw with his own eyes ("quae vidit oculis facta, scivit et facere"). He himself made eyeglasses, which another person had made first without sharing the secret, and showed everyone else how to do so with an open and joyful heart.[5]

Here we have to digress for a moment, because the words quoted above from Giordano's sermon and the convent chronicle, which were scrutinized with learning, but in bad faith, by two seventeenth-century scholars and frequently twisted in meaning, have given rise to such a swarm of hypotheses, or rather certainties, about the putative inventor of eyeglasses—some of them still accepted by scholars of the early twentieth century, and our own contemporaries[6]—that it is necessary to set things straight. The scholar Edward Rosen will guide us,[7] for he has traced the whole tangled story, laying to rest a number of deliberate untruths and also (not without a certain punctilious satisfaction) a heap of

involuntary errors and oversights passed down from the seventeenth century to our own day.

The first to cite Alessandro della Spina and the *Chronica antiqua* of Santa Caterina was the learned author and scientist Carlo Roberto Dati (1619–1676), a follower of Galileo. In an essay entitled "The invention of eyeglasses; whether or not it is ancient; and when, where, and by whom were they invented? A vigil dedicated to the illustrious Francesco Redi,"[8] Dati pretended that an imaginary interlocutor had recalled how "as a young man, having gone to Pisa to study law more in obedience to another's command than [his] own inclination," he preferred to spend his time in the library hunting for manuscripts. From one of these he cites the passage from the *Chronica*, but with a significant variant: Alessandro della Spina immediately grasped "any made object he saw or heard about." Dati continues: "Since it happened that another person was the first to invent eyeglasses but did not want to share his invention with others, he [Alessandro] fabricated them on his own, and happily made the knowledge available to all." So the good Dominican did not just use his intelligence to copy an object he had in front of him: he is represented as the true inventor in a certain sense, or at least the reinventor, because of his ability to fabricate a new instrument purely on the basis of a verbal description. The imaginary interlocutor supposed that the author of the invention was in all likelihood Pisan, noting that Alessandro della Spina also came from a Pisan family; hence Pisa could claim, one way or another, the glory of having been the home of the inventor.

Dati had not seen the manuscript of Santa Caterina for himself, but had instead used a transcription made by his friend Francesco Redi, a famous scientist and writer, who on February 26, 1674 had sent Dati a deliberately altered version of the passage in question. What Redi did was to substitute the phrase "quae vidit oculis facta, scivit et facere" ("he was able to reproduce any made object he saw with his own eyes") with "quaecumque vidit aut audivit facta, scivit et facere" ("he was able to reproduce any made object he saw or heard about").[9] The point was to give more luster to Alessandro della Spina and his power to conceive things with the mind's eye. Redi was no novice at this kind of erudite falsification, and no doubt took great pleasure in using his friend to deceive the whole learned world.[10]

Yet Dati cannot be said to be innocent either, because he knowingly kept silent about information he had received in a previous letter from Redi written on November 8, 1673, in which the latter, while claiming to cite only the *Chronica antiqua* (whereas in fact he was copying from the later *Annales conventus Sanctae Catharinae de Pisis ordinis praedicatorum*[11]) had indeed specified that Alessandro della Spina had produced a pair of eyeglasses, though no one had shown him how, simply and exclusively because he had seen a pair, thus overcoming the reluctance of the first, anonymous inventor to communicate his secret.[12]

Why the omission? Because Dati, who had known Galileo Galilei from youth and publicly expressed his admiration for him despite Galileo's condemnation by the Inquisition, wanted to include an impressive parallel in his essay, to frame his account of the discovery of the telescope by the great astronomer.[13] The *Vigil* does in fact tell how Galileo, when told that Count Maurice of Orange had been offered the gift of a telescope, and with no other assistance, was able "on the basis of this bare relation"[14] to make his own instrument—just like Alessandro della Spina, who had not needed any actual model to copy either.

Upon the death of Dati in 1676, Redi published a *Letter Concerning the Invention of Eyeglasses* in which he repeated the parallel between Spina and Galileo and naturally included the falsified passage from the *Chronica*.[15] Nor did he stop there, for we find him perpetrating another deliberate omission: in quoting the passage from the sermon of Giordano da Pisa about the invention of eyeglasses, Redi left out the sentence "And the reader added: I saw the man who first invented and made them, and spoke with him." Yet Redi was citing a manuscript of Giordano's sermons then owned by Filippo Pandolfini, a linguist and student of Dante, in which the sentence is very much present.[16] Redi, however, through a series of agile leaps, had reached the conclusion that Alessandro della Spina, "frater Pisanus" (though Pisa was not his birthplace[17]) *had actually been* the inventor of eyeglasses. In that case, though, the "reader," whoever he was, Giordano himself or another Dominican, would not have failed to state the fact, so it was better just to suppress the inconvenient remark.

The temptation to give a name and a birthplace to the man who had benefited mankind in this way was nonetheless irresistible, so in 1684 an ardent Florentine patriot, Ferdinando Leopoldo Del Migliore, first insinuated that Alessandro della Spina might after all have been a fellow Florentine, then ripped the veil of anonymity off the true, first inventor, whose burial site he even managed to trace in Santa Maria Maggiore in Florence: a noble named Salvino degli Armati. Del Migliore claimed to have a compilation of old funereal monuments in his possession, though no one else was allowed to see the manuscript of this "*Sepoltuario antico.*" Here is what he had to say about the inventor of eyeglasses:

> There is another memorial that was lost when that church was restored, but is faithfully recorded in our *Sepoltuario antico*, all the more precious in that through it we discover that the first inventor of eyeglasses was a gentleman of this our city, so richly endowed with genius in all matters that require penetrating understanding. . . . It was messer Salvino degli Armati, son of Armato, of noble lineage. . . . The figure of this man was shown supine on a slab, in civil habit, with a text reading as follows: + HERE LIES SALVINO D'ARMATO DEGLI ARMATI OF FLORENCE, THE INVENTOR OF EYEGLASSES. MAY GOD FOR–

GIVE HIS SIN. ANNO DOMINI 1317. This is the very man referred to, with no name or other identification, in the ancient manuscript *Chronicle* of the convent of the Dominican Fathers at Pisa, cited by Francesco Redi . . . where we read how brother Alessandro della Spina, who lived in those times and was perhaps Florentine and not Pisan, attempted to learn the invention of making eyeglasses from one who knew how but did not want to demonstrate it, and so found a way to make a pair on his own.[18]

How had the sagacious Del Migliore proceeded? Noting that in the chronicle of the Pisan Dominicans the inventor was left nameless, he turned to a genuine and reliable compilation of Florentine funereal monuments, the *Sepoltuario* of Stefano Rosselli. In it he hit upon a certain Salvino degli Armati of the *popolo* (parish) of Santa Maria Maggiore, where the family had resided (though their tombs were in Santa Maria Novella). The real Salvino from the Rosselli *Sepoltuario* had died around 1340, but in the epitaph Del Migliore had him die in 1317 so as to make the date agree with the hypothesis of Redi, according to which the first eyeglasses had appeared between 1280 and 1311.[19]

The Armati family were well suited to the purposes of Ferdinando Leopoldo Del Migliore because they had died out, and because no one had established their genealogy.[20] Additionally, an ongoing series of rebuilding projects at Santa Maria Maggiore had caused numerous older monuments to be lost, so the disappearance of the one in question was highly plausible. On the other hand, all the detailed information about Salvino was attested in a document of utter reliability—which Salvino's discoverer just happened to own and which he jealously withheld from inspection by anyone else!

The patriotic forger showed himself a mediocre philologist, though, and studded the epitaph of his chosen candidate with errors: he used the word *inventor*, which was unknown in the Italian language in the early fourteenth century, and in order to give a patina of antiquity to his usage he concocted the artful variant "his sin" ("la peccata") instead of using the correct plural form "his sins" ("le peccata").[21]

Notwithstanding these difficulties, our friend Salvino lived on robustly, fleshed out as a historical personage by a tribe of eighteenth-century antiquarians, and reached the nineteenth century in fine fettle. On the occasion of an important congress, probably in 1841, he even regained a set of features, for a portrait of him—in reality an ancient bust—accompanied by a marble that repeated Del Migliore's inscription was erected in the cloister of Santa Maria Maggiore in Florence, and there it remained until 1891 at least, when Alinari, the famous agency that specialized in art reproductions, photographed it. Not long after the cloister was demolished in order to build a school; and what was it called? Why, Scuola Salvino degli Armati, of course! Within its walls generations of children no doubt were

urged by their teachers to venerate the discoverer of eyeglasses, and count-less essays no doubt were written about this glorious Florentine.[22]

Meanwhile, as the edifice grew, the bust and the marble wandered in-side the church, to the chapel of the Orlandini del Beccuto, where a mod-ern marble (on which "le peccata" took the place of "la peccata") was sub-stituted for the previous one. The bust, placed on a high shelf, must have seemed to visitors who read the opening words ("Here lies . . .") of the epitaph to be keeping watch over itself, for below it a fifteenth-century marble sculpture of a deceased member of the Beccuto family (as the coat of arms on his breast indicates) was used to cover a sarcophagus that bore the date 1272. This sarcophagus had been taken from the cloister and bad-ly mutilated so as to make the cover fit, while the cover itself came from the predella of the altar of the chapel.[23]

Salvino's luck ran out in around 1925 when the school changed its name, perhaps because of a long article five years earlier by Isidoro Del Lungo, in which he traced "the course of an erudite imposture" with pas-sionate indignation and great acumen.[24] With poor Salvino gone, none of the other candidates whose names have been put forth have withstood crit-ical examination, and so we must simply resign ourselves to paying hom-age to the unknown inventor of eyeglasses.

Venice was a major center of glass production, and by the end of the thirteenth century eyeglasses had certainly become an object of general use there, as we can tell from an ordinance dated April 2, 1300 aimed at mak-ers of glass and crystal. It prohibited them from perpetrating a fraud that must have become widespread: "acquiring or causing to be acquired, and selling or causing to be sold, ordinary lenses of colorless glass, under the pretence that they are crystal, for example buttons, handles, discs for kegs and for the eyes ("roidi de botacelis et da ogli"), tablets for altar pictures and crosses, and magnifying glasses ("lapides ad legendum").[25] The penal-ty was a fine and the smashing of the fraudulent object. The precise dis-tinction made in the document between eyeglasses and magnifying glasses establishes clearly just what each of the named objects is, and since words preserve their own past like fossils preserved in amber, I note that the term *Brille*, which means eyeglasses in German, is derived from *berillum*, the me-dieval Latin word for crystal.

It is worth emphasizing what a momentous discovery eyeglasses were. A magnifying glass, whether concave or convex, allows a sufferer from presbyopia to see because it *enlarges* the dimensions of everything. The bi-convex lenses of eyeglasses, on the other hand, make up for the insufficient convexity of the crystalline lens of the eye, and cause objects to appear dis-tinctly *in their real dimensions*; eyeglasses, so to speak, combine with the eye, while a magnifying glass combines with the object viewed.[26]

In the ancient world, even before the invention of magnifying glasses, people had used mirrors to improve visual perception, having observed

that if the mirror were concave it presented an enlarged image. Since it was a reversed or "mirror" image, some practice was needed to be able to read the letters, but it was not all that difficult to do: engravers, and until recently printers, did so routinely.[27] For that matter, Leonardo da Vinci wrote in reverse, and his writings are legible with the aid of a mirror. The mirror was simple enough to survive alongside magnifying glasses and eyeglasses: in the *Book of Messer Gioambattista Palatino, citizen of Rome, in which is shown how to write every sort of letter, ancient and modern* (1545)[28], commenting on an illustration of all the instruments of the scrivener grouped together, the author explains:

> The compass, the square, the ruler, the *rigatorio* with one or two lines, the *mollette* to squeeze the ruled lines under the sheet, all help to write in a measured and equal manner, and to steady the hand, as we said at the start. About the scissors, string, seal, etc. it is not necessary to say anything, since their purpose is known to everyone. The mirror is used to preserve vision and strengthen it during continuous writing. Mirrors of glass are much better than ones of steel. The stylus depicted on the inkwell is used by many when they are writing with diligence to hold the paper in place in front of the pen so that the wind will not make it flutter (figure 1).[29]

In connection with the fabrication of mirrors, we may note that in the West the Venetians were the first to apply glass to a thin layer of lead, imitating a technique they probably learned from the Byzantines;[30] Dante mentions "leaded glass" in the *Divine Comedy* (*Inferno* 23, 25) and at other places in his works.[31]

Glasses in Paintings

The inventor of eyeglasses was probably a layperson rather than a cleric. Since he had to earn a living on his own, he must have hoped to profit handsomely from the new device, and for that reason sought to keep the method of fabrication secret. Even in 1445, a nondisclosure agreement is expressly included in a very interesting contract drawn up among three goldsmiths at Pisa before the notary ser Francesco da Ghezzano. Simone, son of the late Antonio Nerucci, undertook to instruct his two partners, who were to contribute their labor to the enterprise, in the art of making eyeglasses with glass and bone, and to supply the equipment necessary. During the term of the contract, four and a half years, Nerucci promised not to teach anyone else how to make eyeglasses, but his two partners in turn promised not to pass on what they learned to any pupils and future competitors either; the contract was sealed with a solemn oath on the

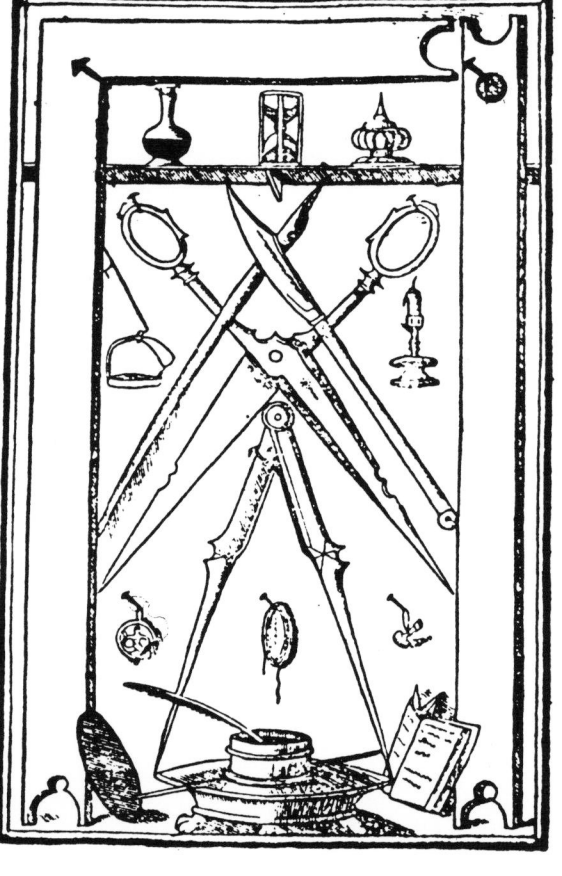

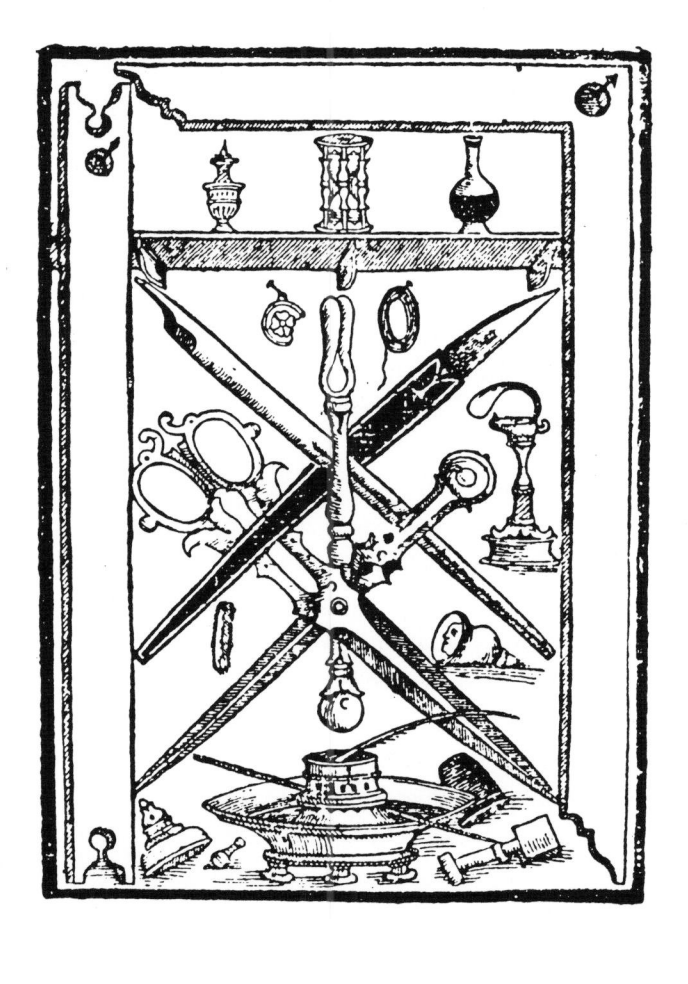

FIGURE 1   The Instruments of the Copyist.
Illustration from *Libro di M. Giovambattisa Palatino, cittadino romano, nel qual s'insegna a scriver ogni sorte di lettere antica et moderna.* Rome, Campo di fiore, by Antonio Blodo Asolano MDXLV (1545)

FIGURE 2   The Instruments of the Copyist.
Illustration from *Lo presente libro insegna la vera arte del Excellente scrivere de diverse varie sorti di litere . . . Opera del tagliente. . . .* Printed in Venice by Pietro di Nicolini de Sabbio, MDXXXVII (1537)

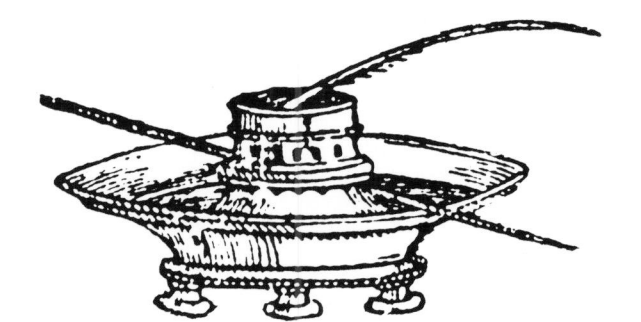

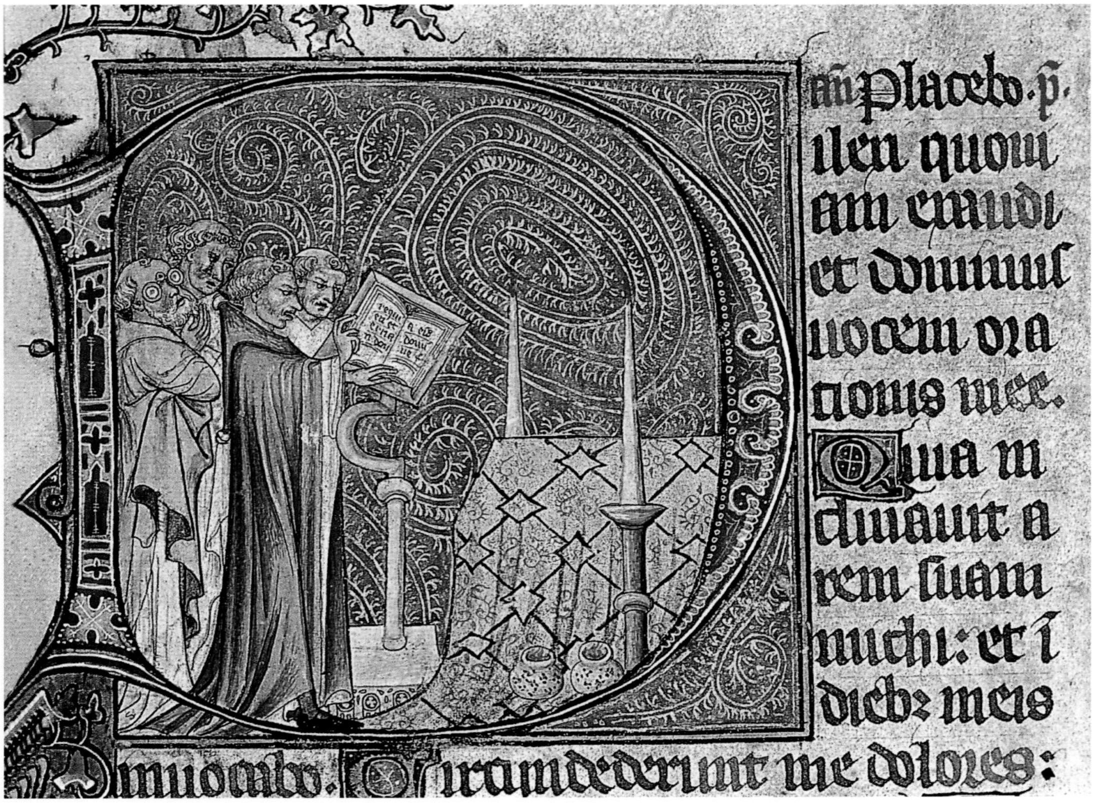

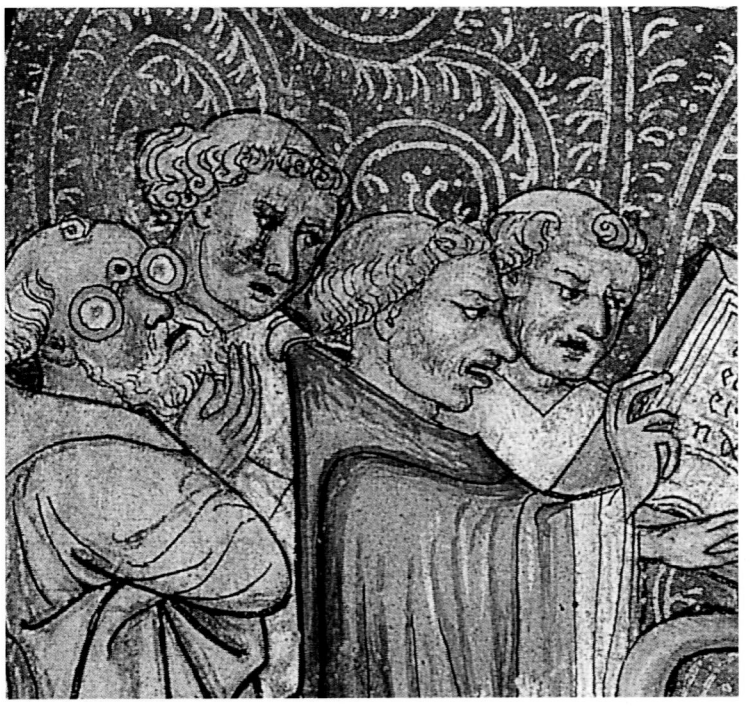

FIGURE 3 The Celebration of the
Office for the Dead.
Miniature, middle of the fourteenth century.
On the left, a detail of the same miniature.
Besançon, Bibliothèque Municipale, ms. 140
(a composite manuscript; the miniature is part
of the *Salterium ad usum Engolismensis diocesis*),
f. 190

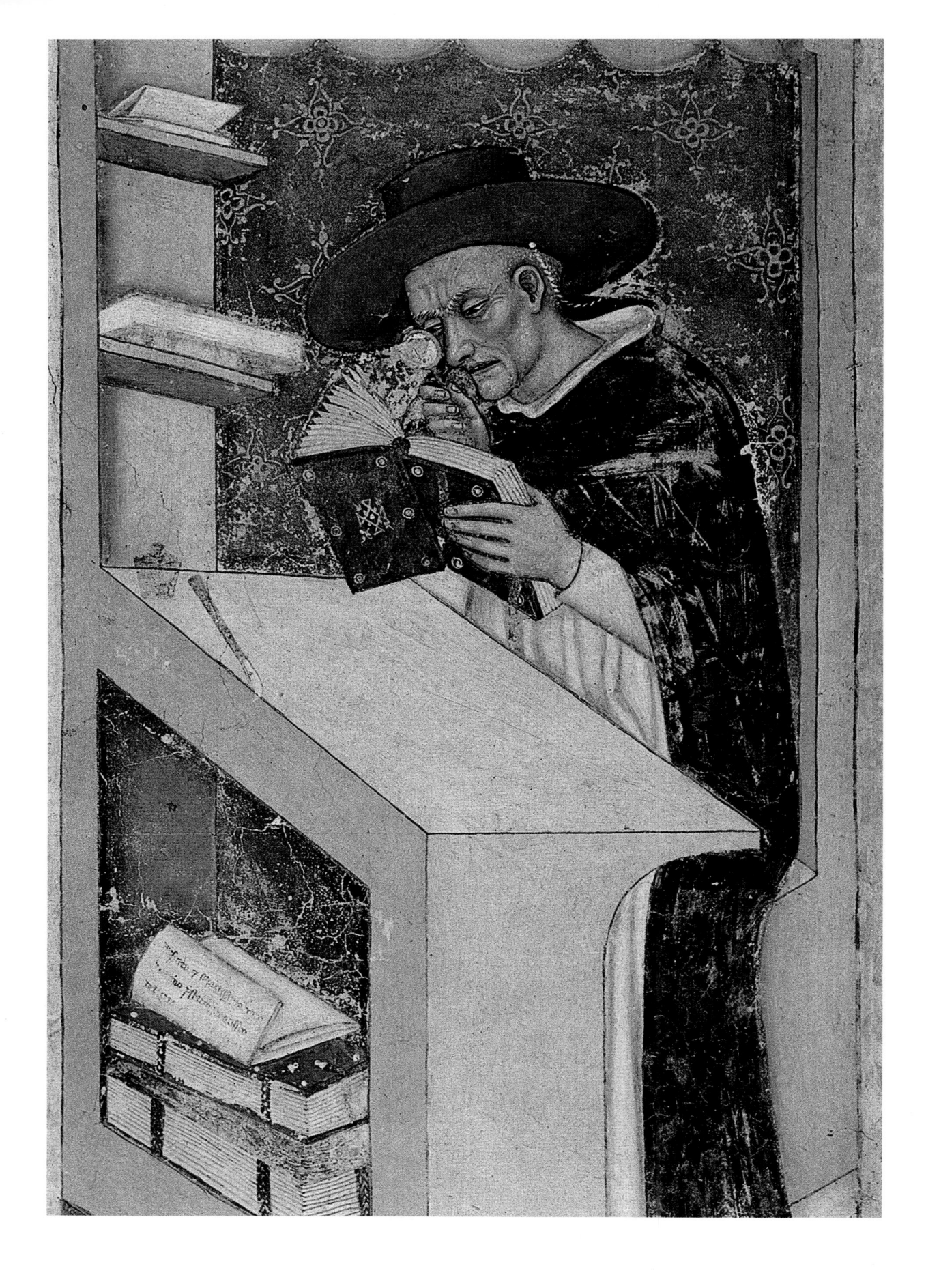

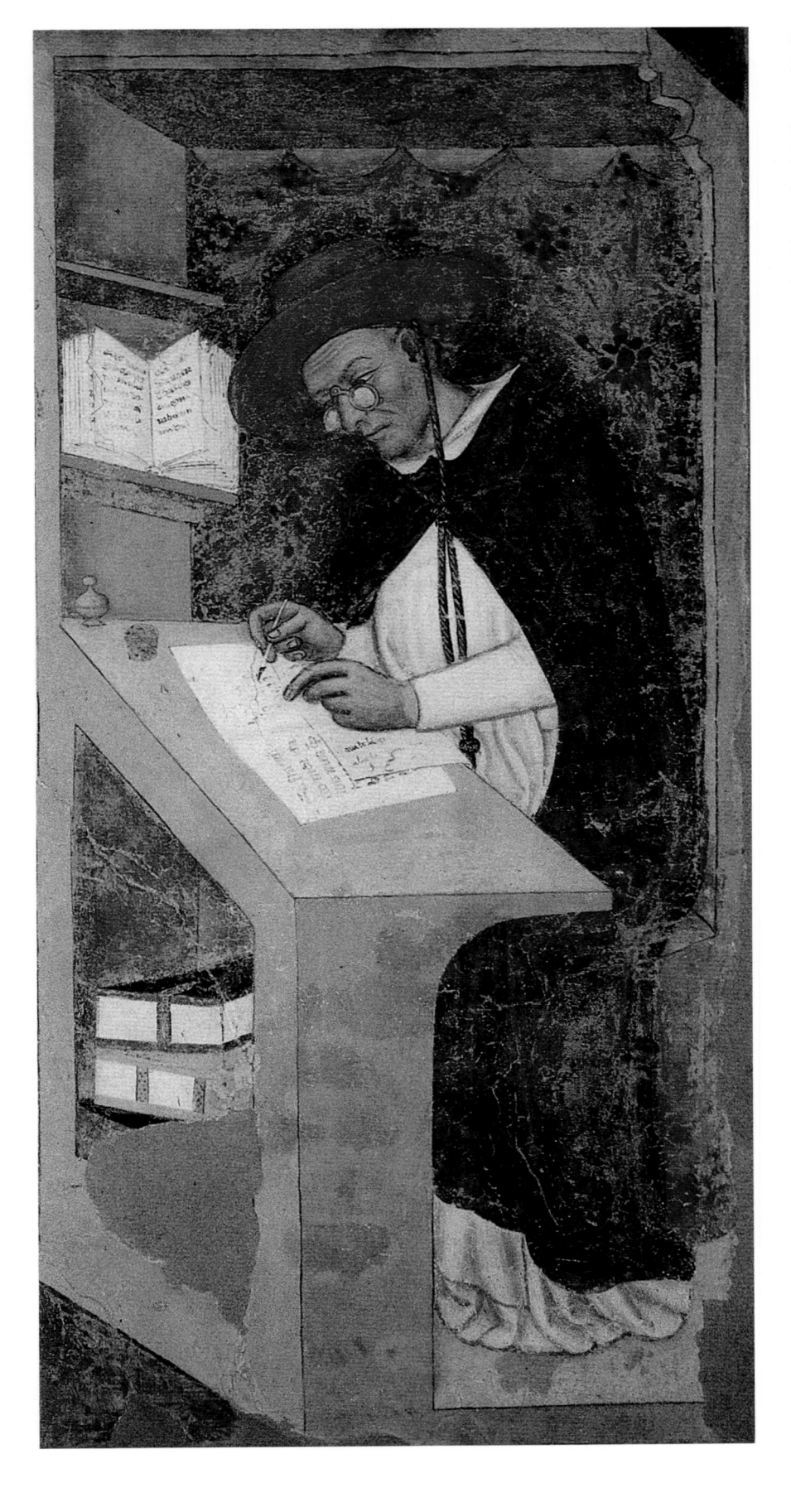

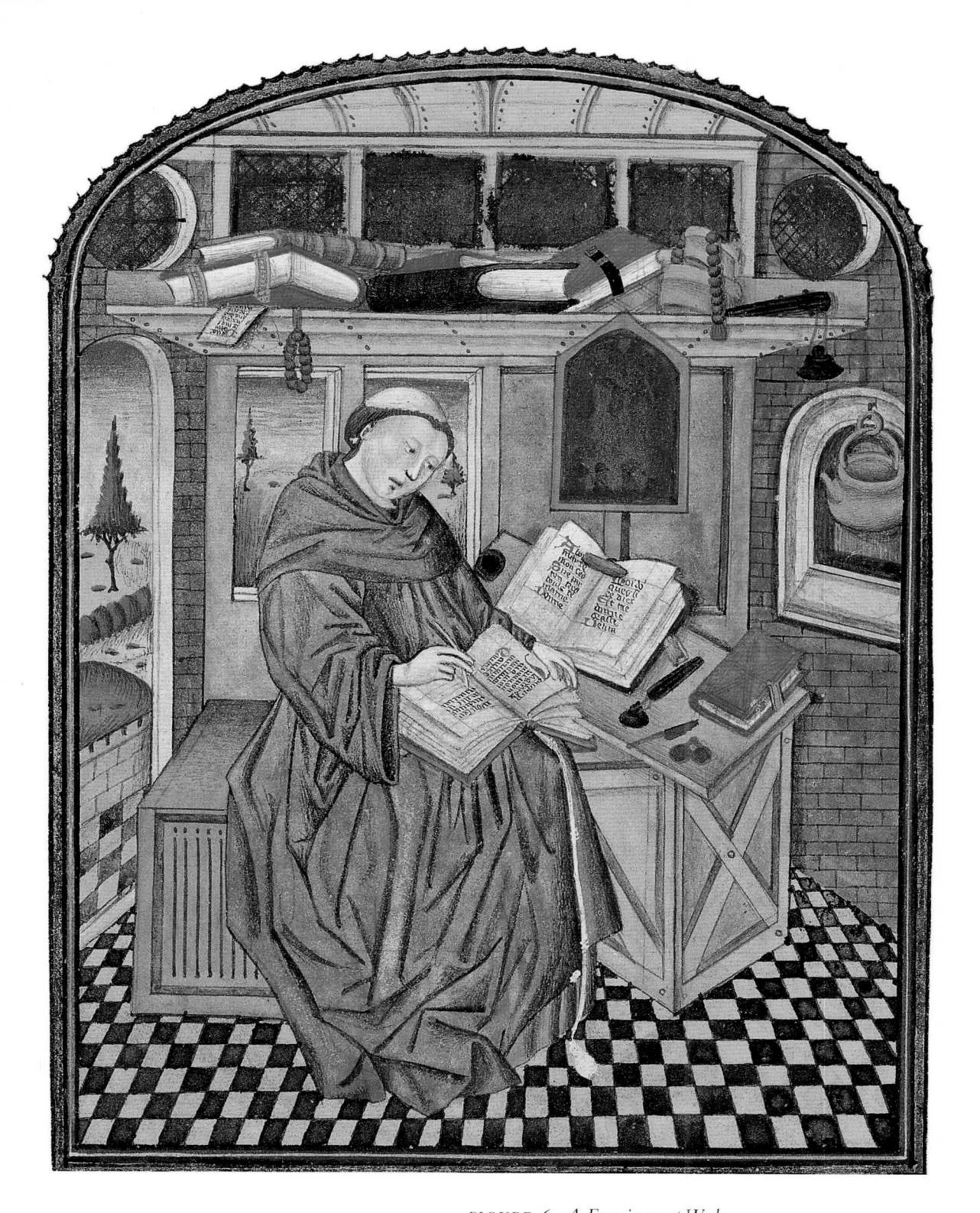

FIGURE 6 *A Franciscan at Work.*
Miniature, fifteenth century. From Jacques de Guyse,
Chroniques de Hainaut. Paris, Bibliothèque Nationale,
ms. Fr. 20127, f. 2v

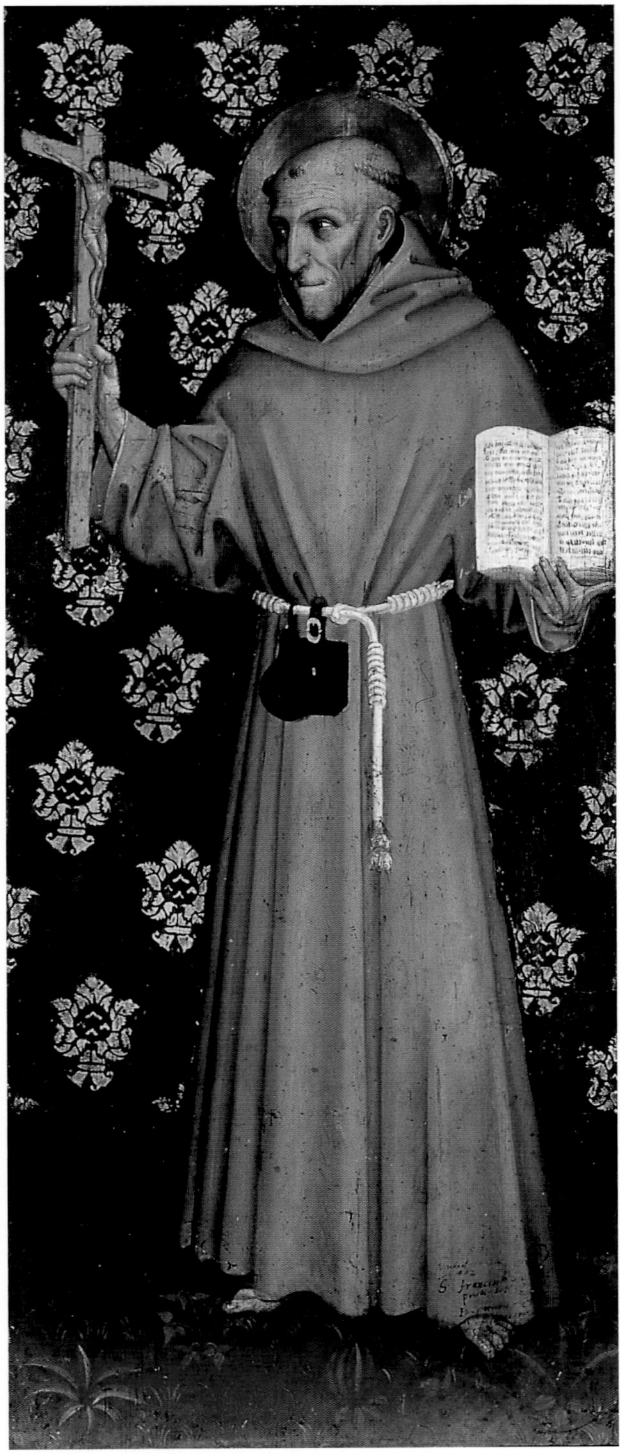

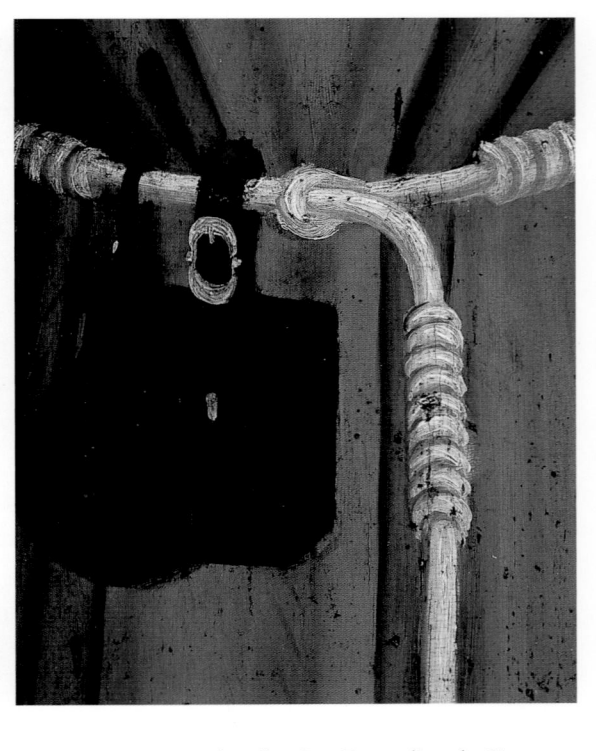

FIGURE 7 Conrad Leib, *San Bernardino da Siena with His Glasses Hanging from His Sash in a Case.* Altar panel, 1460–1465. Ptuj (Slovenia), Pokrajinski Muzej

gospels. The skill necessary to make eyeglasses must have been considered something really special, and to emphasize this the notary mentions not only technical capacity but also knowledge of alchemy: "they have mutually concluded an association among themselves for the purpose of making, constructing, and alchemizing [*archimiandum*] said eyeglasses."[32]

Alessandro della Spina, on the other hand, did not have to worry about income and outgo and the cost of living because he dwelled in a convent, and it was perhaps for this reason, in addition to his natural generosity, that he was ready to impart the results of his own ability freely ("he . . . showed everyone else how to do so with an open and joyful heart"). And it is among the Dominicans that we find the oldest surviving depiction of the use of eyeglasses.

Recently a Francophone scholar has attacked this priority, presenting in evidence a miniature supposedly from the end of the thirteenth century (figure 3): it seems we are back to the erudite disputations of the past! Inside the capital letter D (*Dilexi* . . .), four religious are intent on celebrating the office for the dead before a tomb. A manuscript lies open before them on a large reading stand, and on it we can read the beginning of the prayer "Requiem aeternam dona eis Domine." The oldest of the four is wearing glasses—actually pince-nez with what appear to be very thick lenses—and his mind must be elsewhere, for he is not following the choral chant of his companions and seems to want to draw attention to himself, turning his head in the direction of the viewer.[33] In reality, however, the miniature is from the middle of the fourteenth century,[34] so let's call it a draw and return once more to Italy.

The Dominicans had made learning the cornerstone of their religious life, so as to be able to combat heresy effectively on the doctrinal plane and in public disputations; hence they were professionally inclined to need "vitreos ab oculis ad legendum" (eyeglasses for reading). At Treviso, in the convent of San Nicolò (now the archiepiscopal seminary), Tomaso da Modena painted forty illustrious Preaching Friars (another term for the Dominicans) in 1352, accompanied by an inscription identifying them. Each is seated at a desk in his own cell and occupied in meditating, reading, composing, or transcribing.[35] Among this learned company we find Cardinal Nicholas de Rouen holding a magnifying glass, the forerunner of eyeglasses, in his hand (figure 4),[36] intently studying a page, and Cardinal Hugues de Provence with a pair of eyeglasses fixed on his nose (figure 5).[37] The automatic association at mid-fourteenth century between Dominicans, books, and reading accessories, including eyeglasses, is evident.

Saint Francis of Assisi had a different plan in mind for his brotherhood: they were to live with no fixed address, as poor among the poor, maintaining themselves with the labor of their hands and refraining from study, from "knowledge that inflates [self-importance]."[38] Yet with the entry into the order of Saint Anthony of Padua, the original intention to remain, as

FIGURE 8
Leonhard Wagner at Work.
Miniature, 1511–1512.
Stuttgart, Würtembergische Landesbibliothek, cod. mus. I 2° 65 (Lorcher Chorbuch), f. 236v

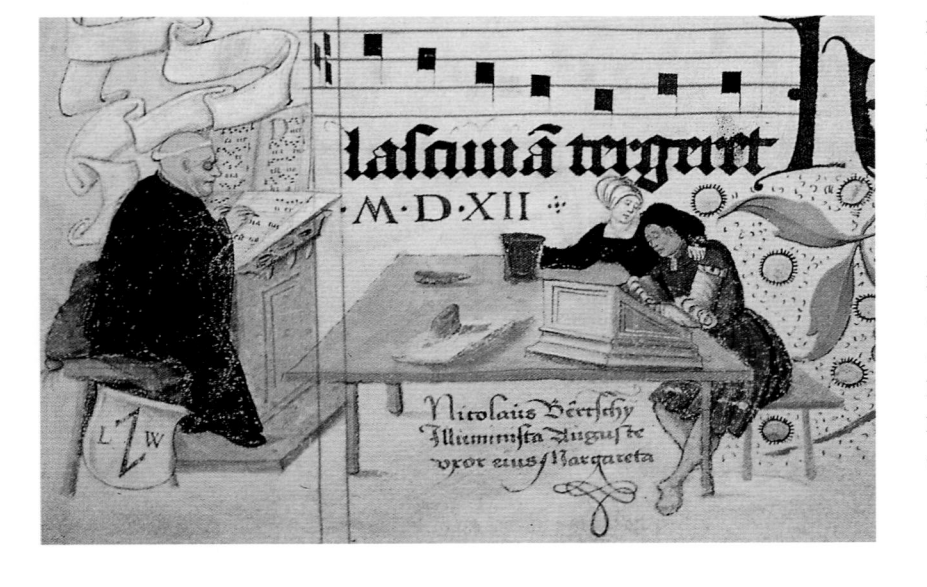

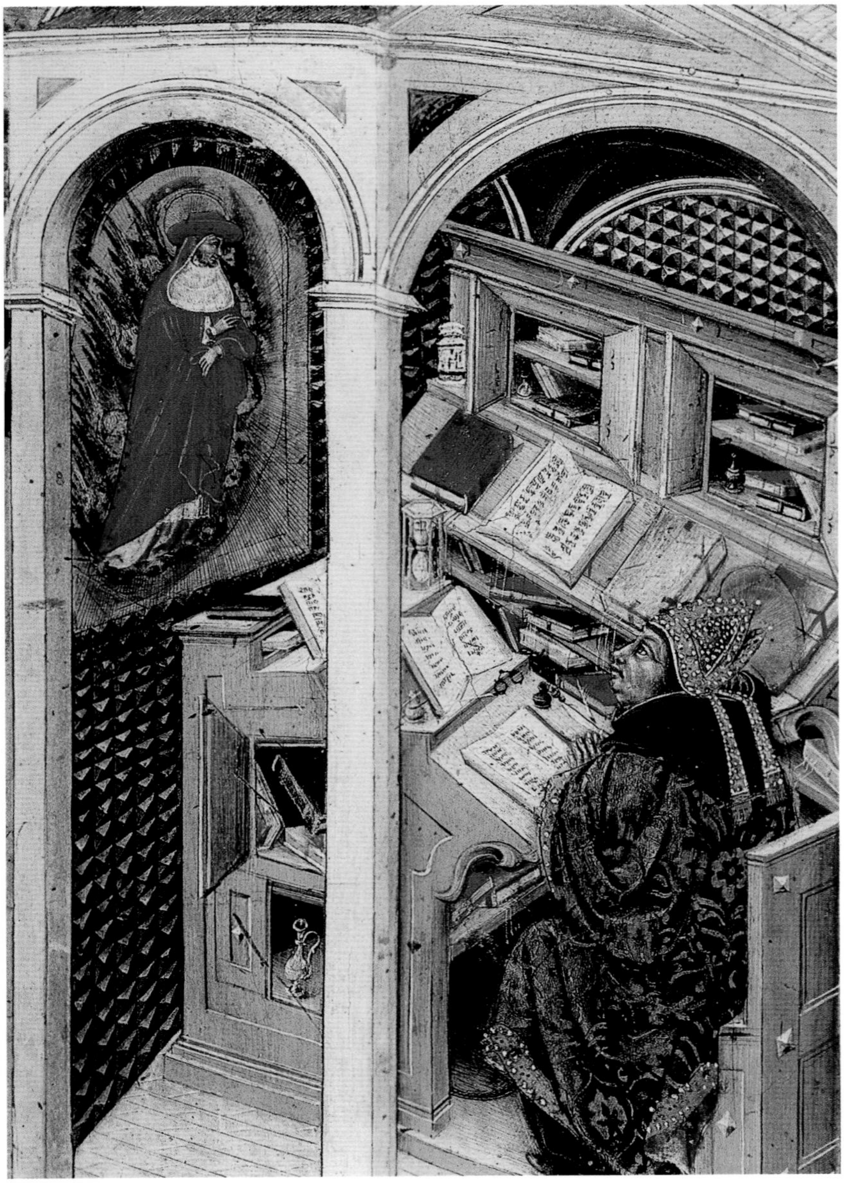

FIGURE 9 Giovanni di Paolo, *Saint Jerome Appears to Saint Augustine.*
Panel, early fifteenth century.
Berlin, Staatlichen Museen, Gemäldegalerie

Saint Francis said, *ignorans* (ignorant) and *idiota* (humble and unacquainted with worldly affairs)[39] was abandoned. In the fifteenth century even the memory of it had faded, as we see in a miniature of a Franciscan wearing a flowing gown of soft material, portrayed entirely at his ease in a handsome, luminous room filled with objects, a room in no way inferior to that of a wealthy prelate (figure 6). A piece of lead has been placed on the manuscript from which our Franciscan is copying to keep the page firmly open, and on the surface of his writing table are laid out a scraper and a movable inkwell, in addition to a pair of glasses with red rims.[40]

If one was traveling, glasses were kept in a case that was hung from the belt. In an altar panel painted by Conrad Leib between 1460 and 1465[41] (figure 7), we see them dangling from the sash of a famous Franciscan preacher, San Bernardino da Siena. In the case of Leonhard Wagner, on the other hand, who was considered the eighth wonder of the world in his time because of his ability to write in one hundred different calligraphic styles without needing to refer to a sample, it was essential to show him with his spectacles on his nose: in a miniature (figure 8) from the early sixteenth century, we see him at work in the company of the painter Nikolaus Bertschi and his wife.[42]

Even Saint Augustine must have needed glasses, on account of the strain on his eyes: so at least thought Giovanni di Paolo, who at the beginning of the sixteenth century depicted the fourth-century Church father absorbed in contemplation of Saint Jerome (figure 9). According to the famous Dominican preacher Jacopo da Varazze, Saint Remigius is supposed to have said of Saint Augustine: "Although Saint Jerome claimed to have read six thousand volumes of Origen's books, nonetheless Augustine wrote so many that no one else, even working day and night, would have been able to write, or even to read, them."[43] Augustine in this painting has no need for the moment of any help in perceiving the supernatural apparition of Jerome clearly, because he is seeing it with the mind's eye.[44] His glasses, which are propped upright by the inkwell, will serve him when he returns to his beloved studies, comparing the numerous manuscripts scattered on various levels of his desk, on shelves, and in compartments and cubbyholes providentially exposed for the pleasure of the viewer. Let us note in passing that the painter, having cast off all restraint in the matter of anachronism, has not only made Jerome (the saintly hermit of the desert and translator of the Bible into Latin) a cardinal but has also dressed him up in the bright red hat and garments that go with this status—a costume the use of which is securely attested only from the middle of the fourteenth century.[45]

If a father of the Church could use glasses, then why should an evangelist like Luke, intent on writing his gospel, not put them on too? In a miniature from a missal in use at Châlons-sur-Marne (the modern Châlons-en-Champagne in France), probably by a painter from Troyes who worked

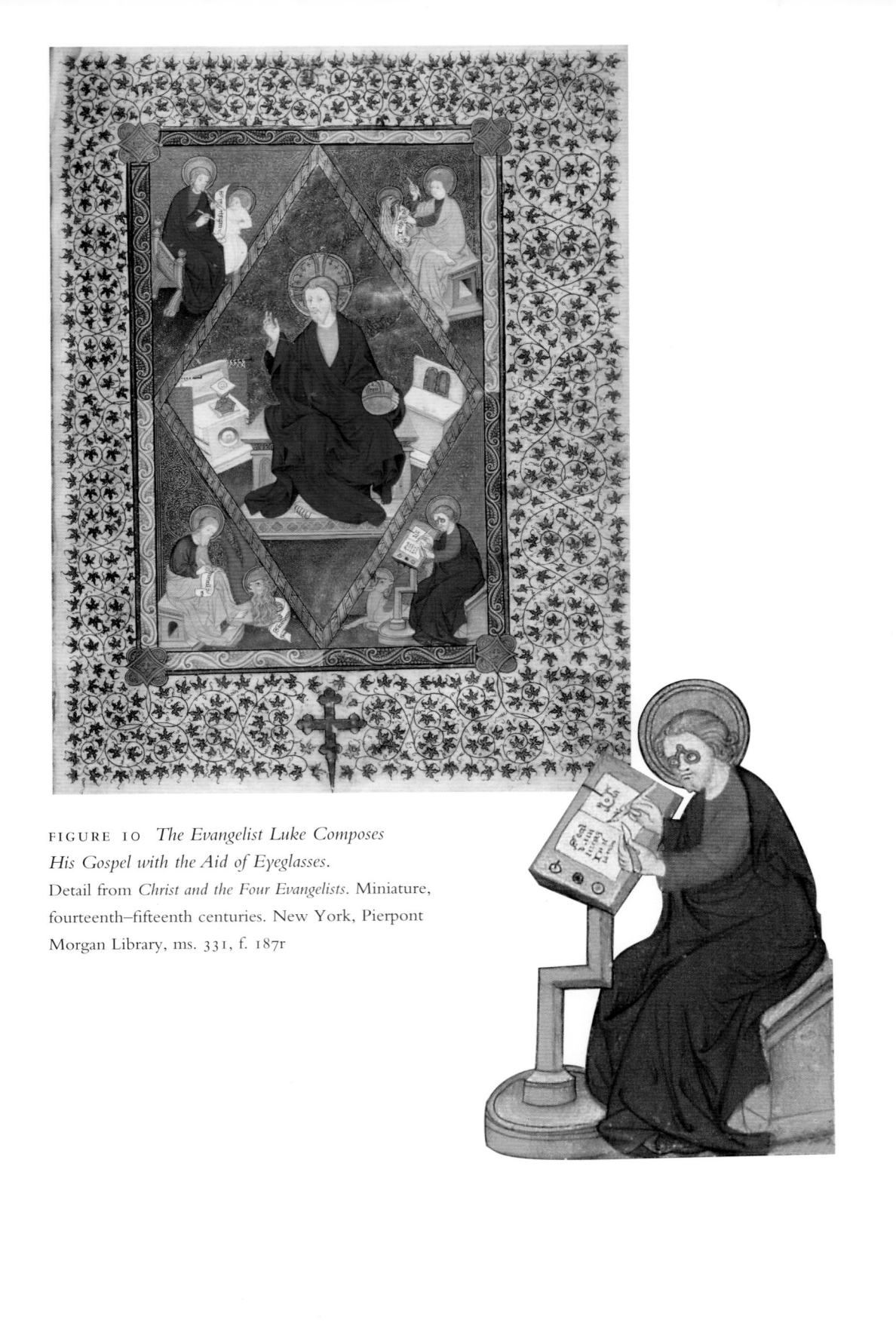

FIGURE 10 *The Evangelist Luke Composes His Gospel with the Aid of Eyeglasses.*
Detail from *Christ and the Four Evangelists.* Miniature, fourteenth–fifteenth centuries. New York, Pierpont Morgan Library, ms. 331, f. 187r

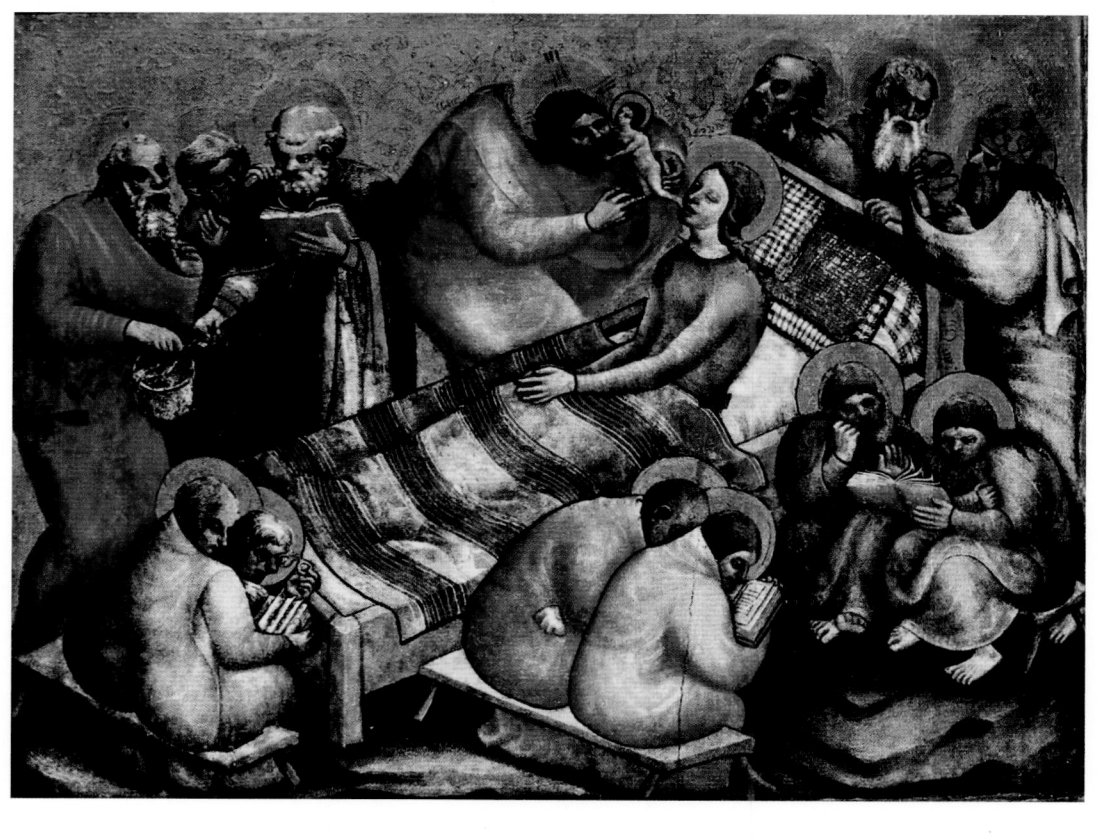

FIGURE 11 *The Death of the Virgin.*
Altar panel, 1370–1372. Detail below: An apostle
reads from the prayer book of his companion with
the help of eyeglasses. Innsbruck, Tiroler
Landesmuseum Ferdinandeum

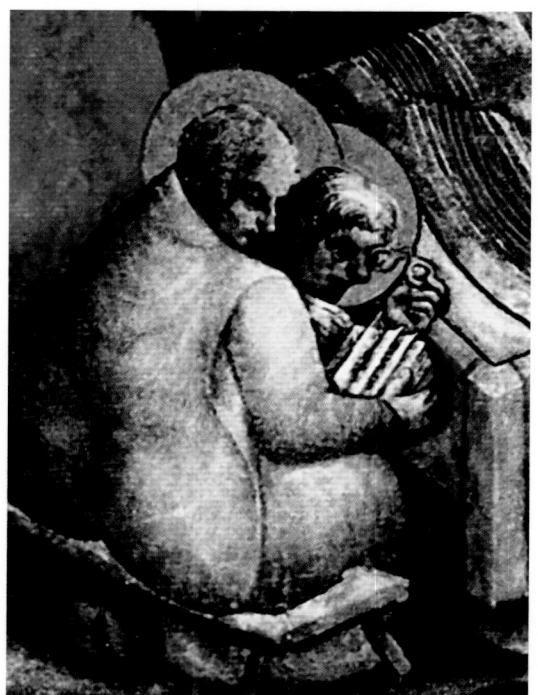

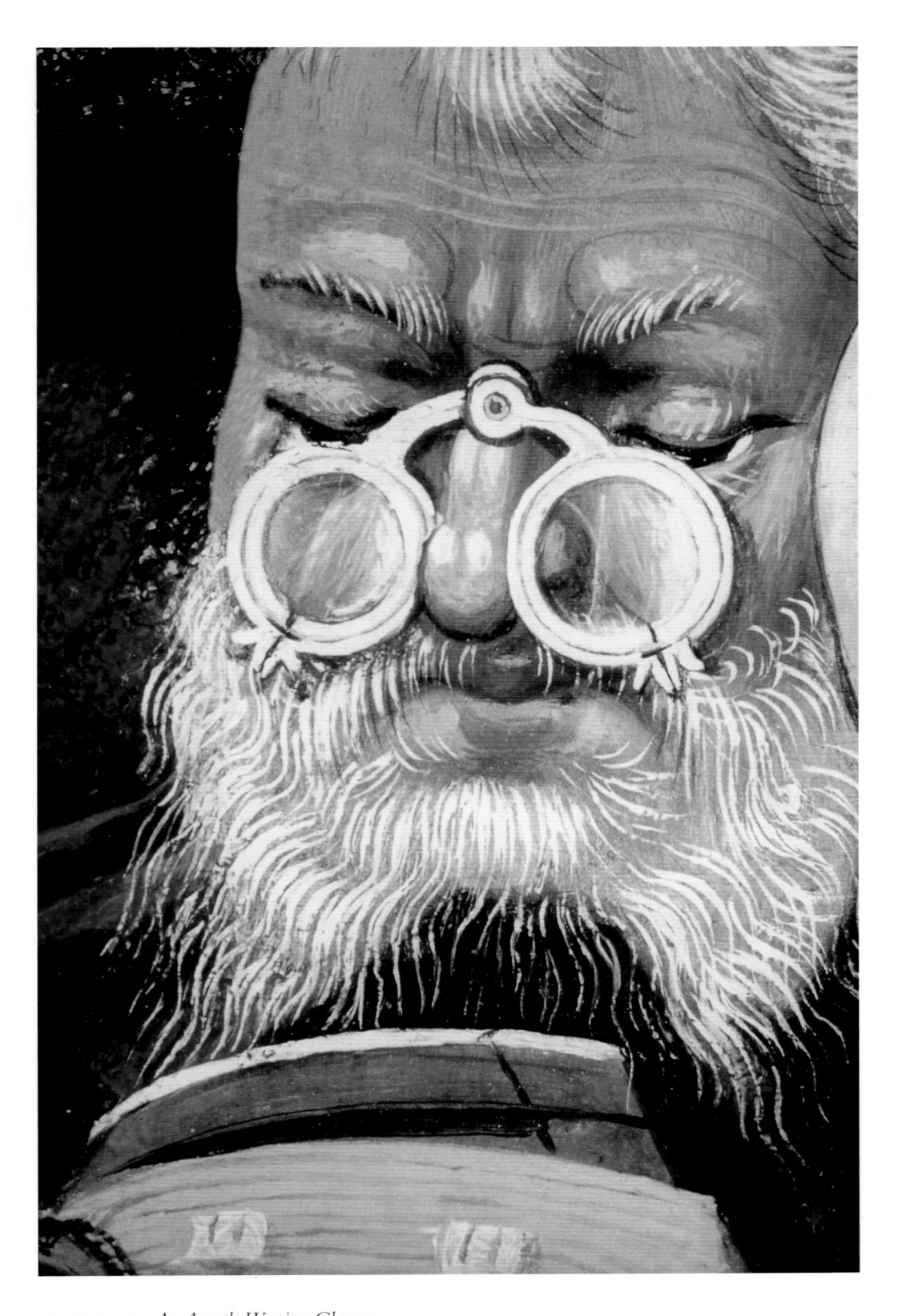

FIGURE 12 *An Apostle Wearing Glasses.*
Detail from *The Death of the Virgin.* Polyptych (Albrechtsaltar),
1439. Klosterneuburg, Stiftsmuseum Klosterneuburg

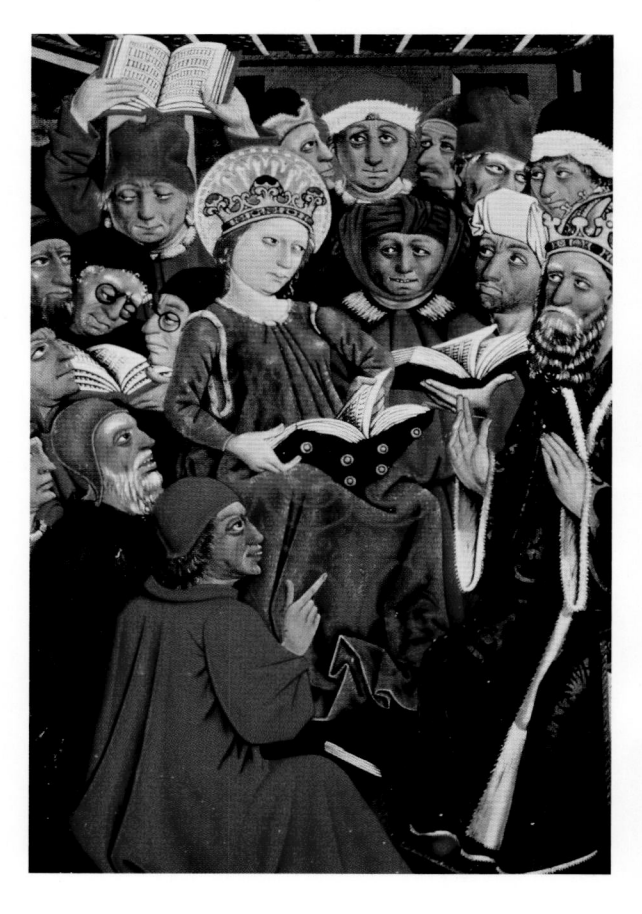

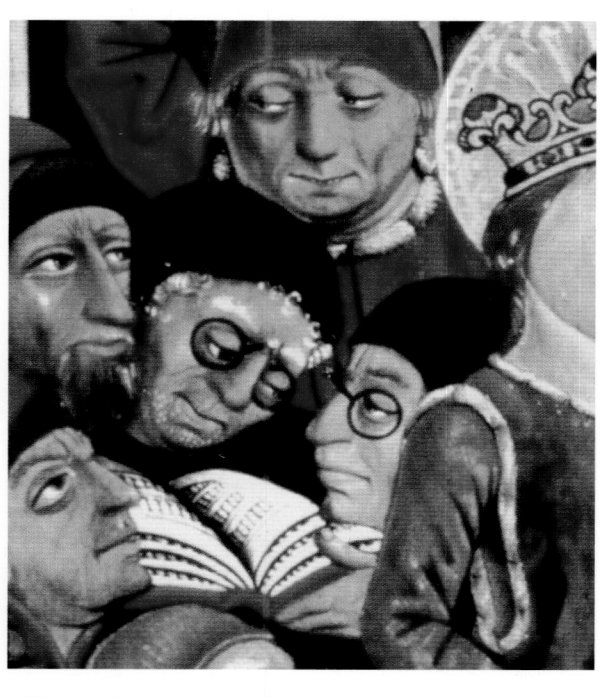

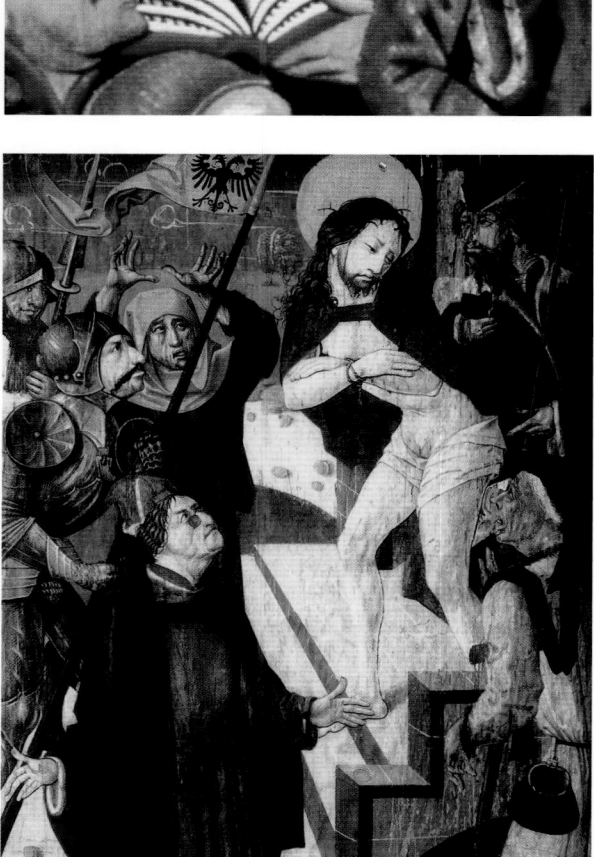

FIGURE 13 *The Disputation of Catherine of Alexandria.*
Panel, fifteenth century. St. Lorenzen ob Murau Styria

FIGURE 14 Michael Pacher, *Ecce Homo*, with the detail
of the pharisee wearing glasses with emerald-colored lenses.
Panel, c. 1475. Gries (Bolzano), Parish Church

around 1400 (figure 10), we see Christ enthroned at the center, framed by a rhombus,[46] and the four evangelists, each with his own telling symbol, in the corners. Three of them are intent on writing their own names on scrolls they are holding, but Luke has been given special attention, since he has an adjustable writing desk with two inkwells and a container for colored ink, all for his personal use. He is writing with a pen and a scraper on a double sheet of parchment on which a magnifying glass rests. Since Luke was a painter according to legend, the illuminator of the missal, himself accustomed to squint for better focus, must have thought of the evangelist as a colleague, and has furnished him with a remarkable pair of glasses that have a hinge on the bridge over the nose so they can be folded up.

Even an apostle might need a pair of glasses when he had to find the text of a prayer quickly, at the moment Christ was greeting the soul of the Virgin on her deathbed. The thought occurred to a couple of anonymous painters from the German-speaking world: one of them painted an altar panel representing the *Death of the Virgin* between 1370 and 1372 (figure 11), the other a largy polyptych from around 1439, in which the same subject constitutes one of four scenes from the legend of the Madonna (figure 12).[47]

Much less benevolent are two scribes with glasses perched on their noses, searching intently in a book in the evident hope of finding a passage with which to confound Saint Catherine of Alexandria, whose learned disputation with the pagan philosophers[48] is shown in a fifteenth-century altar dedicated to her and still to be seen in the Church of St. Lorenzen ob Murau in Styria (figure 13). The green-tinted glasses in a gold frame[49] worn by a pharisee with a curved nose who is deriding Christ, depicted in clothing contemporary with the painter (Michael Pacher, c. 1475; figure 14),[50] partially hide the expression of his eyes and impart a deliberately disquieting appearance to the face of the persecutor. Tinted lenses, normally used to shield the eyes, here combine with strongly characterized somatic features to connote active aggression and open hostility.

Anti-Semitism, since we have touched on the subject, is a sentiment that arose at a certain point in the Middle Ages: the aftermath of the First Crusade, to be precise. The iconography of the Synagogue (an allegorical figure representing the Jewish people as a whole, in opposition to another figure standing for the *Ecclesia* or Church) aiming a blow from a lance at the mystic Lamb was invented at the same time that numerous trials were launched, and tragically concluded, against Jews accused of having profaned the host. In a miniature from the beginning of the thirteenth century (figure 15), the Synagogue, with a veil over her eyes because of the failure to recognize the Messiah, pierces the Lamb at the center of the cross with a banner, the shaft of which is already broken to symbolize lost glory; the divine blood is gathered in a cup held by *Ecclesia*, who holds her attribute, a model of a church, in her other hand.[51]

per quem maieſtatem tuam laudãt
dominationes. tremunt poteſtateſ.
tuteſ. ac beata ſeraphyn. ſocia exulta
Cum quibʒ & nraſ uoceſ ut admitti i
ſupplici confeſſione dicenteſ. Sanctu

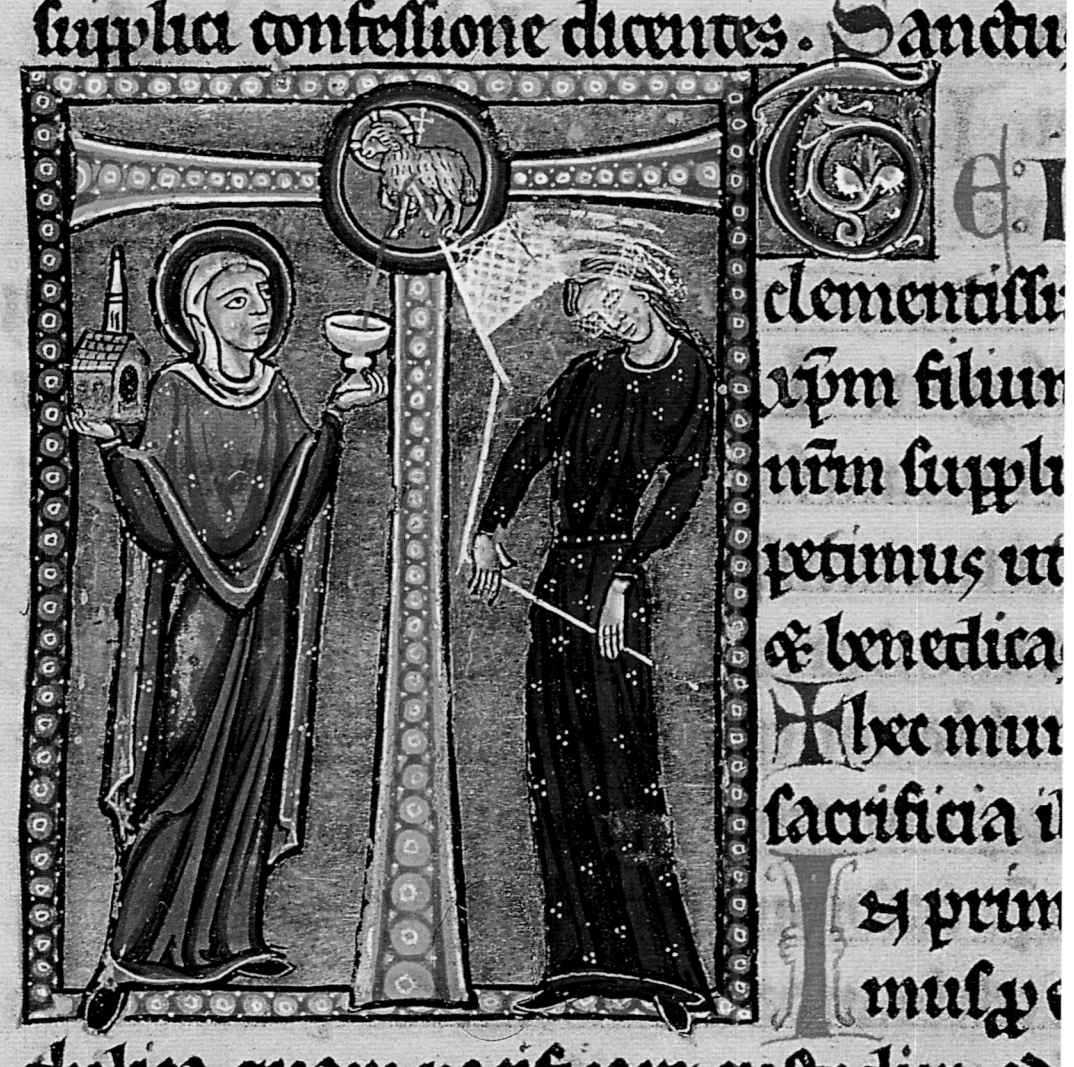

clementiſſi
xpm filiũ
nrm ſuppl
petimuſ ut
& benedica
Hec mun
ſacrificia i
ʒ prim
muſ p

be tra tholica. quam pacificare. cuſtodire ad
digneriſ. una cum famulo tuo papa
nro. ⁊ rege nro. ⁊ omnibʒ orthodoxiſ atq

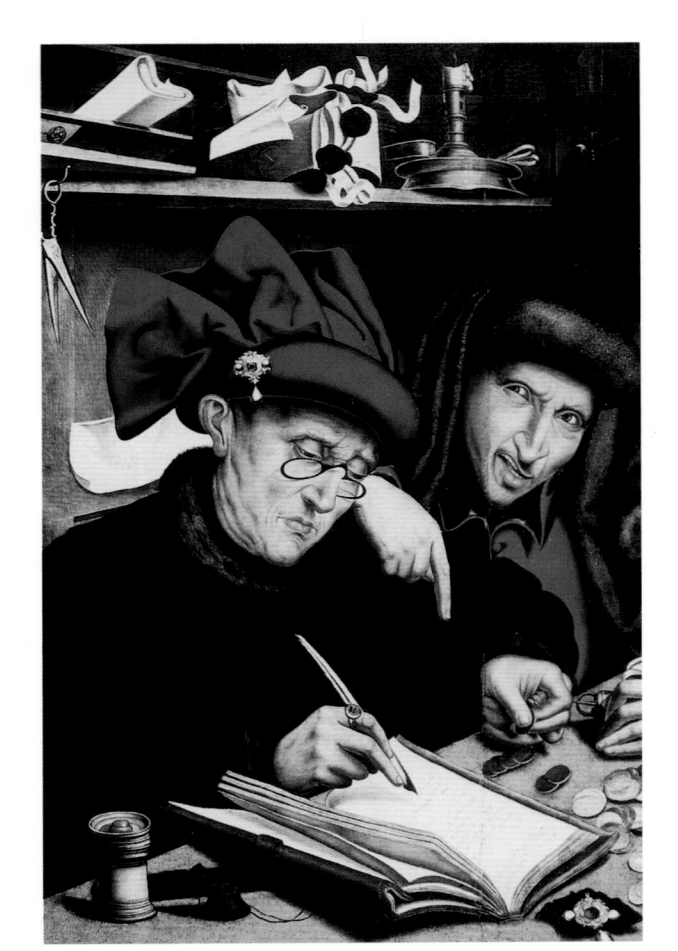

FIGURE 15 Church (*Ecclesia*) and
Synagogue personified.
Miniature, beginning of the thirteenth century.
Montpellier, Faculté de Médecine, ms. H 399, f. 108

FIGURE 16 Marinus van Roymersvaele, *The Usurers*.
Panel, sixteenth century. Florence, Museo Stibbert

The Jews were often accused of being usurers. In a painting of the Flemish school from the beginning of the sixteenth century, a Jew with the customary hooked nose is anxious to see all the money lying scattered about on the table entered in the books, and rests his hand in a familiar fashion on the shoulder of a merchant bent on doing the writing; the surface of the table is cluttered with pledges (figure 16). The second individual is certainly not a Jew, but he is a crony of the usurer and has to be given a negative visible trait: a pair of glasses with black rims, which make it easier for him to perform a role deemed reprehensible, fit the bill nicely.

A satirical poem of Franco Sacchetti deplores the decadence of the knightly class, because in his time even people of low condition had crept into it, "astute traders, wearing glasses, with pens behind their ears, doing sums in their books, making deceptive transactions, buying and selling, trading and lending, seizing and grabbing, robbing the widows and orphans."[52] "The art of making eyeglasses," which the Dominican Giordano da Pisa had embraced with so much enthusiasm because it would enable him to meditate more deeply on holy scripture and compose edifying sermons, now helped to keep track of the debts of others and one's

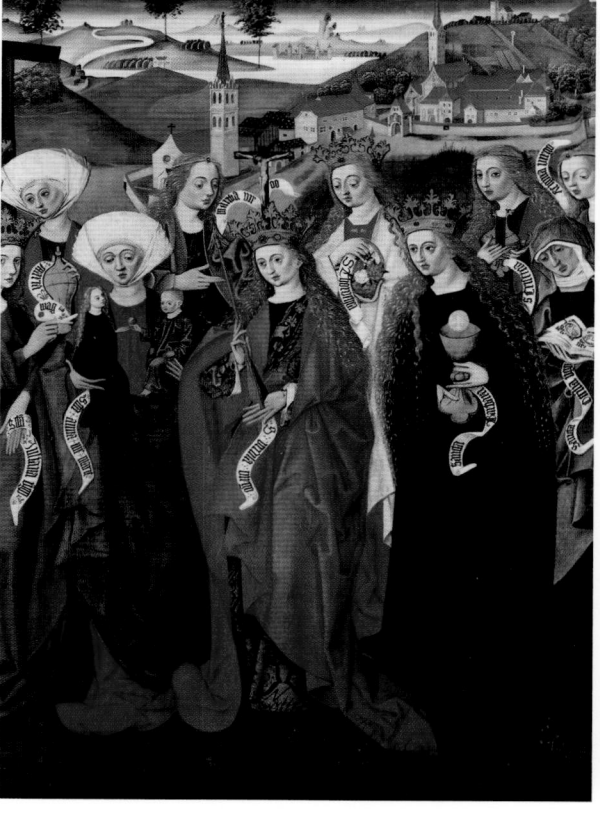
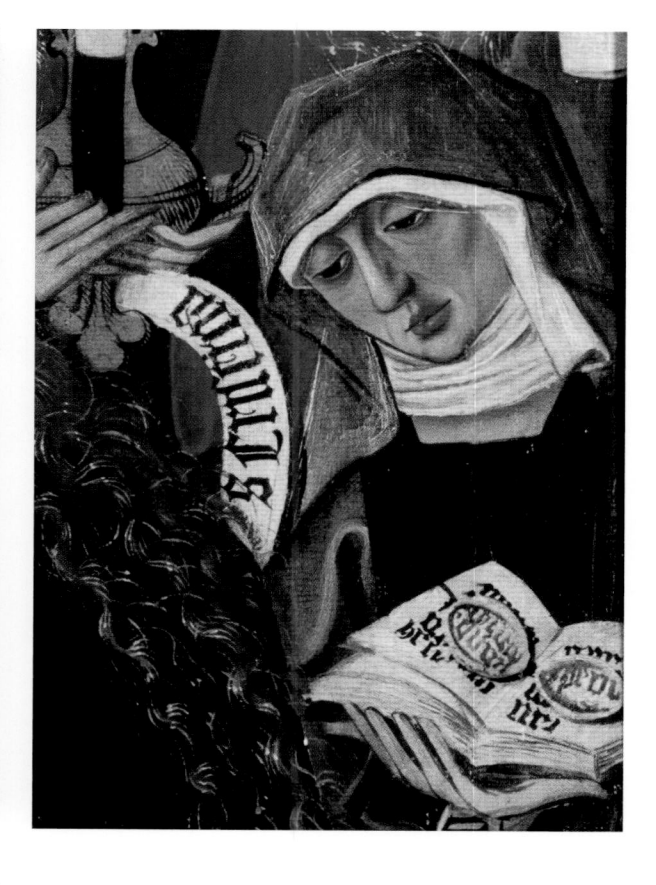

FIGURE 17

Ludwig Konraiter, *Saint Anna,
Madonna with Babe, Saint
Ursula, and Virgin Saints*.
Panel, 1485–1490. Detail:
Saint Ottilie in meditation.
Wilten (Innsbruck),
Stiftsmuseum des
Prämonstratenser
Chorherrenstiftes

own illicit gains. What began as an instrument of the church had become
a tool of the merchant, though in any case the use of glasses remained a
male prerogative.

One exception is a late image of Saint Ottilie (c. 660–720), an erudite
abbess who had been born blind, but had regained her sight upon being
baptized and was considered the patron saint of the eyes. In the panel,
painted between 1485 and 1490 by Ludwig Konraiter, the court painter of
emperor Maximilian I, Ottilie accompanies a saintly cortège, among
whom Saint Ursula stands out; its members cluster around Saint Anna, the
Madonna, and the Baby Jesus. Ottilie has her head bent over an open
book, on which her glasses lie, and the painter, in an excess of realism,
shows the line of writing visible through them as if enlarged by a magnifying lens (figure 17).[53]

In the course of time women gladly adopted eyeglasses too, making
them an instrument of intrigue and seduction, as they were inserted into
perfume bottles or between the folds of fans.[54] But these details carry us far
beyond the Middle Ages, indeed down to the time of Louis XVI, so we will
merely cast a brief and distant glance at those amiable ladies and pass on.

On their way to becoming a pure fashion accessory, eyeglasses underwent a few changes to make them easier to use, for keeping them perched
on your nose or having a handle fitted so you could hold them in one

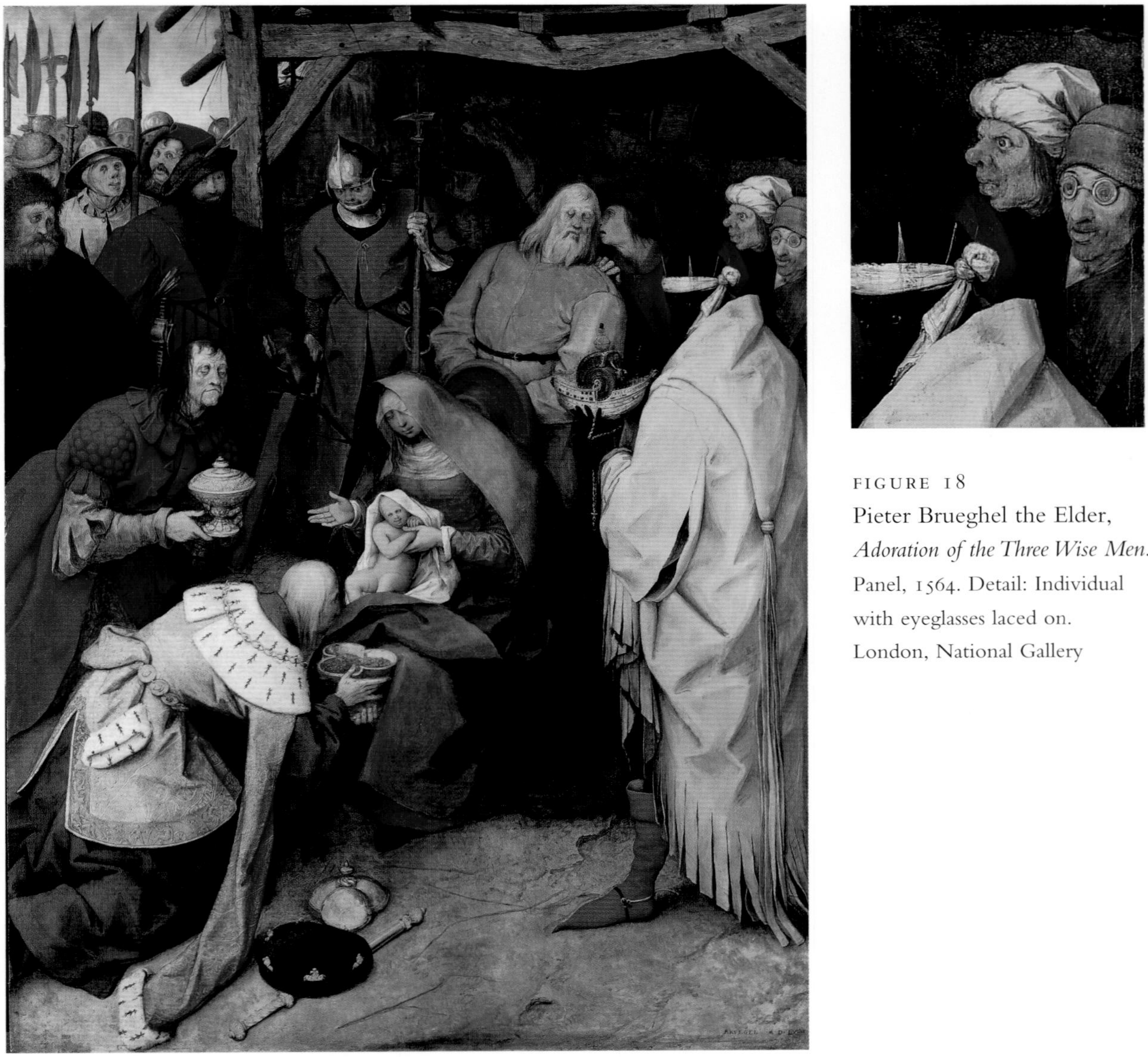

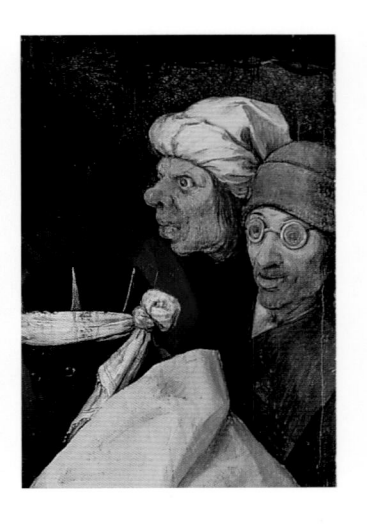

hand was not very practical. Savonarola and San Bernardino da Siena wore their glasses with a *berrettino* (cap) that had a special hook to which their glasses could be attached, and the glasses and cap of the Sienese preacher were felt to be such an integral part of his outfit, so to speak, that they were considered precious relics.[55] A great advance in functionality was made when earpieces were introduced, which at first were made to clasp the temples and later were adapted to rest on the ears.[56] Though the earliest surviving examples are from the mid-eighteenth century, the *Adoration of the Three Wise Men* by Pieter Brueghel the Elder (1564; figure 18) already contains a clue to their evolution, in the form of a goofy-looking individual on the extreme right, wearing glasses that are held in place on his nose by some kind of lateral support; whether it is a cord or a rigid arm is unclear.

In and Around the Learned Man's Study

Giordano da Pisa, our most important witness for the invention of eye-glasses, was an alert observer of the world around him, and in describing how Noah had built his ark, he involuntarily put another medieval invention on record: glass-covered windows (though a few scattered references do indicate that they may have been tried in ancient Rome):

> This ark was entirely enclosed, you see; that's why it was called an ark, not a ship, for a ship is open on top, but this vessel had a roof and was enclosed. The doors below were closed, and the window overhead was closed as well, but was glazed with crystal, which was useful to keep the water out, and to let the light in.[57]

Panes of glass, especially stained glass, had already made their appearance some time before this in churches: as early as the end of the tenth century, Guzbert, the abbot of the monastery of Tegernsee in Bavaria, had written a letter of profuse thanks to the aristocratic donor who had banished the cold and the dark from the naves:

> Up till now the windows of our churches were not covered except by old cloths; thanks to you, for the first time the sun, with its golden mane, passes through the panes of glass tinted in various hues, and gleams on the pavement of our basilica. An inexhaustible joy fills the hearts of all who are able to admire the extraordinary novelty of this exceptional accomplishment.[58]

The church of the abbey of Saint-Denis, which was rebuilt at the behest of Suger, the head of the abbey from 1121 to 1151, still stands at the outer rim of modern Paris, and Suger's proud words as he celebrated the completion of the project are famous: "It was the year of the incarnate Word 1144 when the church was consecrated. . . . The new apsidal area is now linked to the frontal portion, and the basilica glows because the central portion has been made luminous. Whatever is harmoniously joined to the light shines, and the edifice, pervaded with new light, shines indeed."[59] The most innovative part was the ambulatory, due to which "the whole church shines thanks to the marvelous, constant light coming through the transparent panes of glass."[60]

Suger had himself portrayed in one of the panes, which fortunately survives; he in turn holds in his hand a pane on which appears the Tree of Jesse (figure 20). The shoot that sprang from the loins of Jesse was interpreted, in medieval exegesis, as the prophetic annunciation of the incarnation of Christ (on the basis of Isaiah 11:1–2 and 7:14); in the images (figure 19), a majestic tree emerges from the sleeping prophet, its branches

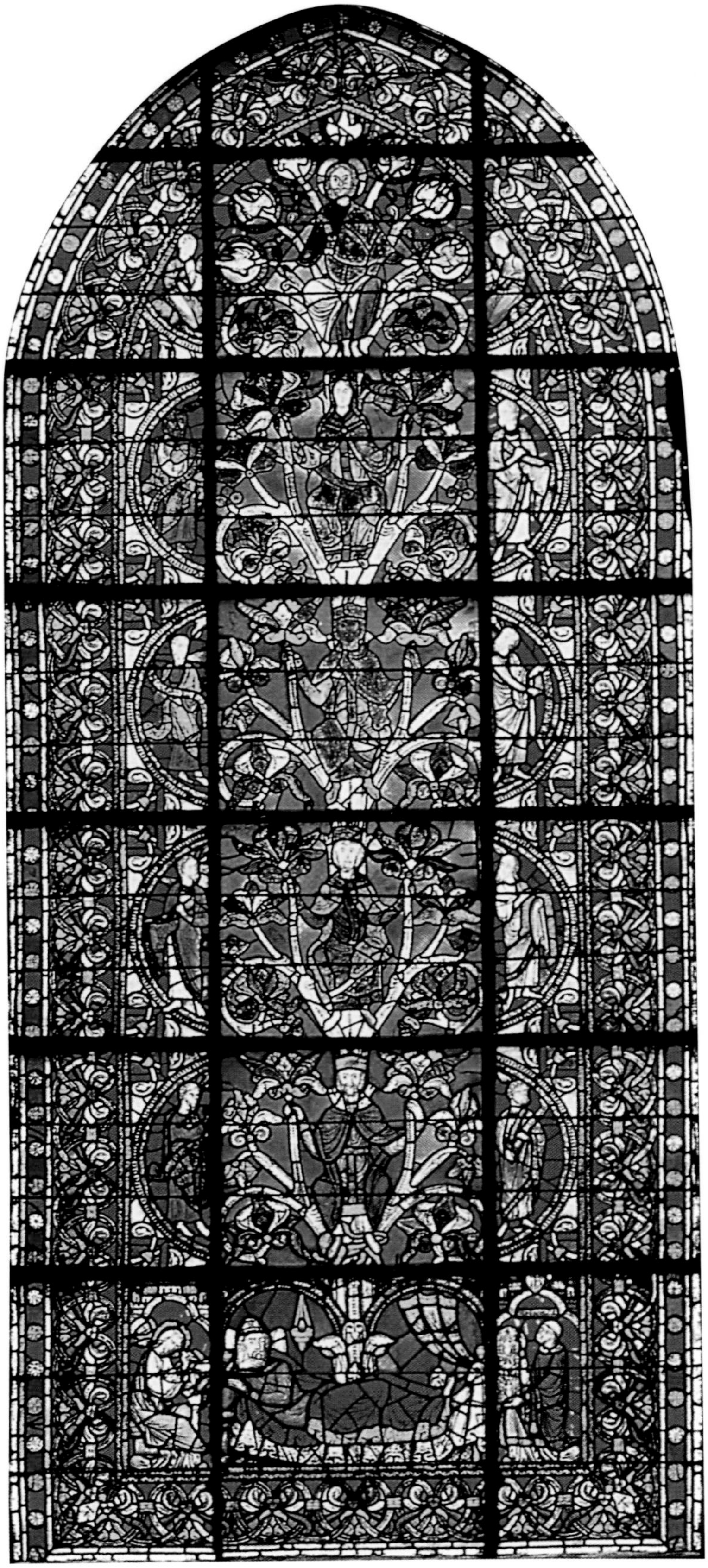

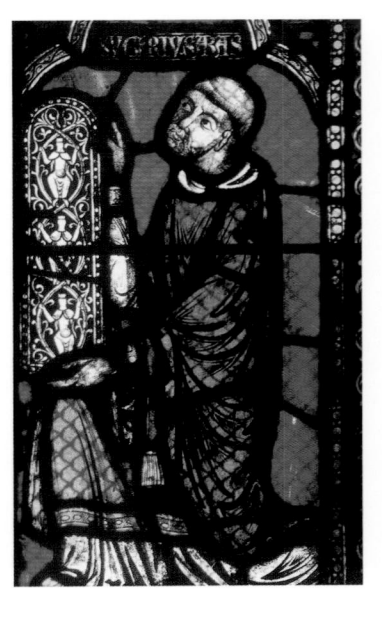

FIGURE 19 *The Tree of Jesse.*
Stained-glass window, c. 1145.
Saint-Denis (Paris), Abbey Church

FIGURE 20 *The Abbot Suger*
Offers a Windowpane.
Stained-glass window, c. 1145.
Saint-Denis (Paris), Abbey Church

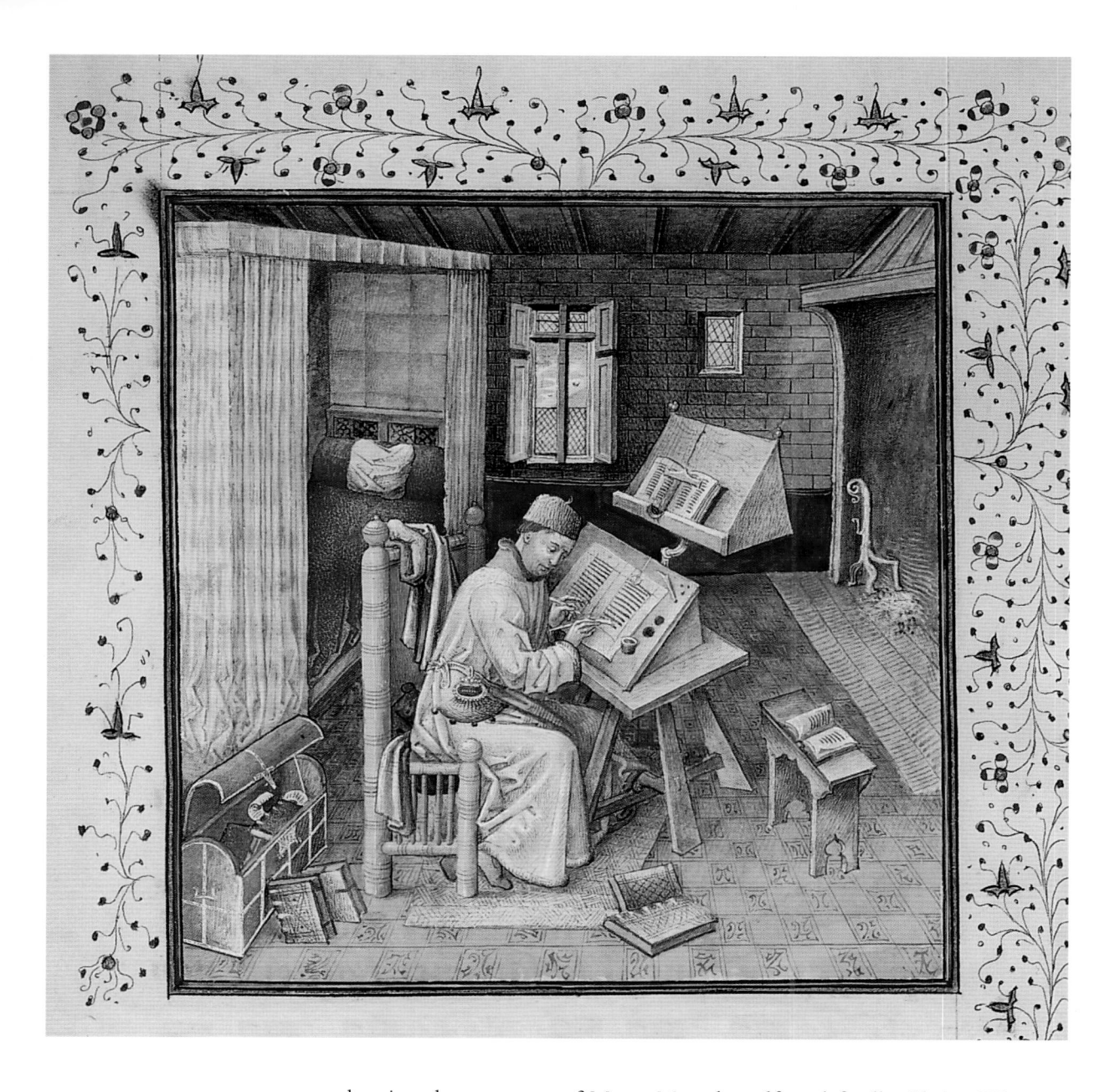

bearing the ancestors of Mary, Mary herself, and finally Christ. What we have here is a family tree of a special kind (because of the thorny problem of accommodating Joseph, for one thing), which nevertheless shows how important it was to be able to trace a lineage back to its founder.[61] Even to visualize the "shadow of our forefathers"[62] was entirely a medieval innovation. The use of family trees spread widely as members of the nobility, who achieved undisputed hereditary status by the twelfth century, found themselves obliged to document their line of descent through ordered branching charts of successive generations.

In the late fourteenth and early fifteenth centuries, glass began to appear in the windows of city buildings, first in the imposing houses of the rich, called *palazzi* in Italian, then in the houses of the comfortably well-off. (In

the countryside, glass greenhouses facing south protected flowers against frost.[63]) For the first time it was possible to look out beyond the window-frame, which before that was usually covered by a wooden shutter or a piece of waxed cloth. Though the glass used was not as translucent as the modern sort, it still created a passageway to the world outside, making it possible to work longer and more comfortably inside the house, in warmer rooms lit by natural light.

Let's take a look at Jean Miélot, who functioned as assistant and translator to Philip the Good, duke of Burgundy (1419–1467), in the room that served as his bedchamber and study[64] (figure 21). The warmth of the crackling fire is retained by the glazed windows, which the sunlight turns to gold as it pours through them into the room. Jean Miélot, who wants to feel good and warm, has put on a heavy gown lined with fur and covered his head with a woolen cap, and is resting his feet on a woven mat. He is hard at work, surrounded by manuscripts and holding a pen and a scraper; a piece of lead, as usual, holds the page of the manuscript from which he is copying firmly open on a movable reading stand, and there is a magnifying lens above the page on which he is writing.

The glazed windows are not, however, the only thing we can spot that is new in this room, which is full of medieval inventions. The fireplace is one of them, for although the ancient Romans used complex heating systems in their public baths, with tubes of hot water running under the floor tiles, they made do with simple braziers in the small, dark rooms of their houses. We can only begin to picture the crackling of burning wood in a handsome fireplace in a few private homes belonging to the very, very rich in the thirteenth century, while in the fourteenth fireplaces spread to the houses of those who were simply well-off. But they never arrived in the humble dwellings of the peasants, who had to fill their rooms with smoke in order to keep warm. In comfortable urban houses the hood of the fireplace not only channeled the smoke into the chimney but also reduced the risk of the fire spreading out of control. Since wood was used everywhere in the construction of multistory medieval houses, the best place for the kitchen was on the top floor, right under the roof. Pity the poor women who were forced to drag logs and bundles and water and food up one flight of stairs after another in such houses! Even a man might have to trudge up and down quite a bit before finding someone to welcome him. That's what happened to Ferrantino degli Argenti, one of the characters in a novella of Franco Sacchetti, who got soaked in a sudden rainstorm:

> Sticking his head in one door after another, and climbing the stairs, he went about poking into other people's houses and brazenly trying to find a fire at which to dry himself off. Going from one to another, by chance he came upon a door, entered, and went up. In the kitchen he found a large fire with two full pots, and a spit of

capons and partridges, and a beautiful young servant girl who was turning them while they roasted.[65]

Ferrantino was very lucky to come across a young maiden, for most often the keepers of the kitchen were elderly women no longer able to busy themselves about the house, and with their youthful beauty gone, confined to "watching the ashes around the fireplace" and "telling stories to the cat and counting the pots and pans."[66]

Even the cat is a medieval animal, in the sense that although it was known in the ancient world and turns up—sporadically—in ancient art, it became common in the West only in the early Middle Ages. Like the horse (to which we shall return), the cat is at home in two different stylistic registers: the cultivated word for it, *musio*, was used by clerics writing in Latin[67] and does not appear all that often. In the register of popular speech, the word *cattus* is attested from the fifth century and leads to our word *cat* (and the cognate terms in the modern European languages: *gatto*, *gato*, *chat*, *Katze*). The fact that the word *cattus* prevailed indicates that the domestic feline became widely known rather later than earlier. Householders must have begun to appreciate the cat more when the redoubtable black rat first appeared in Europe (perhaps in the eleventh century), for cats were willing to take it on. And at around the same time, crusaders returning from the Holy Land began to bring back feline specimens of great beauty, for example the ones called *soriani* in Italian (from Syria, which was called Sorìa in the Middle Ages).[68]

While dogs hunted outside and were only rarely welcomed inside domestic walls, the doors were thrown open to the cats, for they were chasers of mice, and they were permitted to roam where they pleased, even (no doubt to their satisfaction) in the dining room. For the painter Stefano di Antonio (1407–1438) it was perfectly natural to include a couple of cats, who are eyeing the tidbits scattered on the floor (figure 22), in the drama of the *Last Supper*. All but one of the apostles are sitting upright; only John has allowed his head to sink almost to the table and seems to be asleep, resting on the breast of Christ. There is an iconographic misunderstanding here, deriving from the lines of the gospel of John (13:23–25) that recount the moments just after Christ has announced to the assembled guests that there is a traitor among them. The evangelist writes: "One of his disciples, whom Jesus loved [i.e., John himself] was reclining in the lap of Jesus. Simon Peter made a sign to him and said to him, 'Who is it he speaks of?' And he, leaning close to the breast of Jesus, said to him 'Lord, who is it?'"

We can understand (as Stefano di Antonio did not) the true sequence of events in this dialogue if we remember that, like the Greeks and the Romans, Jesus and the apostles were eating in a reclining position, resting on

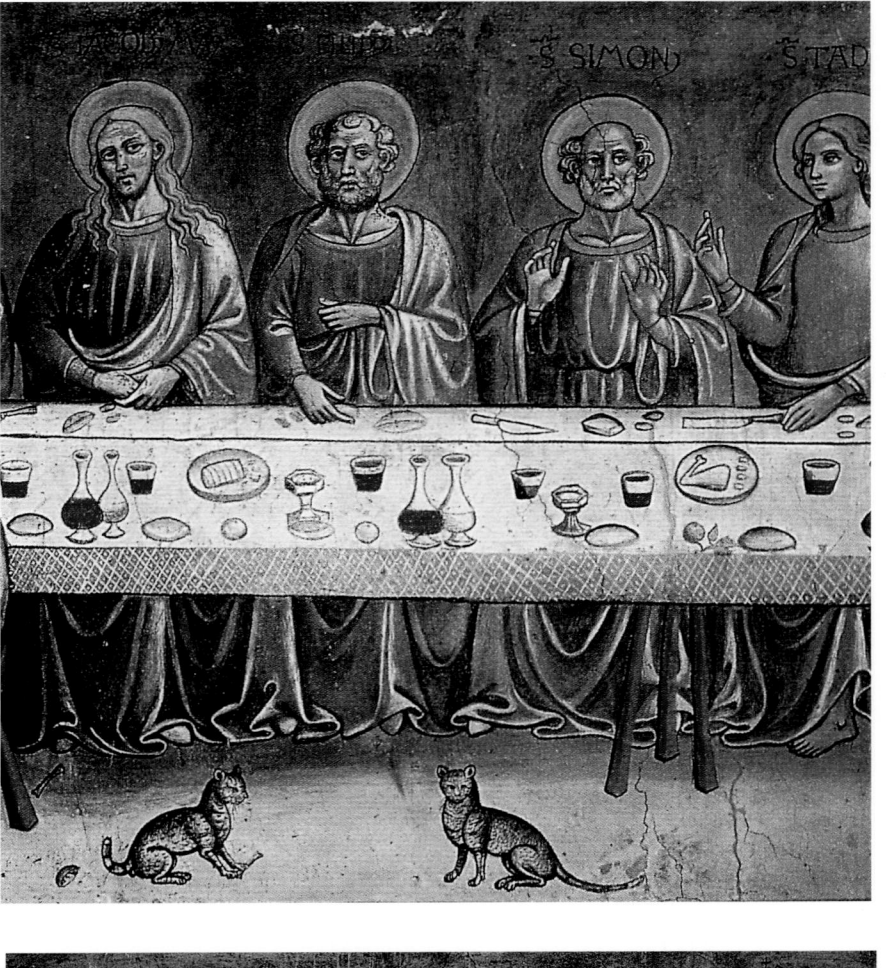

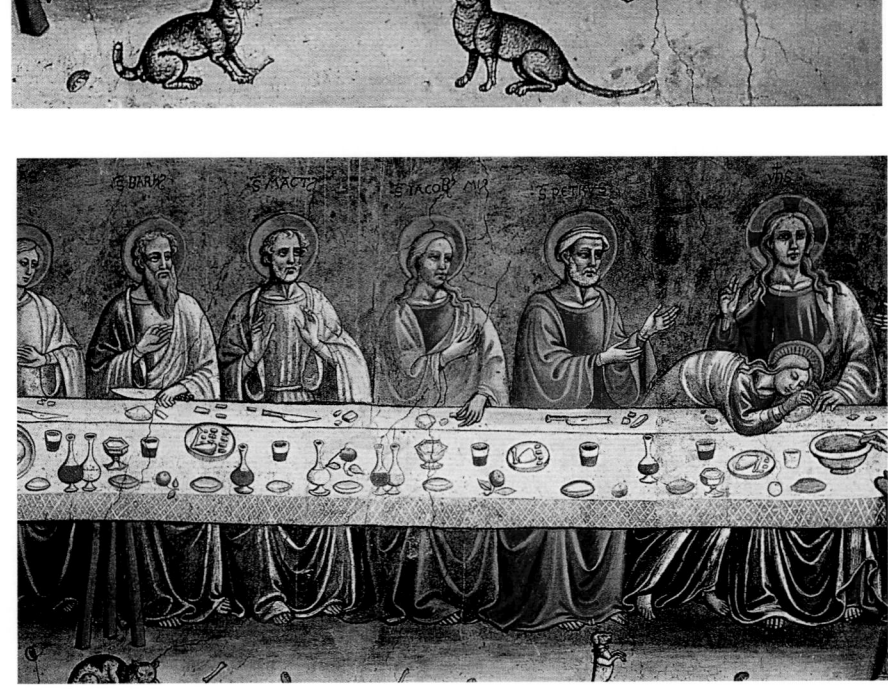

FIGURE 22
Stefano di Antonio
(1407–1438), two
details from *Last Supper*.
Fresco. Cercina (Florence),
Sant'Andrea

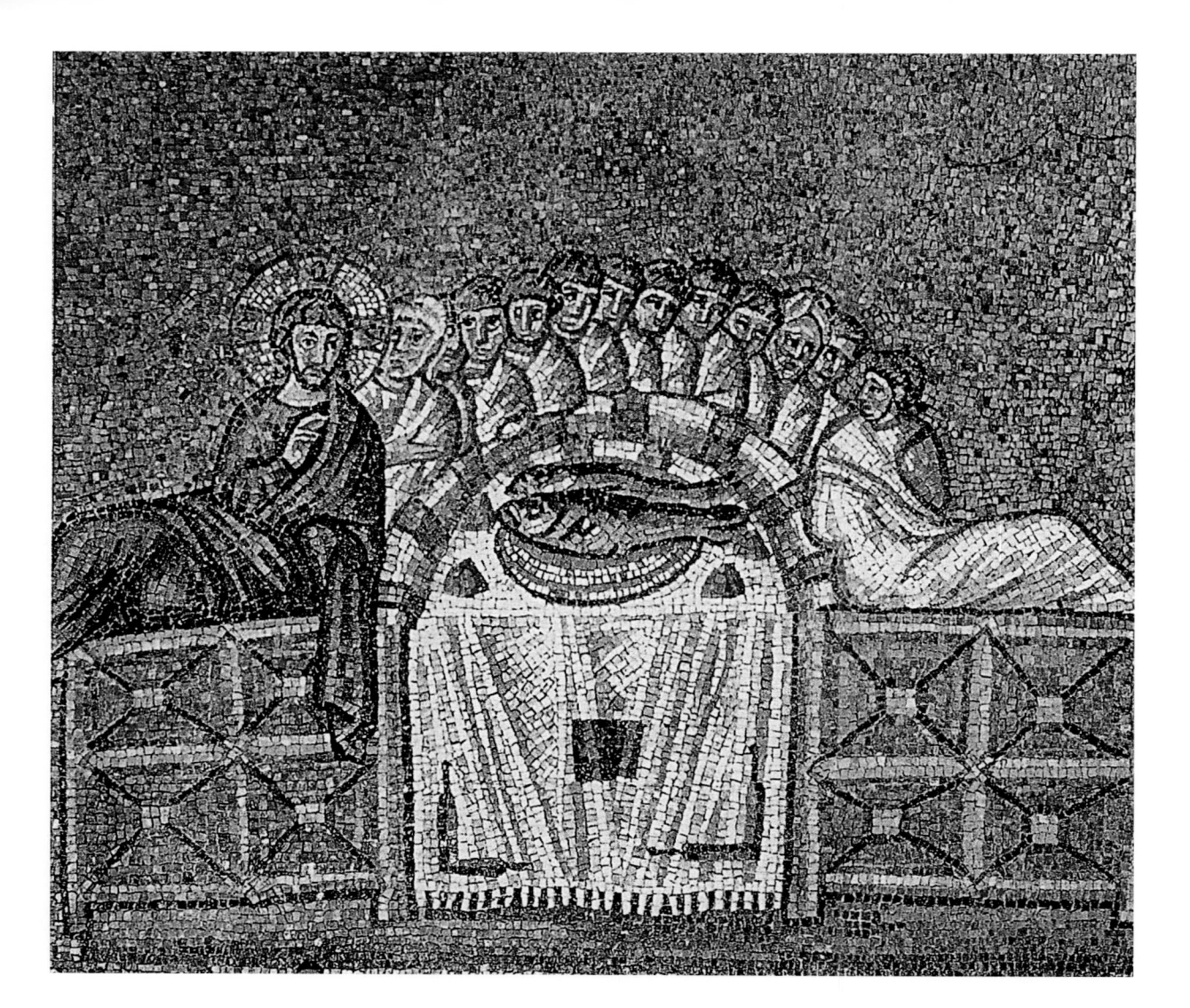

FIGURE 23 *Last Supper.*
Mosaic, sixth century. Ravenna,
Sant'Apollinare Nuovo

their left elbow. Peter was lying in the place of honor, to the left of Jesus, and John was lying to his right, so that Peter could make a gesture to John over their master's shoulder, and John in turn, by rolling his head back a little, was in a position to whisper the question discreetly in Christ's ear. But the custom of banqueting while reclining on couches, widespread in classical antiquity, disappeared with the arrival of the Germanic peoples: our way of eating at table goes back to the dawn of the Middle Ages. By the time of the composition of the mosaics of S. Apollinare Nuovo at Ravenna, at the beginning of the sixth century, Christ and Judas are still depicted reclining on a couch (a *stibadium* perhaps), but the true significance of all the phrases in the gospel, the complex play of glance and gesture, were no longer fully understood (figure 23).[69]

In only one—rather obvious—case did a meal taken in bed continue to be represented: when John the Baptist is born, or the Virgin Mary, the two mature mothers, Elizabeth and Ann respectively, are brought food to re-

store their strength by their friends, so they do not have to leave their beds. It is even possible to find a little table set up on top of the inevitable long low chest, in an inadvertent reconstruction of the iconography of the classical banquet: for example, in the *Birth of the Virgin* painted by Ugolino di Prete Ilario between 1370 and 1380 in the cathedral of Orvieto (figure 24). The setting is a typical fourteenth-century room, to which a pair of cats, ready to pounce, give a touch of easy familiarity.

But let us resume the visit we were paying to the solitary, silent Jean Miélot. The books lying about everywhere, even on the floor, are so much a part of our everyday reality that it needs a certain effort to recall that they too were an invention of the Middle Ages.[70] The Romans wrote on leaves of the papyrus plant. These leaves were glued together in a row and then

FIGURE 24
Ugolino di Prete Ilario,
Birth of the Virgin.
Fresco, 1370–1380.
Orvieto, Duomo

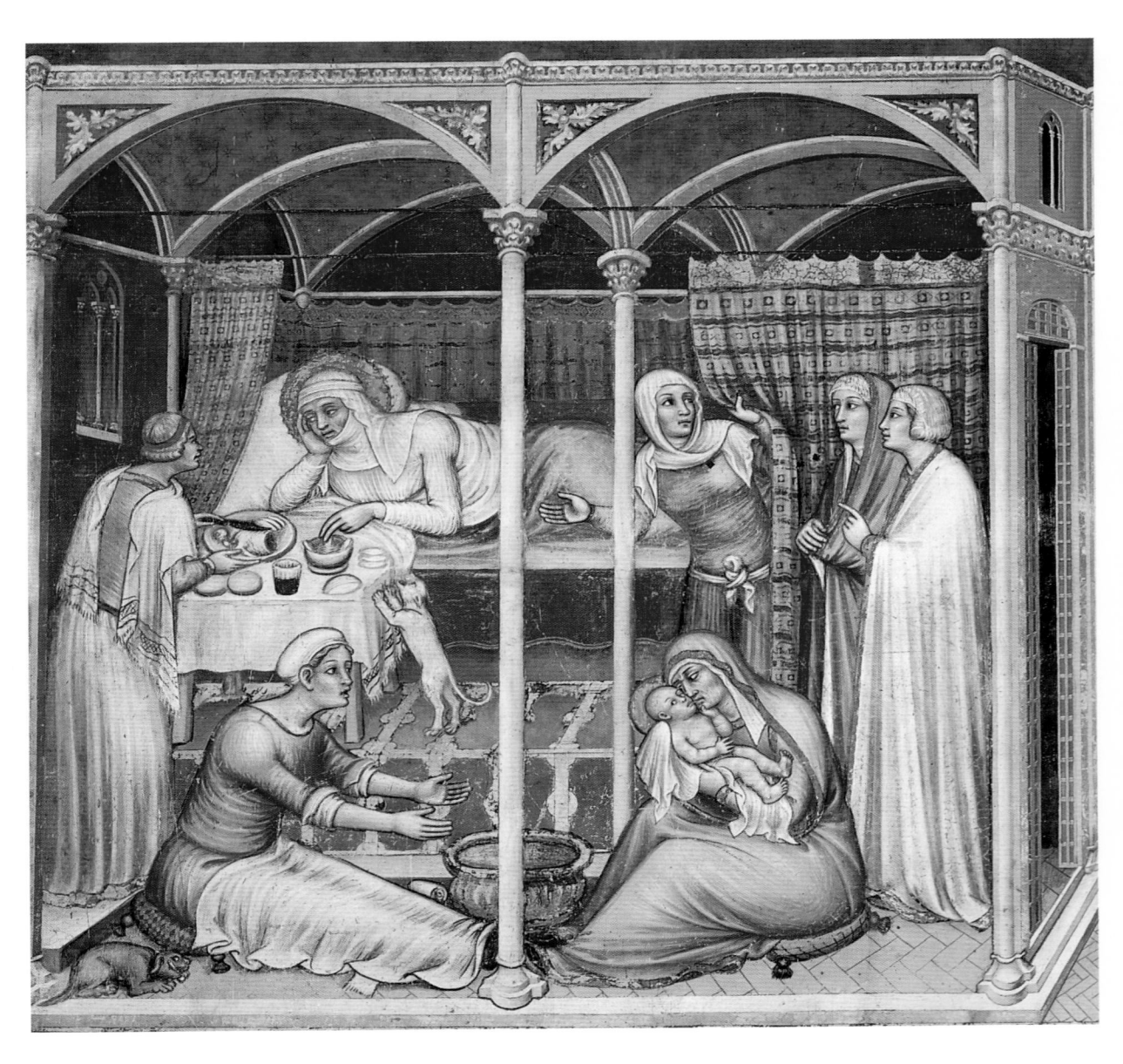

rolled up into a large scroll called a *volumen* (from the Latin *volvere*, to wrap). The papyrus scroll was difficult to read, and if you wanted to look something up, you might have to unwind it right to the end to find the item you were after. The very nature of the support made illustrations difficult and permitted only one side to be written on.

The Middle Ages used very different supports: first parchment, and then from the twelfth century on, paper produced from recycled rags. Parchment was made from the skin of calves, or more often from that of sheep and goats; the skin was tanned and subjected to a series of operations to make it soft, smooth, thin, and white. Then the skin was cut into sheets; these were normally folded twice to produce a quarto sheet with four pages on each side. These were gathered into fascicles, sewn together, and bound inside hard protective covers, and the result was the manuscript codex—essentially the book as we know it. You could write on both sides of a piece of parchment, although the outer side from which the animal's hair had once protruded was always rougher and darker. The beautiful miniature illustrations that make "the pages beam" ("ridon le carte," *Purgatorio* 11.82) were usually painted only on the inner side, which was much brighter and softer, allowing the ink and the colors to be applied evenly. Such manuscripts not only consumed numerous livestock—for a large Bible a whole flock of sheep was required—but demanded a lot of time and a lot of careful labor to make. Not only were they costly, they were meant for a literate elite, since for a long time they were written only in Latin. Monks, as we know, needed books in order to meditate and attend to their liturgical duties: even in the cloister, they could turn to God with codex in hand, for there were niches, opportunely placed, that functioned as miniscule libraries (figure 25). The work of the monks consisted principally of transcribing sacred texts, a task that constituted a slow and continuous form of prayer.

So what did people use for making quick memoranda, rough drafts, accounts, literary scribbles, love poems, hasty notes while listening to sermons or university lectures—in sum, for all those things that were not meant to be kept for long? Ever since antiquity, waxed tablets had filled this need.[71] Even Charlemagne used them to try to learn to write,[72] though with limited success. This kind of support for script, which could easily be found even in private houses, constituted a valid alternative to expensive parchment, until the emergence of paper shouldered both of them to one side. The tablets were made of pieces of wood (or as a luxury item, ivory) in which a hollow was made and then filled with a layer of wax, the surface of which could be marked with a stylus of bone or metal. The writing area could be reused only by smoothing away whatever was written on it, using the rounded end of the stylus. We read in *Floire et Blancheflor* that some youngsters "when they went to school took tablets of ivory and

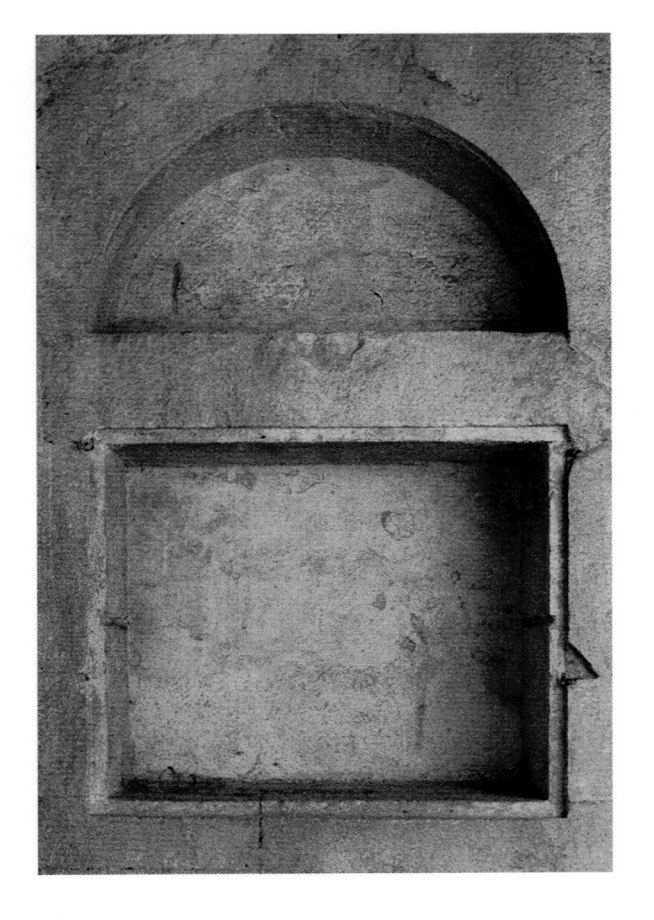

FIGURE 25 Niche for books in a cloister. Stonework, beginning of the thirteenth century. Fossanova (Latina), Abbey

traced on the wax letters or verses of love."[73] Sometimes the tablets, which, because they were rigid, functioned as both writing desk and manuscript at the same time, were themselves bound together to make a "book"; those that recorded important computations were especially likely to have their life prolonged in this way. So in the Middle Ages, along with parchment books, there were wooden books as well.

The birth of the written *volgare* or "vulgar tongue" in Italy (the first sample of which is probably the so-called "Indovinello veronese," a riddle from the second half of the eighth century; but the oldest secular lyric was composed only between 1180 and 1220[74]) broke the linkage between the culture of writing and religious culture, broadening the hitherto restricted circle of users of manuscripts. The urban takeoff and the evolution of political forms that led to the flowering of the communes brought new social actors to the fore. Society, no longer divided into the traditional threefold structure of the early Middle Ages (the clerics, the nobles, and those who labored, meaning the peasants) had to make room not just for artisans but also for merchants, jurists, teachers, bankers, and notaries. The members of these new occupations talked, bargained, amused themselves, engaged in disputes, tried to persuade and maybe even to cheat, if they were merchants. But above all, they wrote.

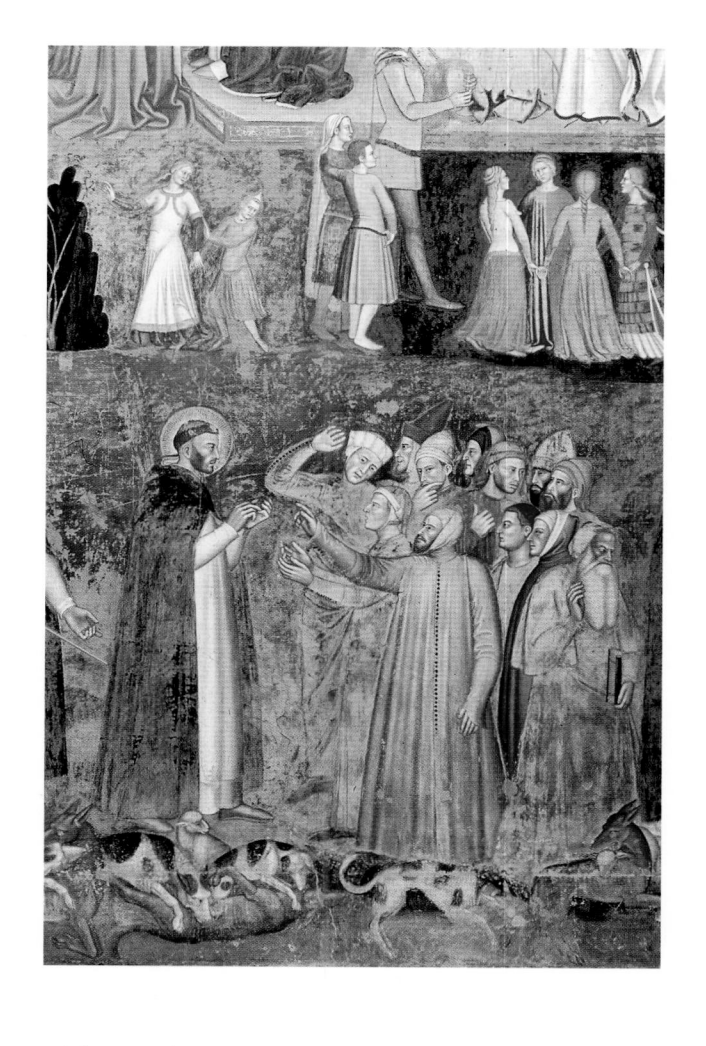

Making a Living with Book in Hand: The Universities

A new force arrived in the thirteenth-century cities: the mendicant orders of Dominican and Franciscan friars. They preached in the vulgar tongue and busied themselves with translating ancient texts from Latin, in line with their pastoral program of establishing close bonds with the faithful and creating a new consensus. The commitment to the study of the Bible in the monastic schools had resulted in a strong conservatism and subservience to tradition, for the holy word could not be made the subject of debate. Schooling in the cities, in contrast, was based on disputation and sought contradictions so as to go beyond them; it nurtured the idea of progress.[75] Hence it is a gesture denoting the syllogism[76] that defines the apostolate of San Pietro Martire, engaged up to the moment of his death in disputing with the heretics, in the great fresco celebrating Dominican triumph in the Cappellone degli Spagnoli at Santa Maria Novella in Florence (figure 26).

"Today there are so many masters," declares our Dominican preacher Giordano da Pisa, "all the cities are full of them: so many preachers, and so

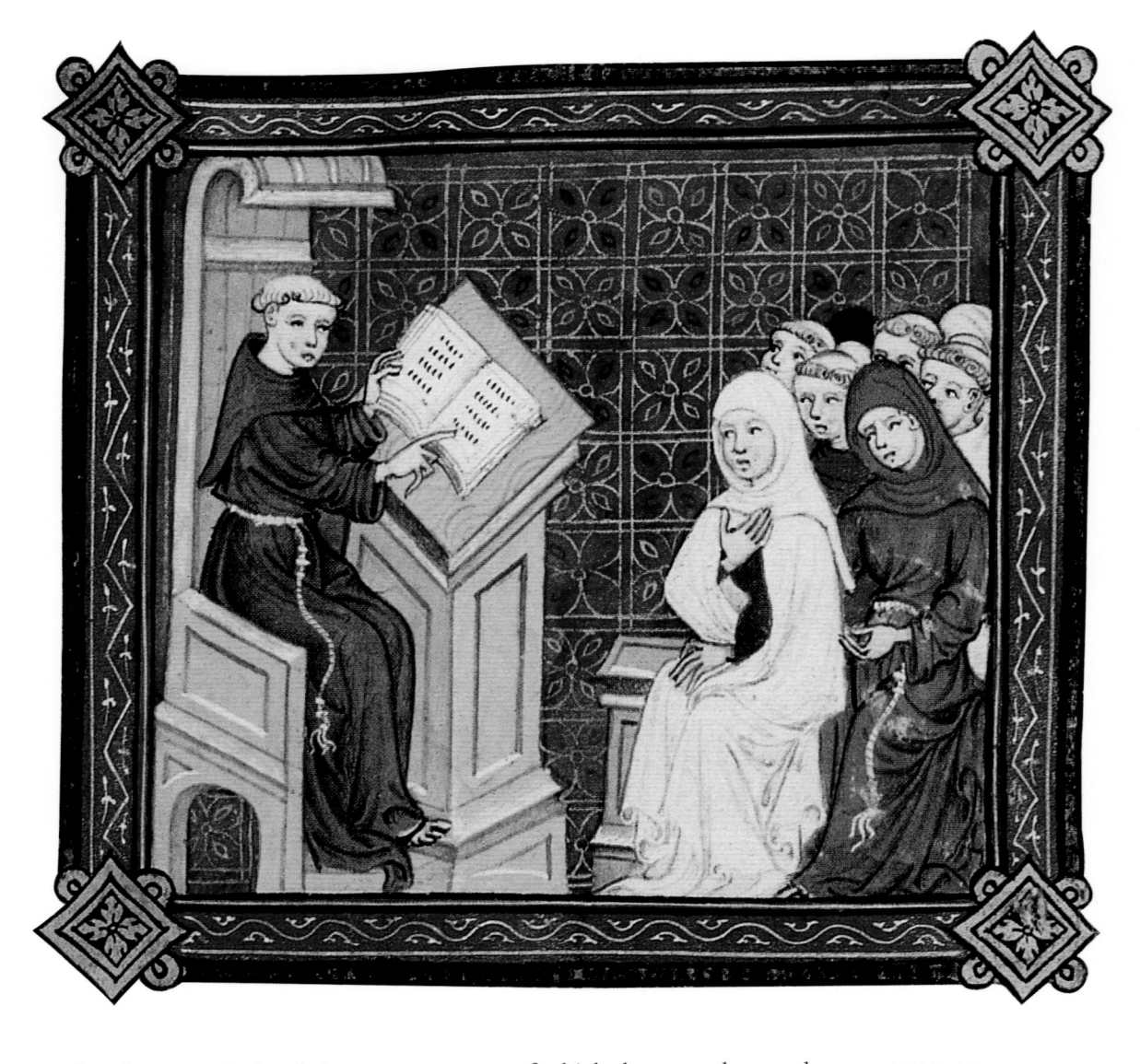

good and true; and schools in every convent, of which there are thousands, in which every day wisdom is sought, and clarified, and mastered." And as for books, "the religious orders, the friars, produce books every day; at Paris books are produced daily."[77] In a miniature of the fourteenth century (figure 27) we do indeed observe a Franciscan in the role of instructor, and among the audience, in the front row are seated a nun from the Poor Clares (recognizable by her sash) and another from the Carmelites.[78]

The urban schools produced a new class of people with intellectual training, and consequently a larger population of readers with the capacity to become copyists themselves, not as professionals perhaps, but simply in order to have their own copy of a text they cherished. Manuscripts were no longer confined within the walls of monastic *scriptoria* (copying rooms) where no one could acquire them: they circulated in a flourishing market of booksellers and customers.

FIGURE 27

A Franciscan Lecturing from a Professorial Chair.

Miniature, fourteenth century, from Nicholas de Lyra, *Postillae*. Reims, Bibliothèque Municipale, ms. 178, f. 1

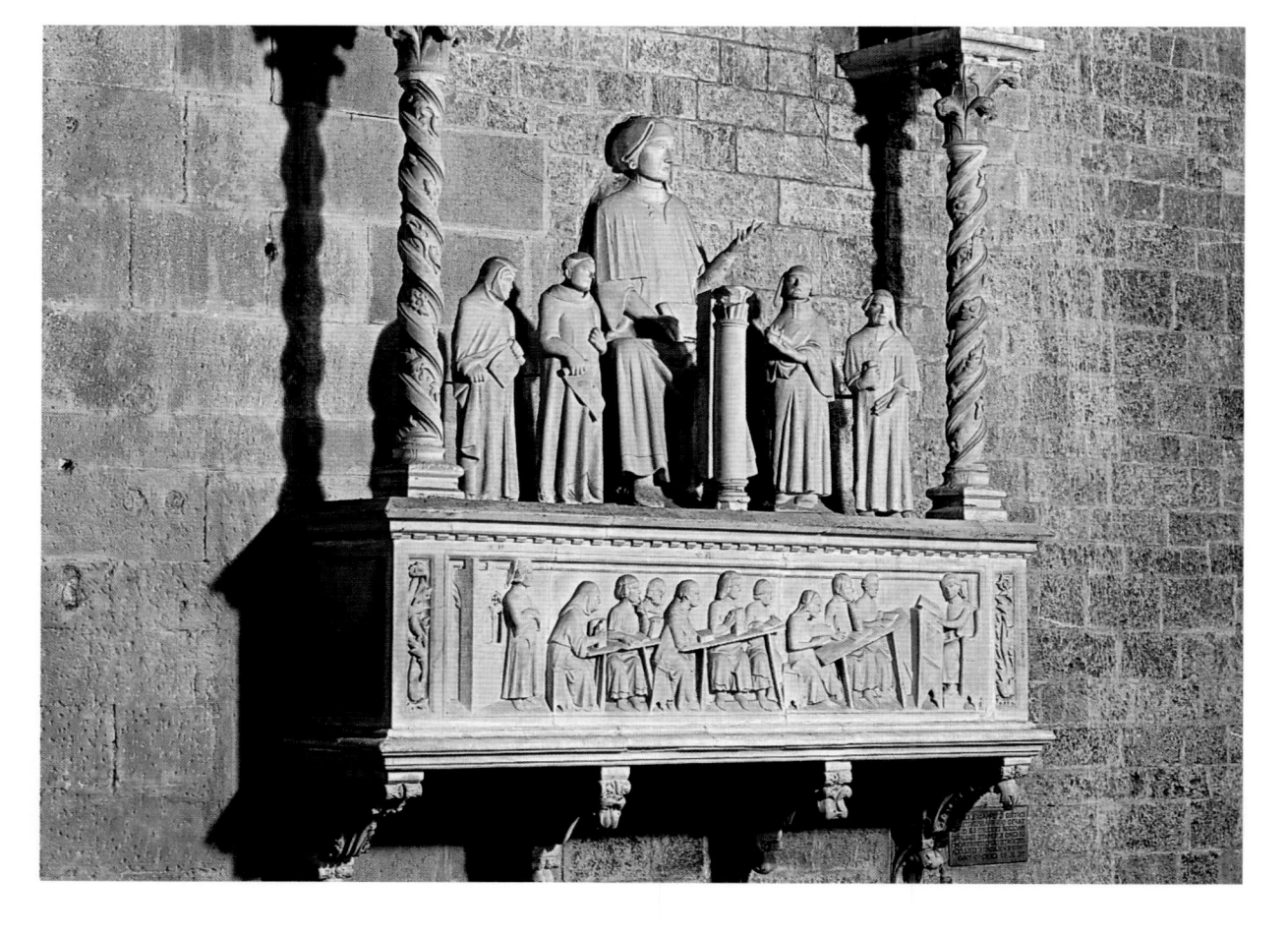

FIGURE 28
Tomb of Cino da Pistoia.
Sculpture, beginning of the
fourteenth century.
Pistoia, Duomo

A sign of growing esteem for the value of the urban professions is the spread of elaborate tombs commemorating teachers. The custom of publicly celebrating the most famous professors of the University of Bologna by dedicating large monumental tombs to them in city churches goes back a long way—the tomb of Matteo Gandoni is from 1330[79]—and indicates recognition of the public and social role of university teaching in drawing economic resources and prestige to the city.

In the tomb of the jurist Cino da Pistoia, in the city from which he took his name, a Sienese sculptor of the early fourteenth century carried off an audacious emulation of elements from Christian iconography (figure 28). In a lunette in a typical church doorway, the architrave beneath is dedicated to the narration of events, and the actual lunette itself to the devotional celebration of the sacred personage in question; an example (figure 29) is in Benedetto Antelami's baptistery of Parma, with the story of John the Baptist underneath and the Madonna enthroned in the lunette.[80] At Pistoia, Cino is first depicted on the "architrave" below lecturing to his students from his chair in a university lecture hall, and then again in the "lunette" above in a frontal position flanked by his learned audience, like Christ flanked by the apostles. The impression is reinforced too by the fact that in the latter group the figure of Cino is enlarged to gigantic propor-

tions, in accordance with a medieval convention that related the proportional size of figures to a scale of values—except that this difference in size is normally used to emphasize the difference between a towering saint or biblical character in a painting or sculpture, and the humble and minute human donor who commissioned it.

Even the poet Virgil is represented as a legal scholar in a statue from the first half of the thirteenth century at Mantua, the city that claimed to be his birthplace. On the façade of the Broletto, a municipal palace, we see him protecting the liberty of the commune (a protection taken so seriously that some important decisions could only be taken *ad sculpturam Vergilii*, literally in front of this sculpture), seated in a professorial chair in the act of writing, wearing the robes of a judge and a cap trimmed with costly fur of vair (figure 30).[81]

The life of teaching and study became a paid occupation, and time itself, which the Church had always declared could never be given or taken in exchange for anything else because it belonged to God, began to be treated as a commodity. The universities were born, an educational institution that was another innovation of the Middle Ages.[82] Free associations of students (*universitates scholarium*) and teachers (*universitates magistrorum*) were formed in cities that had had a local tradition of teaching ever since the eleventh century, like Paris and Oxford with their famous schools of theological studies. The most widely renowned masters of jurisprudence

FIGURE 29
Benedetto Antelami,
*The Virgin Enthroned, and
Stories of the Baptist.*
Sculpture, end of the twelfth
century. Parma, Baptistry

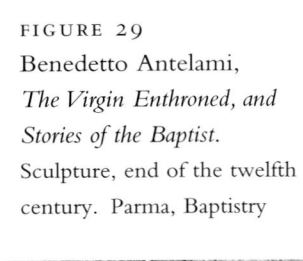

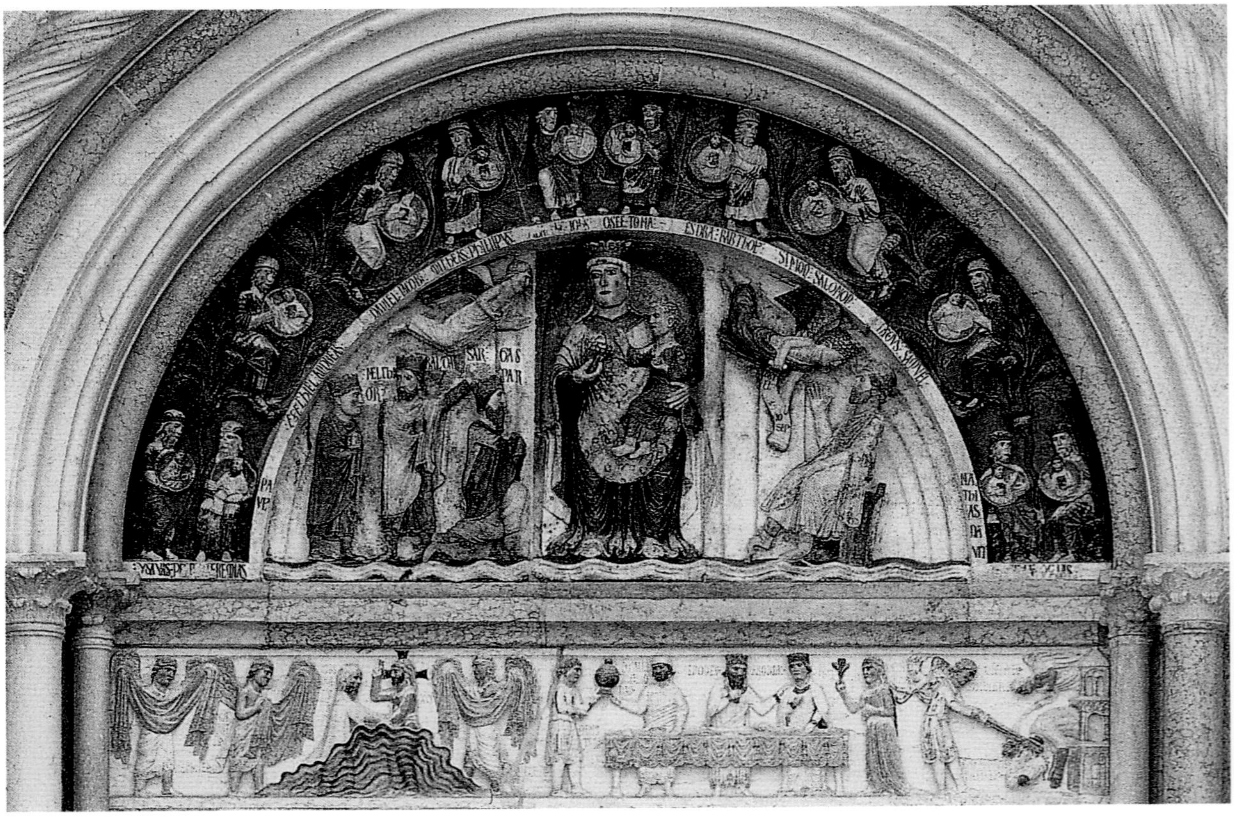

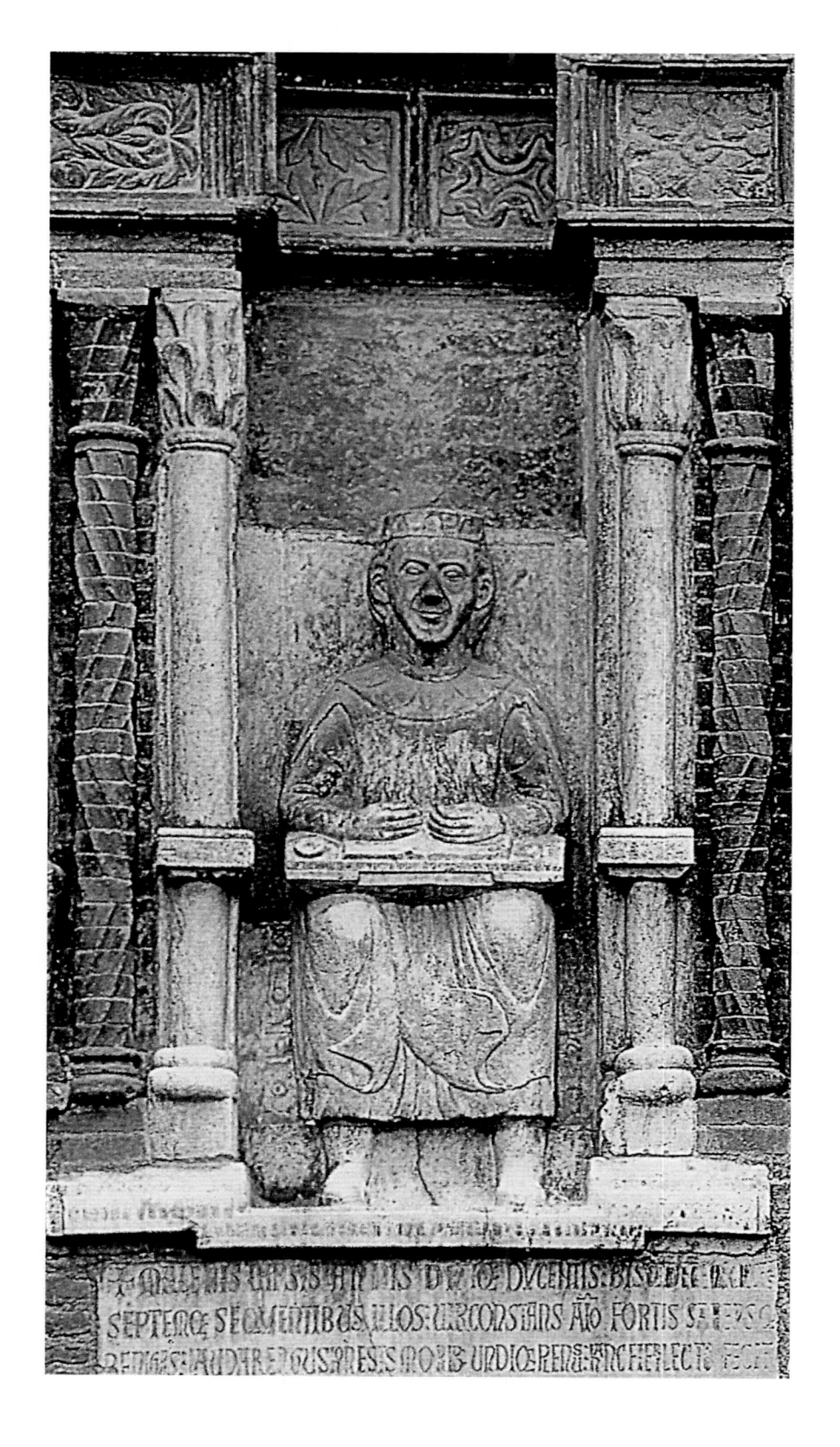

FIGURE 30
The Poet Virgil in the Guise of a Jurist.
Sculpture, first half of the thirteenth century. Mantua, Palazzo del Broletto

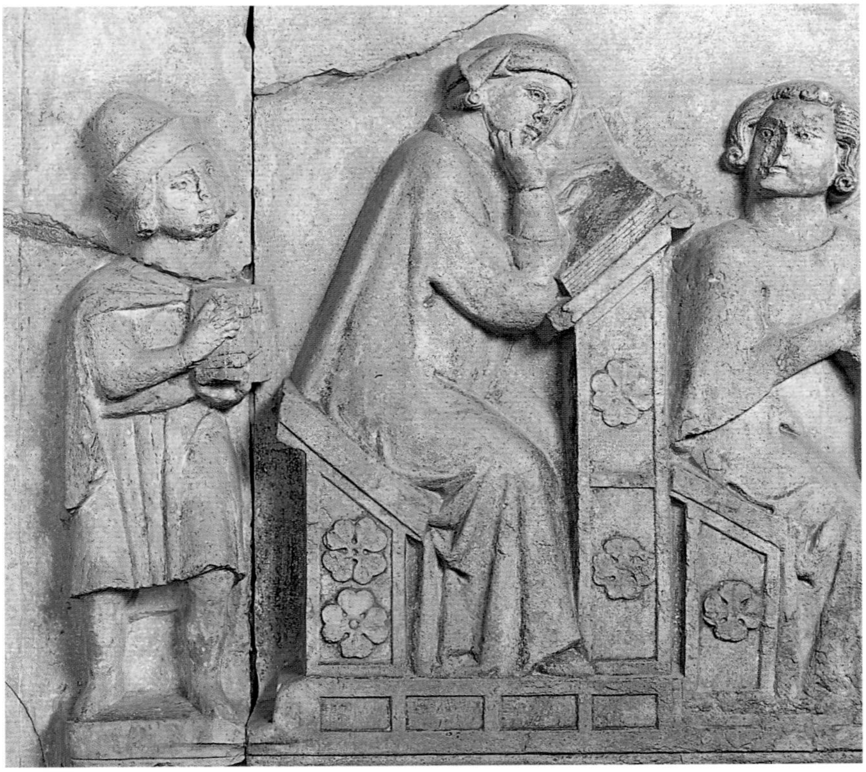

FIGURE 31
*The Beadle and the Student
Reading.* Detail from the
tomb of Matteo Gandoni.
Sculpture, 1330. Bologna,
Museo Civico Medievale,
Palazzo Ghisilardi-Fava

taught at Bologna, the city that contends with Paris for the title of the old-est university center. The whole complex of courses, with all the attendant activities of teaching and research, constituted the *Studium*, the medieval word for what we call a university today. At Paris and Oxford the *Studia* were integrated into the ecclesiastical structure and subordinate to the au-thority of the bishop, but at Bologna the *Studium* was entirely independ-ent of the Church, and in a position to deal with the commune (the city government) on an equal footing.

In the first place the *Studium* provided instruction (to those who had al-ready been schooled in Latin) in the fundamental areas of knowledge through courses in the liberal arts.[83] At the next level one could choose among theology, law, and medicine, though not every university offered the complete range of faculties. The various disciplines were in fact called faculties (*facultates*), just as they are today. At Paris the instructors were called *magistri*, while at Bologna they took the title of *doctor* to indicate their lofty status, or even *domini* (lords), an appellation of feudal origin giv-en only to the professors of law that shows us how much respect they en-joyed. The *bidello* or beadle in a modern Italian university is a member of the staff who helps to keep the place running, but the medieval *bedellus* was a much more important individual, who even had the authority to make sure that the professors were carrying out their teaching functions proper-ly. We see a *bedellus* bringing a book into the lecture hall where the stu-dents are already assembled on the tomb of Matteo Gandoni, which was

originally located in the Church of San Domenico at Bologna and is now preserved at the Museo Civico Medievale (figure 31).

The number of *Studia* in Europe increased as popes and emperors, kings and princes promoted new foundations, driven by the need to find greater numbers of personnel qualified to do what we call office work. In 1155 Frederick Barbarossa had already conceded various privileges to a delegation of Bolognese instructors and students who had come to meet him while he was en route to Rome to be crowned emperor. The celebrated Sorbonne, endowed with its own rich library, was founded in Paris by the canon Robert de Sorbon (1201–1274) with decisive help from Louis XI (1226–1270). In 1224 Frederick II founded a *Studium* at Naples, since he did not want his subjects to have to leave his kingdom to study elsewhere.

The presence of a *Studium* brought great distinction to the city that hosted it, and provided the opportunity for the civil administration and the parallel ecclesiastical bureaucracy to recruit locally the trained personnel and the jurists they increasingly required. Lodging the students and supplying all their practical and academic needs offered the citizens a range of opportunities to make a profit as well, and they also gained the chance to have their own sons educated, opening the door to prestigious careers. All these reasons explain the proliferation of universities in the Middle Ages, despite the fact that the students, the majority of them outsiders, created a number of problems. They were often very turbulent, and it was almost impossible to employ strong measures against them because of the privileges they possessed: automatically enjoying the status of clergy, they were able to escape the ordinary justice system by appealing to the ecclesiastical courts. Grown men, flush with money (it was the students who bore the main cost of their professors' salaries, and an endless list of other taxes and duties too), they did not dedicate all their time to study. On the contrary, if we can believe the accusations, they passed a good deal of it in the taverns, drinking, playing games of chance, quarreling, and frequenting women of ill repute. Here is how the preacher and writer Jacques de Vitry recalled them:

> They were always fighting and engaging in scuffles, and not just on account of the different subjects they were studying, or some topic of debate; the differences among the various nationalities were also a source of dissent, hatred, and virulent rancor, and they shamelessly abandoned themselves to every sort of challenge and reciprocal insult. They asserted that the English were drunkards and had tails; that the French were supercilious, effeminate, and as fussy as women about their clothing. They claimed that the Germans were ferocious and bestial at their banquets, the Normans vain and boastful, the Potevins traitors and unfailing scoundrels. Burgundians were considered stupid and vulgar. Bretons were reputedly inconstant and voluble, and were often charged with the death of Arthur.[84] The

Lombards were characterized as money-grubbing, vicious, and cowardly; the Romans as seditious troublemakers and slanderers; the Sicilians as domineering and cruel; the Brabantines as bloodthirsty and quick to burn, wreck, and snatch things; the Flemish as fickle, megalomaniac, greedy, as spineless as butter, and indolent. And when they had exchanged insults of this kind, they often passed from words to blows.[85]

And for further testimony, let us listen to a stylized rendition of the words of a father writing to a son who was studying at Bologna at the end of the thirteenth century:

> Your great madness makes my heart ache. You have left aside all the things you ought to be doing at university, and I have it on good authority that you take pleasure in nothing but playing at dice, and that you often visit the most disreputable places. For this reason, if you do not cease this kind of behavior and apply yourself strongly to your studies, as you are supposed to do, you should know that you will lose all my support and all my grace; and also that you cannot deceive me with your phoney letters.[86]

On the other hand, a father might become overanxious if he learned that his son was studying too hard, and write him a letter of a completely different tenor, as in this example:

> They tell me that, unlike everyone else, you get out of bed before the first bell sounds in order to study, that you are the first into the classroom and the last to leave it. And that when you get back home you spend the whole day going over what you were taught in your lessons. You are thinking of them while you eat, and even in sleep you dream about what the professor said and repeat the lectures, moving your tongue unconsciously. . . . But you ought to remember that if you force something to expand to the limit it will burst, and that you have to learn to tell the difference between too much and too little. Nature condemns both and demands moderation. Many people make themselves permanently ill through excessive study; some of them die, and others, their humoral essence dispersed, waste away day after day, which is even worse. Others actually lose their minds and spend the rest of their days either laughing or sobbing. Yet others ruin the optic nerve through which the rays of vision pass and become blind. So I beg you, my son, to find the golden mean in your studies, because I don't want to have someone say to me, "I hear your son has come back wearing the garland of knowledge," and have to reply "He has indeed gained a

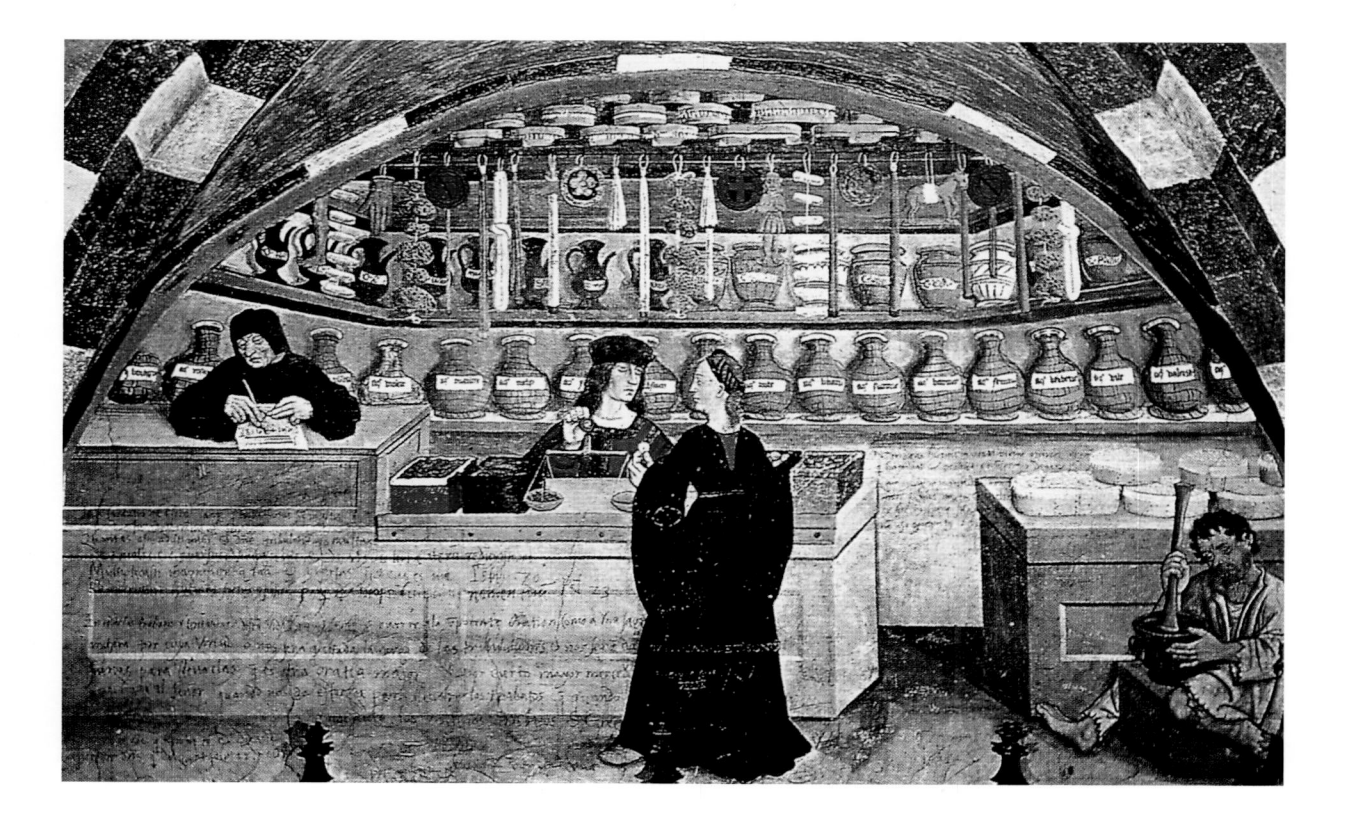

doctorate, but he studied so much that he died," or "He's hope-lessly ill," or "He has lost his sight," or "Yes, but now he's out of his mind."

In sum, if this poor father were to employ more down-to-earth lan-guage, he might have used the Italian proverb "Better a live donkey than a dead doctor."[87]

"To sleep, to dream, perchance to die"[88]: *The Effects of Anesthesia*

Can we at least assume that a living doctor did prolong the lives of his pa-tients in the Middle Ages? Not always, for the medical repertoire includ-ed reckless mixtures, risky surgical procedures, ignorance of the norms of hygiene, and overgenerous doses of anesthetics like opium, mandrake root, common henbane, and hemlock, in which "somniferous sponges" were soaked and then used to daze the patients during operations.[89] We see an example from the beginning of the fifteenth century in a fresco from the Castle of Issogne in Val d'Aosta depicting a pharmacy (figure 32): the goods on offer include a bunch of sponges strung together and suspended like sausages from a pole; they have probably been medicated in advance and are ready to use.

In the ancient world no one conceived that there was a need for anesthesia. Celsus, writing in A.D. 30, describes in great detail the extraction of a bladder stone, in this case from a boy, and takes care to explain that during the operation it was necessary to hold the patient very tightly: two stout fellows were assigned to keep those who actually had the patient in their grip from losing their balance and tumbling on top of the doctor and the youth.[90] There was blood all over the place, and the screams of agony must have been dreadful. In a certain sense the operation corresponded to a performance, like a fight between gladiators. It was because the manifestation of physical pain was considered a form of entertainment that the ancient world was quite indifferent to suffering. But for the Middle Ages, suffering posed a problem. A good example is a novella of Boccaccio featuring a doctor from Salerno named Mazzeo della Montagna, who is getting ready to operate on a patient with a gangrenous leg:

> The doctor, deeming that by reason of the pain it was not possible for the patient to endure the treatment without being doped ["senza essere adoppiato," i.e., without being given opium], caused to be distilled in the morning a certain water of his own concoction, whereby the patient, drinking it, might be ensured sleep during such time as he deemed the operation, which he meant to perform about vespers, would occupy.[91]

A real doctor, however, Guy de Chauliac, recommended great care when using anesthetics because of the risk of total narcosis in his *Chirurgia magna* of 1363: the patients went under and stayed under all right, but reviving them was problematic, for some went out of their minds and some never woke up at all. Only the great Paracelsus, at the end of the Middle Ages, studied the use of ether as a narcotic, explaining how to produce it and experimenting with it on animals. His chickens fell unconscious when they were given "oil of vitriol" and woke up again unharmed, but Paracelsus did not risk the same experiment with human subjects, for fear that he would be unable to control the effects of total narcosis.

The University Book

Let's return to the student who risked not only missing his doctorate but becoming one of the "missing" himself, on account of studying too hard. Given his dedication, he wouldn't have been a habitué of bordellos and taverns. Instead we can imagine him paying frequent visits to the bookshop. The birth of the *Studia* not only stimulated a steep rise in the quantity of books produced, it also brought about a genuine revolution in the way manuscripts were made and used. Every student needed to have in

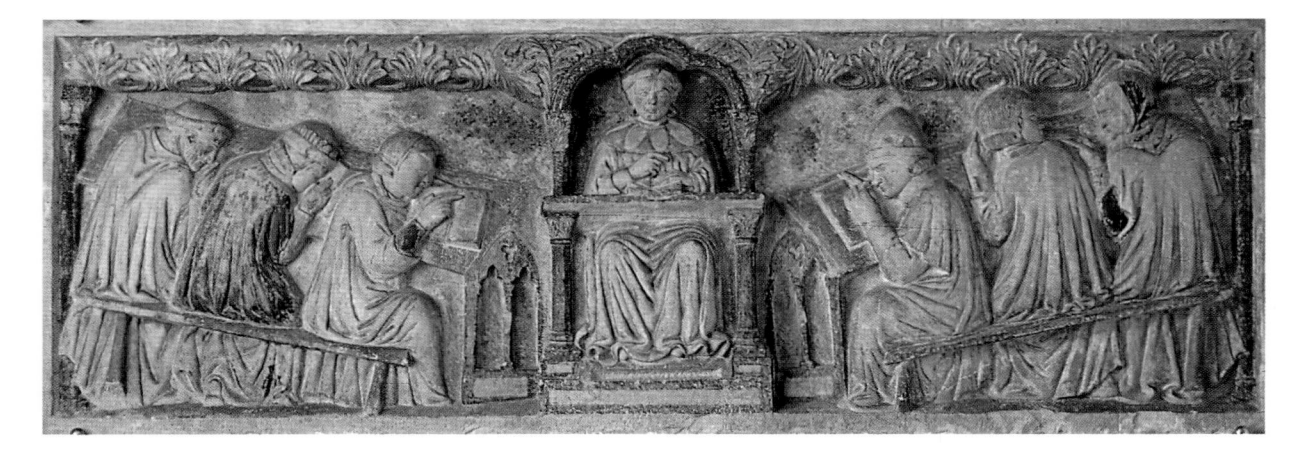

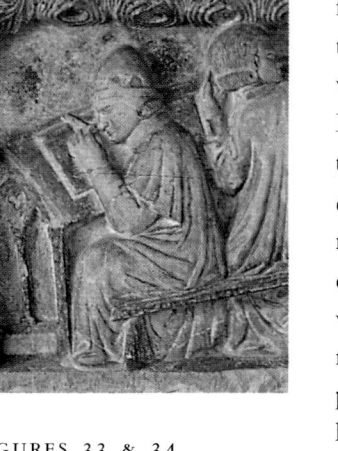

FIGURES 33 & 34
The Tomb of Bonifacio Galluzzi, and Students Reading (detail). Sculpture, 1346. Bologna, Museo Civico Medievale, Palazzo Ghisilardi-Fava

FIGURE 35
Two Notaries Record the Judge's Decision. Miniature, 1375. From the Statutes of the Commune of Bologna. Bologna, Archivio di Stato, Comune-Governo, Statuti, vol. xiii, f. 157r

front of him a copy of whatever text the professor was expounding on in the classroom, which created a demand for multiple copies of the same work. The response was a new method of production, the *pecia* system. Each course text was checked for errors by a committee of professors, and then an official copy, called an *exemplar*, was created. The fascicles of this *exemplar*, each containing the same number of pages and called a *pecia*, were not bound into a single book but were instead distributed to different copyists. The latter were mostly members of the laity, and not all of them were necessarily men: at Bologna, a university city with a bustling book market in the thirteenth and fourteenth centuries, a number of receipts for payment and contracts have been found that bear the names of female illuminators and calligraphers who worked along with their husbands or fathers, from whom they must have learned their trade.[92]

So the same manuscript was copied simultaneously by a number of different individuals—as many of them as there were *peciae* making up the *exemplar*. The copies were delivered to a *stationarius* (bookseller) who rented them out by turns to the students. This innovative system rapidly multiplied the number of available copies of the chosen books, and drastically reduced the cost of obtaining them.

On a carved slab from the sepulcher of a Bolognese *lector* (university professor) named Bonifacio Galluzzi, who died in 1346,[93] a few of the students shown in a lecture hall, one of them a friar, appear to be reading from the pages of a *pecia*, if we compare the thickness of the manuscripts they are holding at their desks with the manuscript of the teacher himself, seated at his *cathedra* (figures 33 and 34). The layout of the text on the page of a *pecia* was also distinctive: two columns, leaving wide margins for *glossae* or explanatory notes, and made visually user-friendly by the introduction of paragraphs and rubrics (initial letters in red ink, from *ruber*, the Latin word for red). Not only that, there were now spaces between the words, making it a lot easier to read and grasp the meaning of the text—the most obvious thing in the world to us, but a great advance from the early Middle Ages, when there were no breaks between the words.

et successionum ab intestato. Et pmo.
¶ De iure reddendo. Rubrica

exceptis diebus feriatis in dei honore ind...

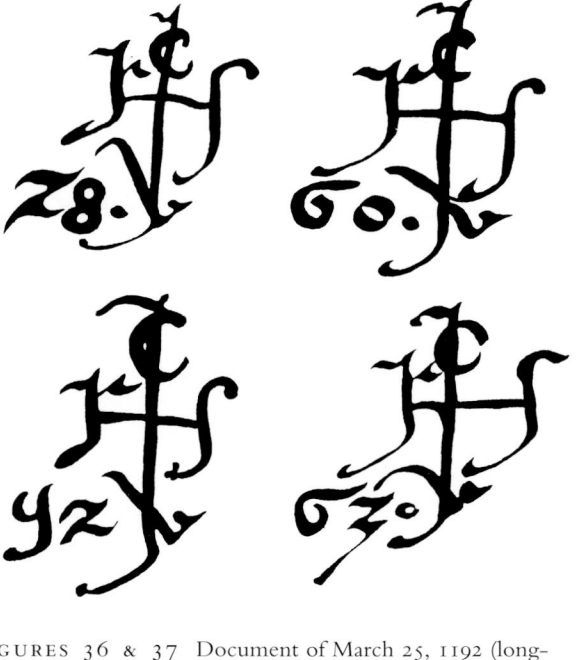

FIGURES 36 & 37 Document of March 25, 1192 (long-term lease of a property belonging to San Paolo di Reschio) on which the notary Raniero di Perugia has marked the number 60 (indicated by the red arrow on the left).

ABOVE: Four versions of Ranieri's seal containing the numbers 28, 60, 52, 63. Pen and ink drawings, dated October 8, 1194; March 25, 1192; November 5, 1187; December 1, 1188. perugia, archivio di stato, fondo corporazioni soppresse, diplomatico di santa maria di valdiponte, parchments 161, 153, 133, 143

In this connection, it is worth noting that the punctuation marks we take for granted only appeared about fifty years after the introduction of the printed book in the 1450s. The apostrophe; the word accents that are still used in the languages of continental Europe; the "stops" like the comma, the semicolon, the colon, and the period all appeared for the first time in Pietro Bembo's edition of the works of Petrarch for the publisher Aldo Manuzio in 1501, while the dot on the lower-case letter I was only introduced around 1450. And even today, in western societies with virtually universal literacy, it is still not easy for everyone to learn to write correctly.[94]

Making a Living with Pen in Hand: The Notaries

There was another professional figure in the Middle Ages who used the pen as readily as scribes and secretaries did, and that was the notary (figure 35). In some of the modern societies of continental Europe, especially Italy, the notarial profession still retains many traces of the juridical profile it acquired in the Middle Ages, while in North America similar functions are now carried out by lawyers.

Before the year 1000, the notary was the person who drafted the official documents emanating from a constituted power, like a king or a count or a bishop. Beginning in the twelfth century, in Italy especially, notaries took on a particular juridical role that made them one of the cornerstones of "communal" (i.e., urban) society: they were the ones who issued a guarantee of "public faith" whenever a written document was required to create a record of a private or public event. Though they still had to be nominated by a public authority, every notary became a public official himself, who not only drafted official documents but also authenticated them by adding his own distinctive professional mark.

The commune did not, however, establish a relationship of trust with the notary because of his membership in a professional category; each individual notary maintained the relationship of trust himself by producing, on demand, documents that were universally recognized as coming from his hand: that was the only thing that gave them legal force. For this reason his mark or *signum* was highly individualized, consisting of certain symbols that corroborated the signature with which he identified himself at the conclusion of every document he drew up; in a sense they "authenticated" the signature. These *signa* are often very elaborate, but the one developed by a former judge and notary, Raniero di Perugia, is not just a gratuitous flourish, for it conceals something that it is no exaggeration to call a coded language: a very early attestation of the knowledge of Arabic numerals in the West.

Beginning in 1184, Raniero began to count the lines of writing on the sheet on which he had written a document, and to include the number in

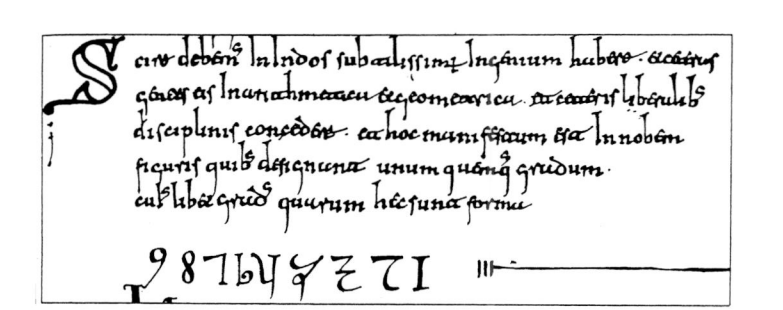

his *signum*, using the numerals from one to ten (figures 36 and 37). With this device he produced a mark that defied imitation and proved beyond the shadow of a doubt that the document was his. Raniero's *signa* were so exclusive that not all of his colleagues could even understand them at first, when they had to transcribe his documents: for example, a copy that was made of a parchment dated March 25, 1192 states that everything has been included "preter signa dicti notarii" ("except for the *signa* of the said notary," i.e., Raniero).[95]

Arabic Numerals and Zero

We are so accustomed to using the numerals of the so-called Arabic system that we find them utterly natural; obviously, however, they aren't. They are an invention that originated far away, in India, and that was picked up and developed by the Arabs in Spain before finally spreading to the rest of Europe: the first attestation is, in fact, a Spanish manuscript of 976 (figure 38).[96] The Romans used a numeric system that was useless for complex operations, even when it was adapted to the abacus, an instrument composed of small beads whose position could be shifted by moving them along metal wires. Addition and subtraction were possible, but it was extremely difficult to accomplish operations that seem elementary to us, like multiplication and division; for those, one had to resort to a professional mathematician. The Romans never did arrive at the idea that underlies the Arabic numerals, which is that any single number, including zero—itself an important discovery—has a different place value according to the position it occupies in a larger number. For example, in the number 222, the single number 2 represents successively two hundred, twenty, and two.

At the end of the twelfth century, a Pisan merchant named Leonardo Fibonacci ("fi Bonacci," or "son of Bonaccio"; he lived from 1170 to c. 1245) became professionally acquainted with some Arab colleagues whom he had met at Bejaïa near Algiers, where his father was a customs employee, and from them he learned the Arabic numerals we still use. Back in Italy, he first wrote about the new method in 1202 in a treatise entitled *Liber abbaci* (Abacus Book) and produced a definitive account of it in 1228.

Thanks to him the new system of numerals spread throughout Italy, and then throughout Europe. There is naturally a high school named after him in Pisa, which, since it is dedicated to a great figure in the history of mathematics who really existed, will never be subjected to the *damnatio memoriae* that toppled Salvino degli Armati, the "inventor of eyeglasses," from his pedestal.

The system introduced by Fibonacci, although greatly superior to the previous one based on the clumsy Roman numerals, had to overcome two prejudices before it could be accepted: for one thing, those numerals had been invented by infidels and might seem to offend the dominant religion; and for another, it might be easier to falsify commercial documents by making changes to the short strokes and gentle curves of the Arabic numerals, whereas the rigid perpendiculars of the Roman numerals were difficult to overwrite. Luckily, neither fanaticism nor traditionalism was able to block an invention that allowed the West to make extraordinary practical and scientific gains.

As well as the Arabic place value of numerals, Fibonacci introduced operations on whole and fractional numbers, trigonometry and algebra, into Europe. Yet he was not just a lucky popularizer but a real mathematical genius, so much so that for the next three centuries very little was added to his solutions and discoveries, and I am very sorry indeed, given my own lack of training in mathematics, that all I can do is relay, to a general readership no more specialized than myself, the esteem that historians of science have for Leonardo Fibonacci.

The Year of Our Lord

Since we are talking about numbers, this question springs to mind: When did we begin to count the years from the birth of Christ? The answer is: very late, for it was a monk of the sixth century named Dionysius Exiguus (literally, "Dionysius the Small") who went about establishing the date of the birth of Jesus, which he fixed as December 25 in the year 753 from the foundation of the city of Rome.[97]

The gospel of Luke (2:1–2) is our source for the chronology of the birth of Christ:

> Now at this time Caesar Augustus issued a decree for a census of the whole world to be taken. This census—the first—took place while Quirinus was governor of Syria, and everyone went to his own town to be registered. So Joseph set out from the town of Nazareth in Galilee and traveled up to Judaea, to the town of David called Bethlehem, since he was of David's house and line, in order to be registered together with Mary, his betrothed, who was with child.

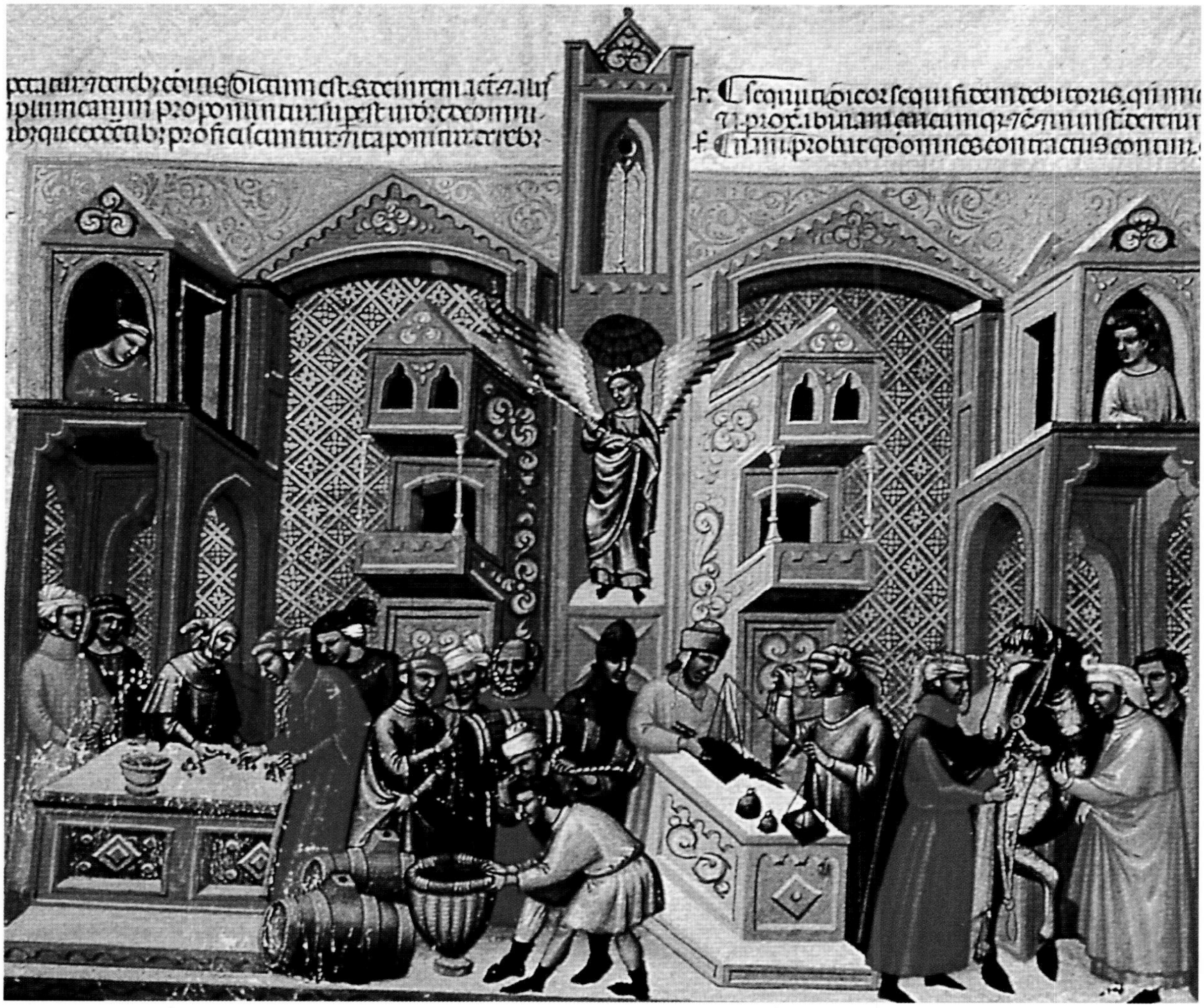

pctatur7catcb;comefdicaur est Sctcintcm actatuf
ipilincatiu pfopomtur super iuid: cccomi
ib; quceccatb; pfofiafcauntur7ctapomtut catcb;

r. Cfcquntudicofscqui ficta debitocie.qumic
ui pfozibui anieaia q:7cauiiuisfcdcitcin
f Cuum.pfobitqdomncscontractuscouatu.

Text and miniature of a scene of commerce in an illuminated manuscript.

FIGURE 39

A Scene of Commerce.

Miniature, 1328.

Turin, Biblioteca Nazionale Universitaria,

Digestum, ms. E.I. 1-c, f. 174r.

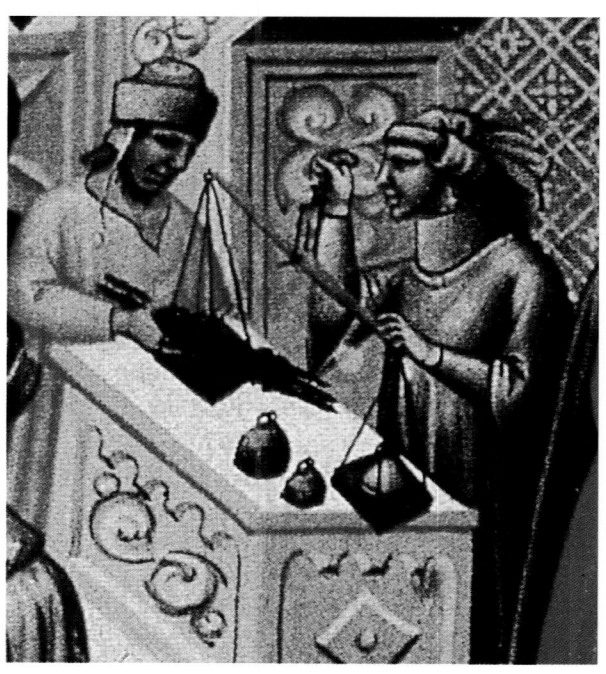

Matthew (2:1–2) adds the star and the wise men to the tale, and most important, he places the birth of Jesus in the time of the reign of Herod, to which Luke (1:5) also indirectly alludes. After many calculations, Dionysius thought he was in a position to establish the exact year in which Herod died, but he was in error, for this sovereign certainly died in 4 B.C. It is more difficult to fix the exact year of the census of Quirinus, but it took place sometime between 7 and 6 B.C.

The system of Dionysius was adopted very gradually, and can only be said to have become widespread in the ninth century, at the time of Charlemagne. Historians today agree that Jesus was born five or six years earlier than Dionysius thought, so the recent millenium actually came to an end before most of us noticed. December 25 became the day on which the year commenced, a date gladly accepted by the Church because it made Christmas coincide with the celebration of the winter solstice, and also with the feast of Mithras, the Persian god of light, which in antiquity was celebrated on the same date.

The western year count from the supposed birth of Christ is now widely used, independently of religious cultures, and with the nonreligious indicators B.C.E. ("before the common era") and C.E. ("common era") increasingly taking the place of the specifically Christian ones, which in English are of course B.C. ("before Christ") and A.D. (*anno Domini*, "in the year of the Lord"). In the Islamic world, however, the years are counted from 622 C.E., the first year of their era.[98] But every single date we specify according to the western system depends on the mistaken calculations of a medieval monk.

Banks, Lending Societies, Charity Pawnbroking

Merchants, both those who took to the road themselves and those who worked from a fixed location, directing a network of associates and employees without leaving their own offices (figure 39), were the ones who spread the system of Arabic numerals and ensured its success. When drawing up contracts of sale and purchase they brought in a notary, while for bookkeeping purposes they adopted the double entry system, in which the credits were entered in one column and the debits in another, so that they could see where they stood at any given time by simply adding and subtracting. The merchants also developed the payment order, a precursor of the modern check: instead of transporting large quantities of actual coin, they drew upon their bank deposits. The banks themselves were only small shops or even stalls, where the banker dealt over a counter or "*banco*": so the medieval institution was the precursor of the modern bank in fact and in name. The receipt a merchant received for his bank deposit represented the value of the deposit itself, and he could use it to pay his bills.[99]

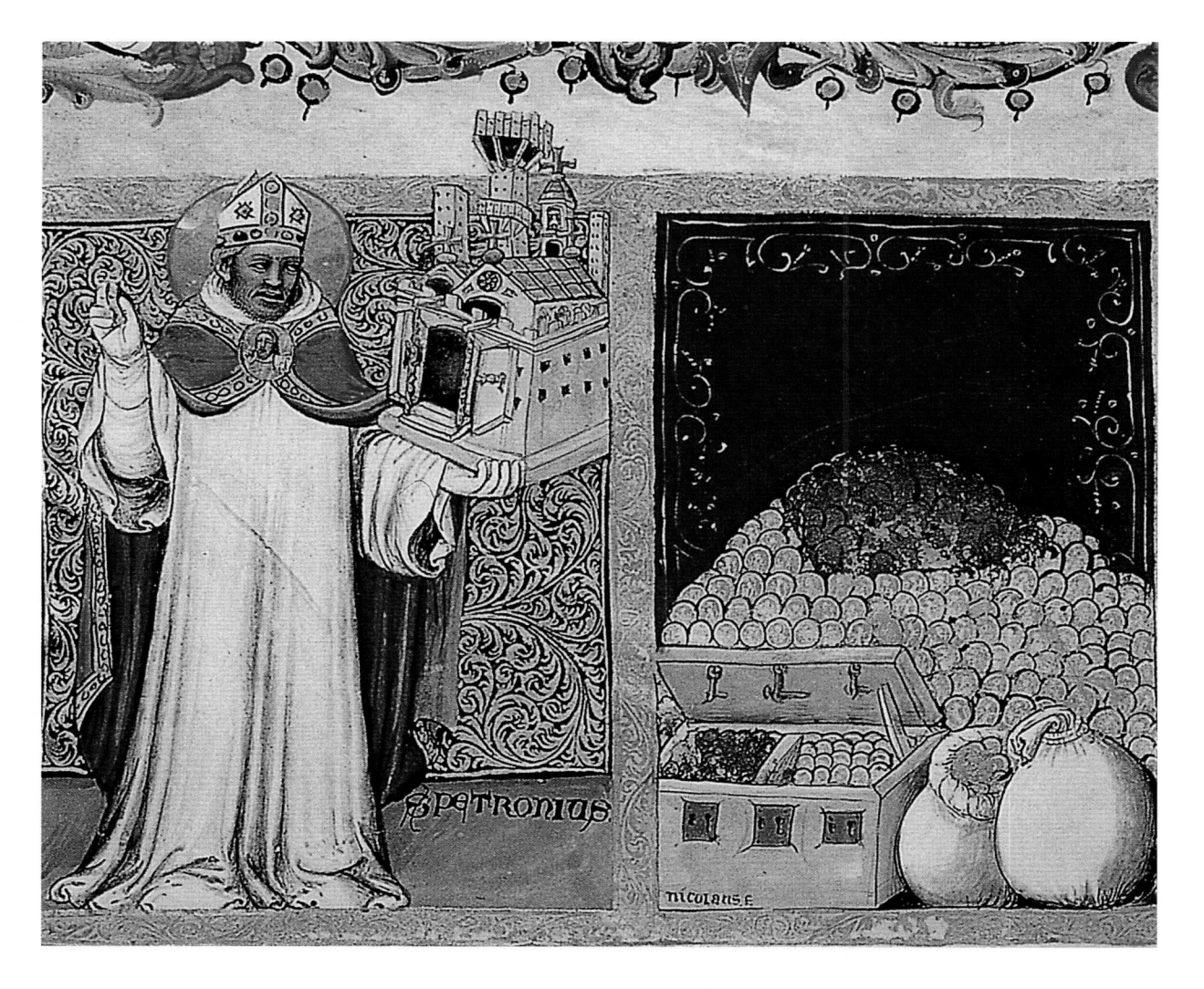

FIGURE 40
Nicolò di Giacomo,
*San Petronio and the Money
Collected by the Commune
of Bologna.*
Miniature, 1394. From the *Libro
dei creditori del Monte di Pubbliche
Prestanze.* Bologna, Archivio di
Stato, ms. Cod. min. no. 25,
f. IV

Some banking companies became so rich that they were able to make loans to clients as illustrious as popes and kings, naturally at a rate of interest, though the Church prohibited the charging of interest as a form of usury. Nonetheless, in the cities of the thirteenth and fourteenth centuries a rate of interest not exceeding 20 percent was tolerated in daily practice. Those whose conscience troubled them could always turn to the Jews, who in the twelfth and especially the thirteenth centuries found their primary economic role in the lending of money at interest (not necessarily usury). Lending at interest was in theory prohibited for Christians and a sin, for interest was viewed as the buying and selling of time, and time belonged only to God.

Bankers were also moneychangers, and always had a balance on their counter with which to weigh coins that were brought to them, which varied greatly in weight and metallic composition, before deciding how much to exchange for them—an operation on which they never failed to make a profit.

The rapid circulation of money may have made more people better off, but it also produced a series of disequilibria and rapid turns of fortune,

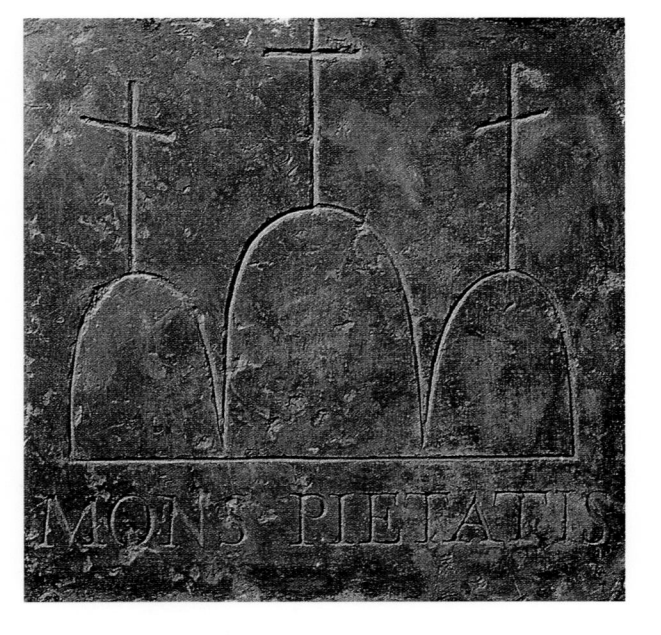

FIGURE 41
Graphic symbol of the Monte di pietà
of Reggio Emilia.
Sandstone, 1612. Reggio Emilia, Bipop-Carire Ltd.

adding new categories of poor to the traditional ones, like peasants, wage workers, the ill, and the bereaved. All it took to be ruined was the failure to pay back money you owed on the due date. The Franciscans Bernardino da Feltre and Barnaba da Terni sought a remedy for this wave of abrupt impoverishment, and found it in a new financial institution, the *monte di pietà* (a "mount" or "heap" or "fund" of "piety" or "pity"). The first of these *monti di pietà* was founded at Perugia in 1462, and they were a great success, especially when in 1515 Pope Leo X recognized that the earning of interest was licit as long as it equaled operating expenses.

Bernardino da Feltre in particular dedicated great effort to making these new institutions a reality until the day he died in 1494, preaching tirelessly and organizing spectacular processions in order to get people emotionally involved and ready to loosen their purse strings. He even claimed to have had a divine revelation, and his homilies give a list of the reasons that led to the creation of the *monte di pietà*. The main goal of the friar, who was known as the "hammer of the usurers," was to see economic transactions taken out of the hands of the "infidel" Jewish lenders. But he also knew all about the social context, in which all sorts of people of relatively modest condition often needed to get hold of money quickly for their small businesses or sudden emergencies, and to him it was intolerable that the only way they could do so produced a profit for the Jews, or in any case for usurers.

So Bernardino da Feltre urged those who were fairly well-off to donate a small portion of their wealth, and with these voluntary offerings a fund or *monte* was set up, upon which those who needed money could draw. The enterprise was launched with the aid of benefactors, testamentary bequests, and the city governments (which often provided a suitable building for the *monte* and earmarked certain revenues for it), and

FIGURE 42 Vicino da Ferrara
(so called), *Bernardino of Feltre*.
Panel, between 1494 and 1507.
Ferrara, Pinacoteca Nazionale, inv. 67

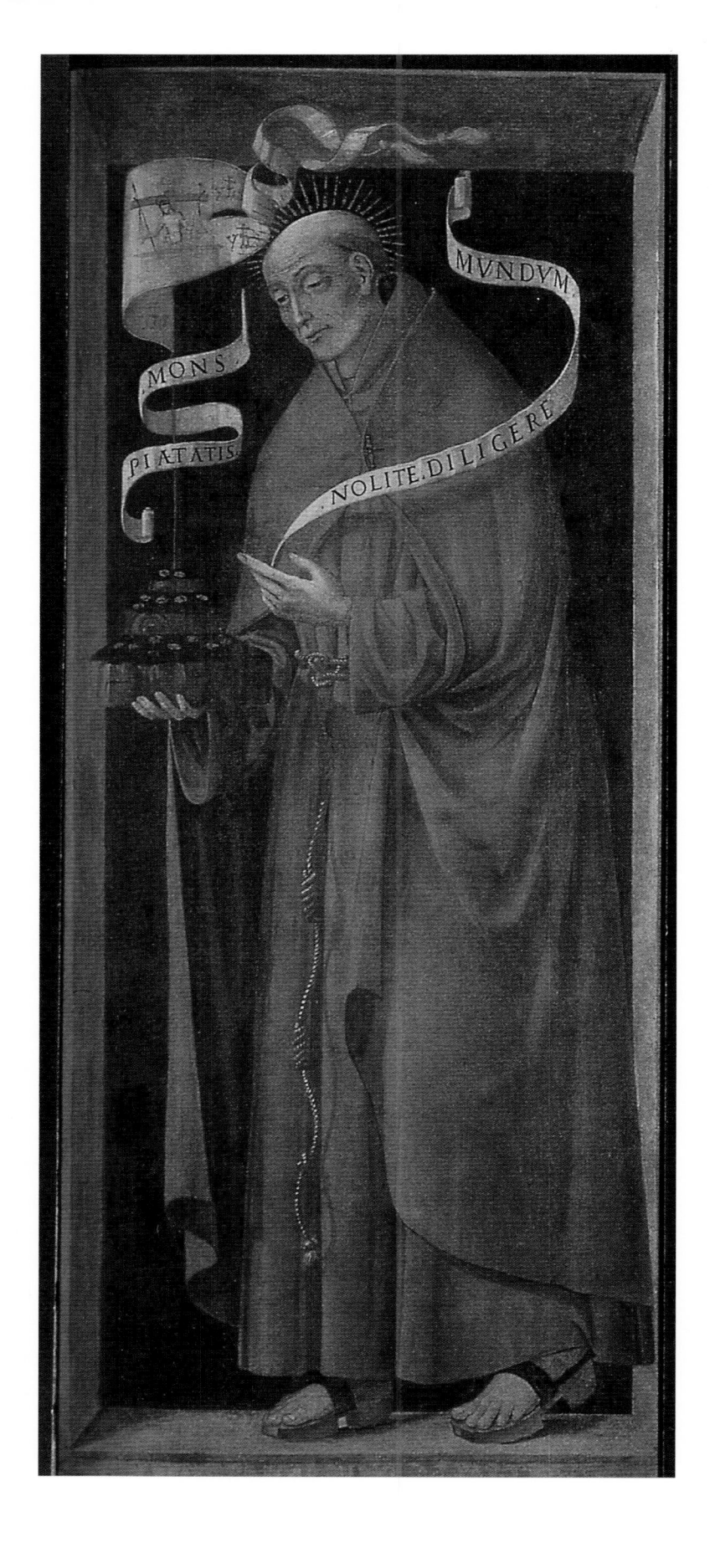

once the statutes were codified and the personnel selected, the institute opened its doors for business. At the *monte* one deposited a pledge, as one does at a modern pawnbroker's shop, and in turn received two thirds of the value of the object pledged: the clients were certainly poor, but not totally indigent.

The practice of pooling resources in a fund was already widespread in the Italian communes, which often needed to have money ready to deal with particular situations. For example, in 1394 the citizens of Bologna had been constrained to subscribe a loan in favor of the commune, receiving interest of 10 percent. In a miniature that decorates one page of a register prepared on that occasion, the *Libro dei creditori del Monte di Pubbliche Prestanze* (Book of the Creditors of the Monte of Public Loans; figure 40), we see the patron saint, San Petronio, holding a model of the city in his hand and demonstrating his approval of the initiative by blessing a heap of money piled up behind a strongbox and a couple of half-open sacks, also full of money.

The new idea of San Bernardino da Feltre was to make such forced loans into voluntary offerings, and shift the purpose from the needs of local politics onto the ethical plane. The faithful were urged to take the pity that Christ had shown for the human race by offering himself up on the hill of Calvary as their model, and direct it toward easing the suffering of their fellow man by donating a bit of money.

The symbol of the new institution, which in the earliest images Bernardino da Feltre displays in his hand, is a rocky mass covered with money, in which a standard is planted displaying the figure of Christ "*in pietà*" (in death following his crucifixion). Later the rocky mass evolves into three hills, with the tallest one always at the center, each topped by a cross, in an explicit allusion to Calvary (figure 41). The banner is completed by inscriptions that invite the observer to practice charity, care for his neighbor, and detach himself from all earthly concerns; in compensation he is promised rich rewards in heaven. Typically they read "Curam illius habe" (take care of him); "Nolite diligere mundum" (rejoice not in the pleasures of this world; figure 42); "Thesaurizate vobis thesaurum in celis" (pile up your treasure in heaven).[100]

Bernardino da Feltre, filled with enthusiasm for his idea, used a mixture of Latin and the *volgare* to explain that giving to the Monte meant accomplishing all seven of the acts of compassion at one go, because the needy man could use the money to find relief for all of his wants at once: "If you give wine, you are not giving bread too; if you give bread, you are not giving clothing too, and so on: you are not giving him money to pay his debts, medicine, and so on. But give to the Monte and you are giving everything. In this way you fulfill the seven acts of compassion. With that money relief is provided for the purchase of bread, wine, clothing, medicine, and everything else."[101]

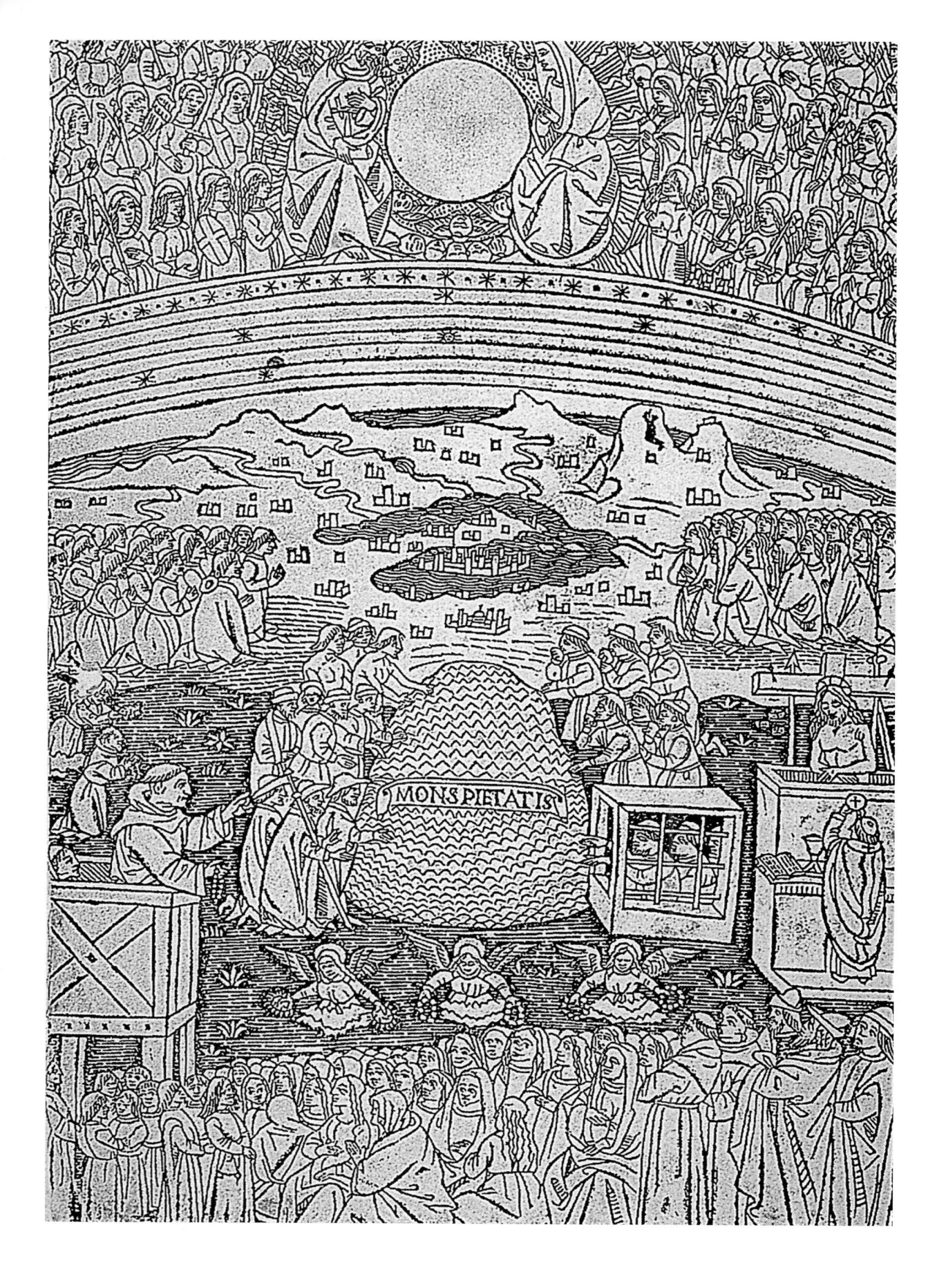

In a woodcut entitled *La figura della vita eterna* (The Figure of Eternal Life) that accompanies the *Tabula della salute* (Table of Salvation) composed in 1494 by Marco da Montegallo (figure 43), we find the whole complex message of the *monti di pietà* represented. The image is to be read starting at the bottom: at the left, a friar addresses a crowd from a pulpit; evidently they are moved by what they are hearing and it is certain that they are about to contribute generously to the *monte*—so much so that a few hovering angels are already conferring the celestial crown upon them. Directly across from the preacher, on the right, a priest is celebrating mass. The elevation of the host evokes the sacrifice of Christ, who in fact emerges *in pietà* above the celebrant, surrounded by the symbols of his passion, in accordance with the iconography of the "mass of Saint Gregory."[102] This is a way to suggest a visual link between the pity of the individual for his fellow man, which is what the friar is urging, and the divine pity sought by the celebrant priest for sinful humanity.

On the next level, and at the center of the composition, a heap of money is piled,[103] which the inscription labels *Mons pietatis* (the Latin for *monte di pietà*), and toward which those at whom the acts of compassion were traditionally targeted—on the left, the poor, the sick, the pilgrims, and the unclothed; on the right, the hungry, the thirsty, and those jailed, probably for debt—are reaching. The road to heaven progresses toward a third stage: in the background is a hilly landscape dotted with towns, while in the foreground two groups, rigorously divided by sex, kneel. They represent the *misericordes*, the compassionate, who enjoy the condition of being the future elect while still here on Earth, and and they are looking forward to their reunion with Christ, the Virgin, and the assembled court of Paradise, who await them out beyond the zone of the celestial spheres. The Savior, bearing the signs of his passion, and the Virgin, whose feet rest upon the apocalyptic crescent moon, are flanking a radiant sphere. The image is incomplete, or was perhaps meant to be colored in later, but it is not hard to fill in the missing part: the monogram of Christ, IHS,[104] which another Franciscan, Bernardino da Siena, had first offered for the adoration of the faithful, goes inside the solar circle. In this way the *Mons pietatis* of the woodcut can be seen as the pedestal of an ideal standard: a symbolic association that finds corroboration in an image of Bernardino da Feltre himself, represented with a "trimonte" (an image of the three hills stacked vertically) in which is planted the fluttering radiant monogram, completed by the usual inscription: *Mons pietatis* (figure 42).

Precious Rags: The Making of Paper

The woodcut we have just been discussing was printed on paper, of course—another very important invention of the medieval West, princi-

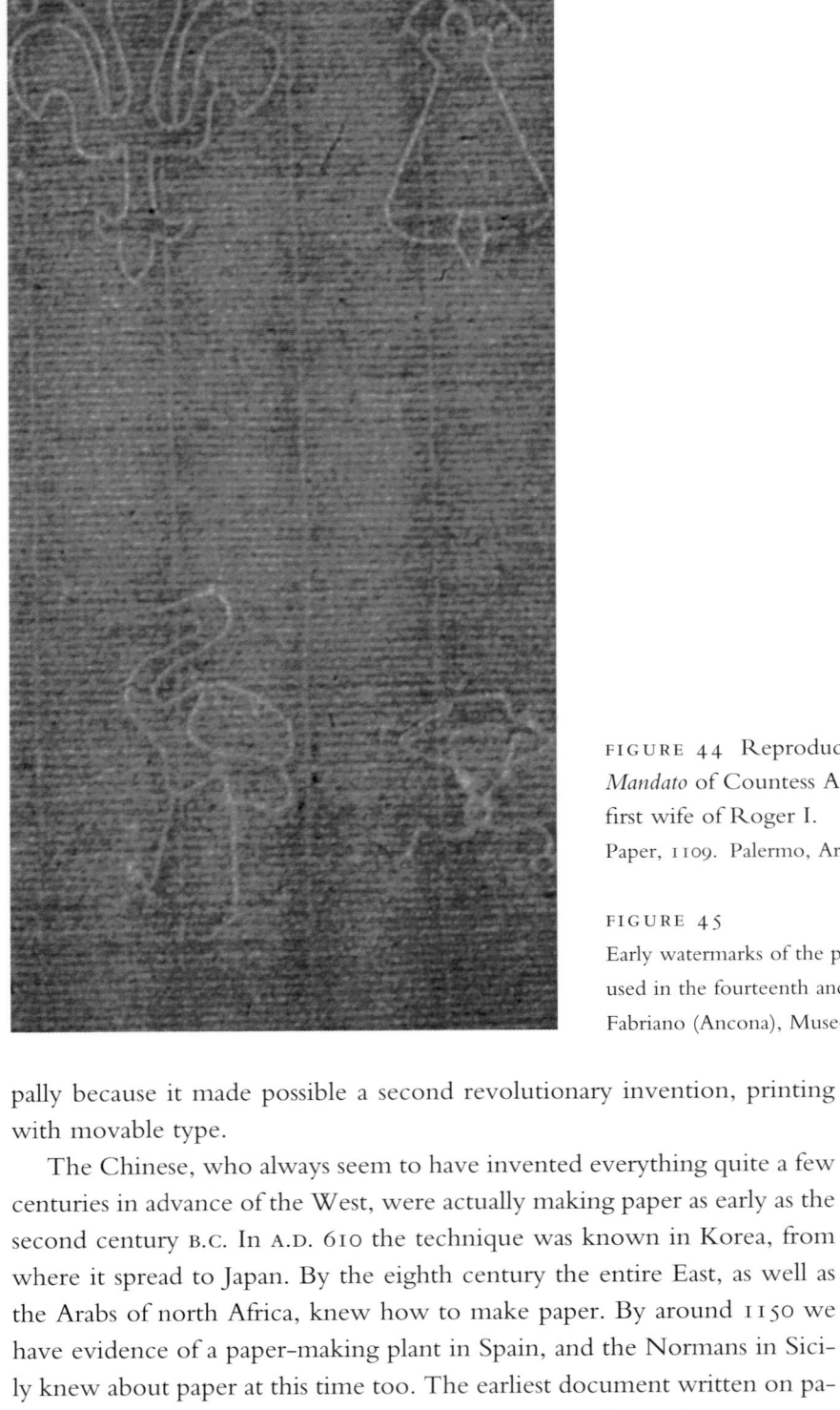

FIGURE 44 Reproduction of the Greek–Arabic
Mandato of Countess Adelasia of Monferrato,
first wife of Roger I.
Paper, 1109. Palermo, Archivio di Stato

FIGURE 45
Early watermarks of the paper makers of Fabriano,
used in the fourteenth and fifteenth centuries.
Fabriano (Ancona), Museo della Carta e della Filigrana

pally because it made possible a second revolutionary invention, printing
with movable type.

The Chinese, who always seem to have invented everything quite a few
centuries in advance of the West, were actually making paper as early as the
second century B.C. In A.D. 610 the technique was known in Korea, from
where it spread to Japan. By the eighth century the entire East, as well as
the Arabs of north Africa, knew how to make paper. By around 1150 we
have evidence of a paper-making plant in Spain, and the Normans in Sicily knew about paper at this time too. The earliest document written on paper that we possess comes, in fact, from the chancellery of the Norman

kings who had occupied the island: it is a mandate from the countess Adelasia, the first wife of Roger I, written in the year 1109 in Greek and Arab and preserved today at the state archive at Palermo (figure 44). Compared to parchment, which was a much more durable substance on which to write and illustrate (all by hand) a book intended for years of use, paper was regarded at first as a fragile material. It was the invention of printing that allowed it to prevail.

How was a sheet of paper made? First you had to gather cloth rags; in China they used rags of silk, and also plant fibers like mulberry and bamboo. The rags were cut into small pieces and pounded to reduce them to a powdery consistency—a lengthy process carried out by hand with wooden pestles until the Arabs introduced a significant improvement, power-driven mallets. These enormous double-headed metal hammers, driven by water power, pounded the rags inside stone vats into which a stream of water was directed. The resulting mash or pulp was diluted with more water, and at this point the paper was almost ready: a finely woven screen (made of strands of bamboo in the East, and metal wires in Europe) attached to a square frame was lowered into the mash, and when it was pulled out a fine layer of mash would adhere to it. As soon as it began to dry and stiffen you could detach it from the screen—and what you held in your hand was a sheet of paper. One notable improvement, called sizing in English, was the application of a layer of a gluelike substance to the sheets to make them partially impermeable, so that the ink would be absorbed cleanly instead of spreading into shapeless blots. When I was a schoolgirl we still wrote using fountain pens and ink pots, and the pen would often deposit shiny black globules of ink on the paper. With trepidation, we used to dip the corner of a piece of blotting paper (paper that hadn't been sized, that is) into these blobs, hoping to soak up the ink and keep it from smearing the whole page. Failure inevitably led to tears!

It was also possible to weave a design or pattern into the fine wire mesh to which the thin layer of pulp adhered, and if you did so the pattern would remain impressed on the sheet when it dried. These designs, or watermarks as they are called in English, can easily be seen if you hold a sheet of paper up to the light, and they can tell us when, where, and by whom the paper was made, and what quality of paper it is (figure 45).[105] The watermark was an innovation of the second half of the thirteenth century and is still important as a way of detecting counterfeit banknotes. In medieval Italy the city of Fabriano, in the province of Ancona, was renowned for its paper-making plants and the high quality of the paper they produced, a renown that still endures. Until a few years ago all Italian banknotes, and those of many other European countries as well, were printed at Fabriano.

Books Get Busy: Printing with Movable Type, a Revolutionary Invention

The great flowering of culture in the Renaissance is connected to the invention of printing with movable type, which made it possible to produce quickly a large number of copies of any given book; they cost relatively little to buy, and they could be circulated widely. It was printing that made the paper industry take off, because books were, and are, printed on paper.

The first typographer was apparently the German goldsmith Johannes Gutenberg (c. 1400–1468) of Mainz: around the middle of the fifteenth century, he had the idea of making "printing types," numerous small square pieces of metal, each of which had the reverse image of a letter of the alphabet carved on its top surface. Soon, however, instead of each piece being individually carved, they were cast from molten metal, so they could be produced more quickly. A complete set of types was called a fount, and it included a number of pieces of type for each letter of the alphabet; naturally you needed more types for letters like E that are used frequently than you did for letters like X that are infrequent. The types were placed in trays in special chests or cases stacked vertically, with the capital letters in the case on top (which is why we still call them upper-case letters) and the small letters in—naturally—the lower case. The types were taken out of their cases one by one (remember, each piece was separate, which is why we call them movable type) and used to compose words and sentences in rows held tightly in place inside a square frame. This frame, which actually contained a number of pages, was then loaded into the press and coated with ink. A blank sheet of paper was pressed firmly against the metal surface of the rows of type, using human muscle power, and the image left by the ink, which reversed the images of the letters on the types to make them readable, was a printed sheet. The first sheet off the press, called a proof, was read for mistakes, and those that were found were corrected by shifting the position of the metal types. After that the printers could turn out as many copies of that sheet and the subsequent sheets as they needed for the book, and since each of the sheets was identical to the others, when they were folded and gathered to produce the right sequence of pages, each page of each of the books that resulted was also identical to all the others. After the printing of each sheet was finished, the metal types were taken out of their frame and put back in their cases, ready to be used again. And that whole process was what we mean by "printing with movable type." The books printed from the beginning down to 1500, called incunabula, are very rare and valuable today. Why do we call them that? Because printing was in its infancy during those fifty or so years, and *incunabula* is the Latin word for the cradles in which newborn babies were wrapped.

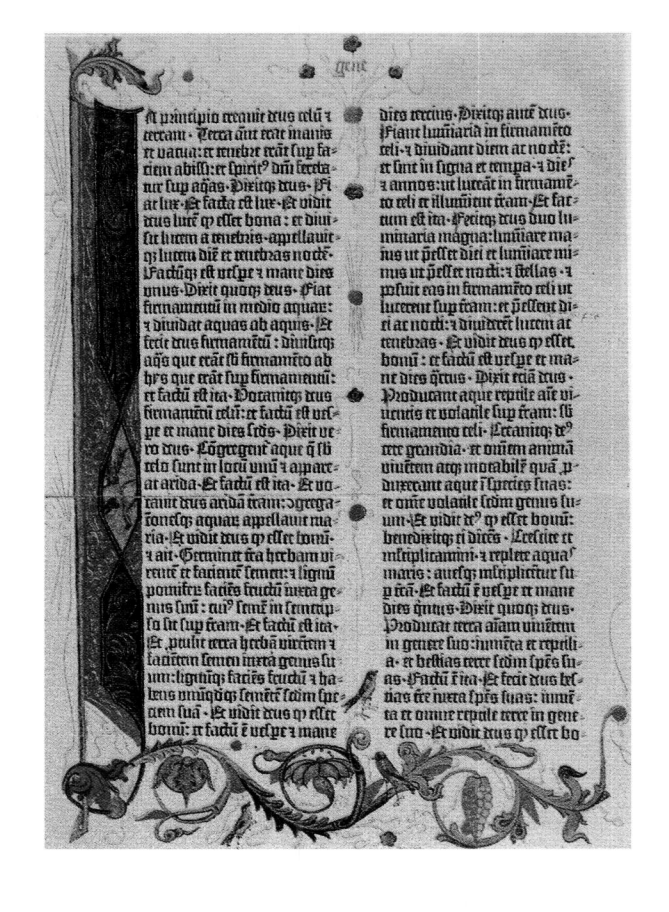

FIGURE 46

A page from the 36-line Latin Bible printed by Gutenberg in 1450.

Sometime in the 1460s Gutenberg's invention, and the equipment needed to make it work, crossed the Alps into Italy, carried by a train of mules and accompanied by two enterprising typographers from Mainz named Sweynheym and Pannartz. The little caravan did not immediately make for Rome, but halted instead at the Benedictine monasteries at Subiaco.[106] In the one named after Santa Scolastica they found all the right conditions necessary to make the new art feel at home: plenty of room, a rich library full of manuscripts waiting to be turned into printed books, and the collaboration of learned monks already skilled in the traditional arts of manuscript book production, like copying, illuminating, and binding. Perhaps there were other reasons that drew the two Germans to that destination: the presence of German Benedictines may have attracted them (Sweynheym and Pannartz were clerics themselves), suggesting that Subiaco was the place best suited to starting up a printing shop in Italy. But we don't really know what their motives were.

At Subiaco the two printers labored intensively, but a few years later, in 1467, they turn up at Rome in the house of a family named Massimo, merchants and bankers who were probably located not far from Campo de' Fiori. The center of Rome was then situated near the bend of the Tiber, between the modern Piazza Navona, Campo de' Fiori, and Palazzo Venezia. The economic heart of the city beat here, and in this district

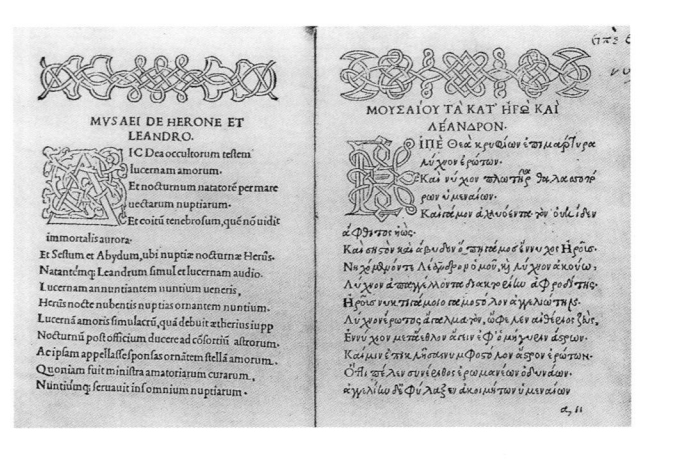

FIGURE 47

A page from Musaeus, *Opusculum de Herone et Leandro*,
in Greek and Latin, printed by Aldo Manuzio in Venice
in small quarto format, before November 1495.
Paris, Bibliothèque Nationale

were to be found the workshops where manuscripts were copied and the
book dealers where they were sold. Those same dealers greeted the products of the new art of typography with enthusiasm, and printed books
spread rapidly, as merchants and bankers quickly saw the potential for
profit that they held.

In the space of 10 years, around 160,000 books were printed in
Rome—books for everyone, rich and poor. Until that time, the written
text had been the privileged possession of a few, and the introduction of
printing with movable type marked an epochal shift similar to the one
brought about in our lifetime by the introduction of the computer. It not
only changed the form of the book, it changed the mentality of readers.

In Gutenberg's time, northern copyists who took up the pen wrote in
Gothic, a type of script in which the letters were fractured at acute angles
and made as narrow as possible in order to save space; in architecture, the
Gothic style, with its pointed arches and ogival cross-vaults, is surprisingly
analogous to similar forms in calligraphy. But in Italy a type of writing very
different from the forms of Gothic made its appearance in the later fourteenth and fifteenth centuries. The Renaissance humanists greatly admired
the nitid and simple script used in manuscripts of the Carolingian age (originating in the ninth and tenth centuries, and remaining in use until the
twelfth), and selected this Caroline minuscule, as we now call it, for use in
their own writing and copying. They, however, called it *littera antiqua* because they were convinced that it was the script used by the ancient Romans themselves. Thus the gracious and rounded forms of Caroline script
came back to life, in reaction against the spiky Gothic that had held sway
in the meantime. And with a few modifications the *littera antiqua* lives on
today, in the form of the lower-case printed letters you are reading right
now in this book, and in most other mechanically produced (typewritten)
or electronically produced (computerized) texts.

At first typographers sought to reproduce the writing of professional
copyists as faithfully as possible, since their books were going to be read by
a public that had never known anything but manuscripts. Customers also

wanted something else they were familiar with and refused at first to do without: the rich colors of the miniatures used to illustrate or "illuminate" manuscripts, and the elaborate capital letters in red that adorned the parchment pages. In 1450 Gutenberg printed his first Latin Bible, called the 36-line Bible (each column was 36 lines deep); printed on parchment and in Gothic letters, it was still strongly redolent of the medieval spirit (figure 46). The production of the text was subsequently completed by the illuminator, who added embellishments and colors in the spaces that, with professional foresight, had been left empty for that purpose.

Around 1500 in Venice, the cradle of the Italian Renaissance, Aldo Manuzio, however, used metal type to reproduce the *littera antiqua*, which spread throughout Europe in the sixteenth century as countless printers followed his example (figure 47). Manuzio was also the inventor of the "italic" typeface, an elegant sloping cursive inspired by the handwriting of Petrarch. He invented something else too, abandoning the imitation of costly, large-format manuscripts: accessible small-format books of great beauty. Books were indeed "getting busy."

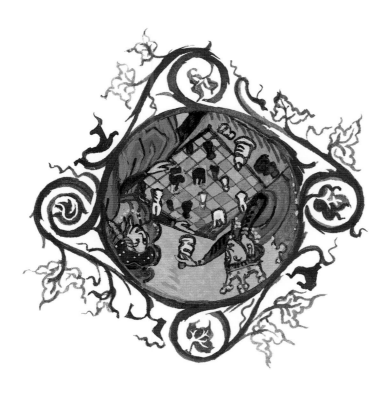

TWO *Time for pleasure and time for Duty*

"Playing cards are the devil's breviary":
Games for Grownups: Cards, Tarot, Chess, and Mock Battles

In 1425 San Bernardino da Siena launched an attack, with his usual vehe-
mence, against gaming in all its forms—the principal means, according to
him, by which men are induced to sin and lose their souls.[1] The preacher
conjured up a diabolical mass in vivid color, with all the liturgical gestures
and implements transformed into actions and things used in gaming.

> The missal is the dice, for just as the die has 21 points, likewise the
> Christian missal is composed of the 21 letters beginning a, b, c. The
> letters of the devil's missal are in the bone. The letters are from the
> devil's excrement, because the ink is his excrement. Cards and *naibi*
> are the devil's breviary. A woman's curls are small *naibi*. The priest
> is the player. You know that breviaries are adorned with miniatures;
> so are *naibi*. The letters are: clubs, things crazy people use; the cups
> signify drunks and those who haunt taverns; the coins, the greedy;
> the swords, conflict and quarreling and killing. The illuminated let-
> ters are: the king, king of the ribalds; queen, queen of the ribalds;
> sodomite on top and sexual extravagance below.[2]

Bernardino distinguishes cards from *naibi*; the first are simple undecorated

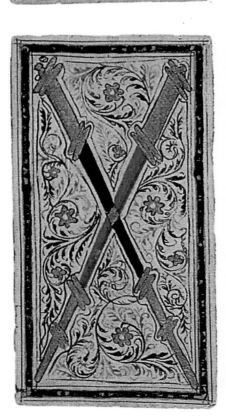
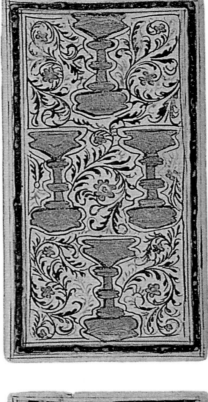

FIGURE 48 Playing
cards from Ferrara.
Woodcut on reinforced
paper, Venice,
Museo Correr

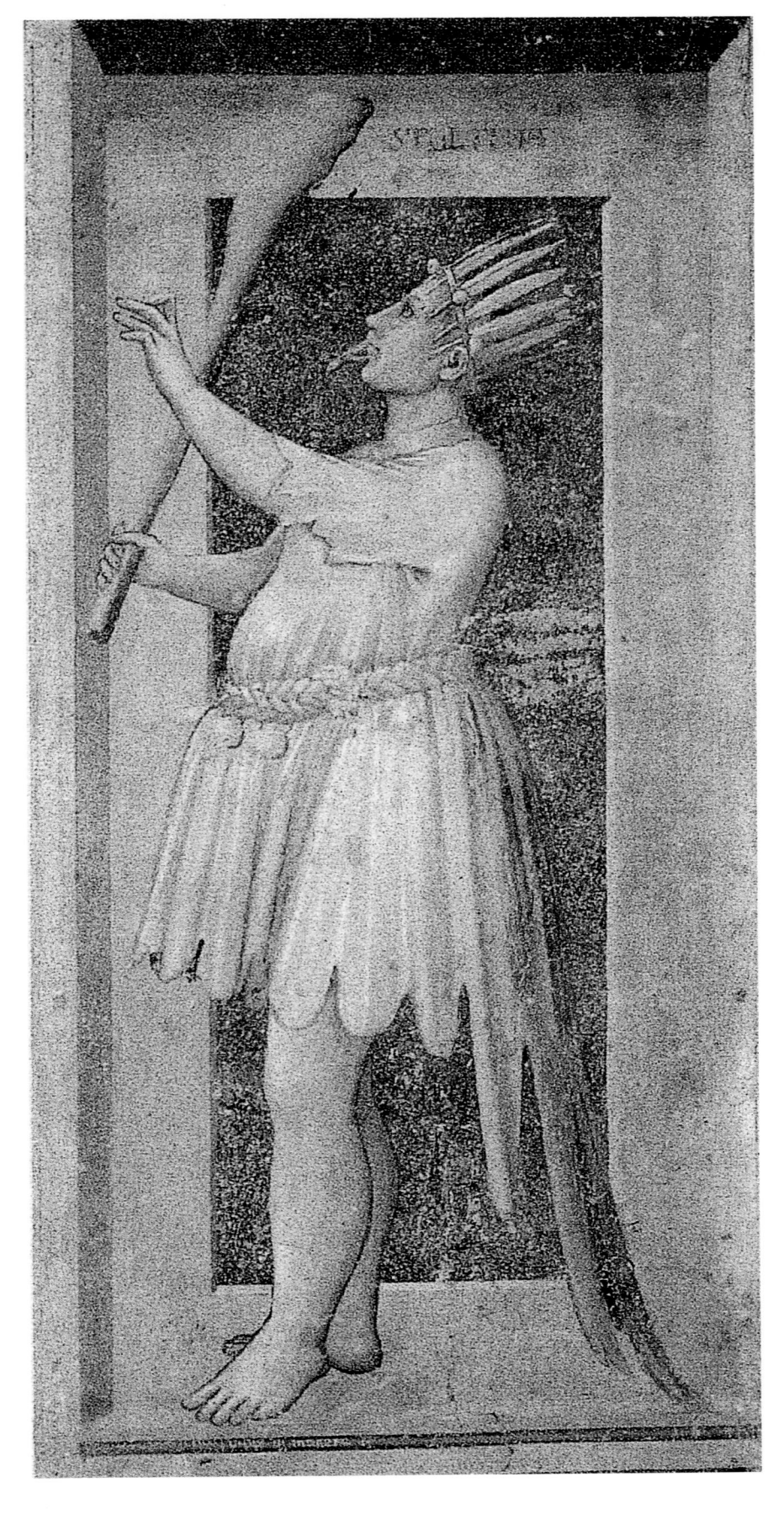

FIGURE 49 Giotto, *Stultitia* (Foolishness). Fresco, 1305. Padua, Cappella Scrovegni

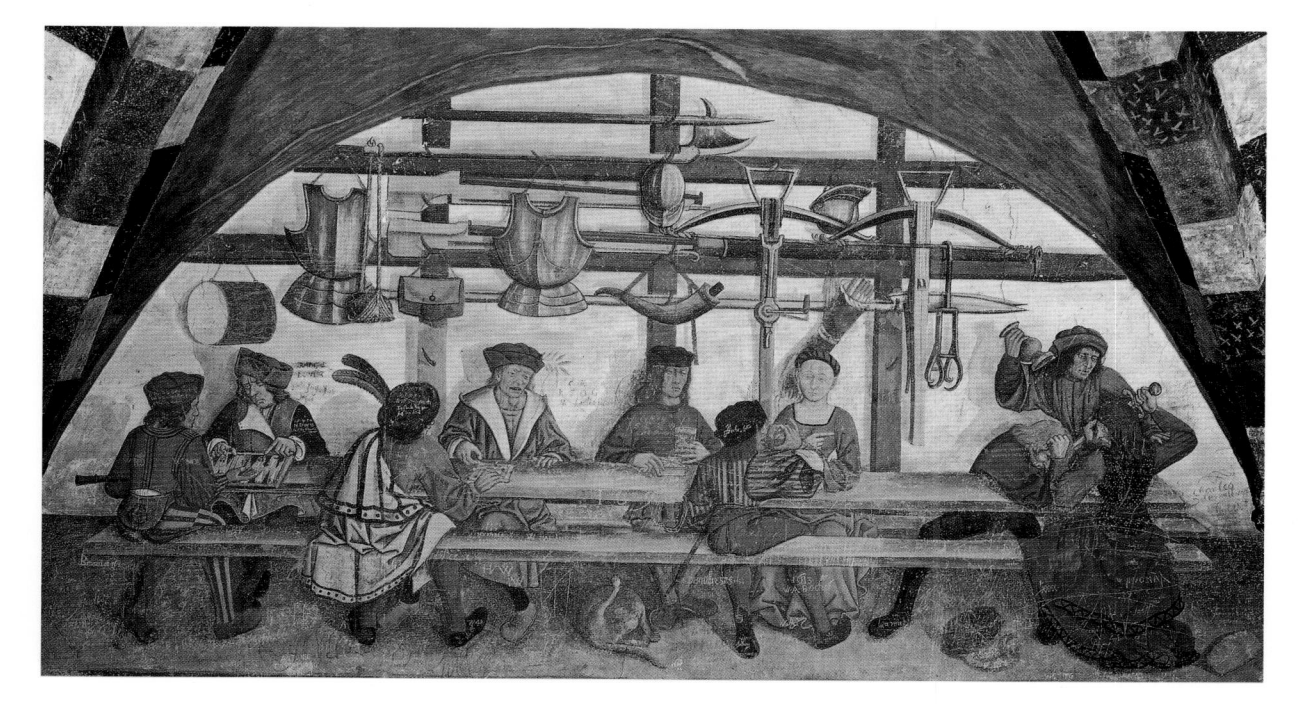

playing cards, whereas the *naibi* are ones that have been decorated by hand. He is thinking of cards of the "Latin" type, with suits of staves, cups, coins, and swords (figure 48). Since madmen and fools were typically represented grasping a club (like the *Stultitia* or "Foolishness" depicted by Giotto in the Scrovegni chapel in Padua, fig. 49[3]), Bernardino says, "clubs, things crazy people use"; the cups, coins, and swords serve as signs denoting three distinct types of sinner.

A group of armed men assigned to guard the Castle of Issogne in Val d'Aosta are realistically portrayed in a moment of relaxation in frescos from the beginning of the fifteenth century in the lunettes of the portico of the castle (figure 50). Their amusements would appear to confirm the words of San Bernardino: some are playing at *tavola reale* (similar to backgammon), some at *filetto*, some at cards; but too much wine has been consumed, and a sword already drawn. The woman seated in their midst has some reason to feel uneasy.

Let us return to our preacher: San Bernardino continues his imaginary "mass" with the figures of the kings and queens identified as leaders of criminal bands ("king of the ribalds . . . queen of the ribalds"). In the late Middle Ages the "ribalds" (*ribaldi*) constituted a precise juridical category: today we would call them vagabonds, individuals with no fixed address or regular source of income. Their ranks included gamblers, pimps, sturdy beggars, strolling players, and mountebanks.

Bernardino takes aim at the sodomites too, a social category at which he rages with special ferocity in all his sermons. He associates them with the two identical half-figures joined at the waist, one head up, the other

head down. In fact, the same card is used to exemplify both sexual extravagance in general and sodomy in particular.

The sermon continues with a close comparison between the successive stages of the Mass, which at that time was still said in Latin, and gaming:

Introibo when he says "Let's play." The cleric answers "yes." *Kyrie eleison*: everyone gets his money out. *Gloria in excelsis deo*: they give glory to the devil and blaspheme God. *Dominus vobiscum*: filth. *Et cum spiritu tuo*: zara [from a game of dice]. Saint Jerome identifies this zara as Lucifer. *Oremus*, the prayer, is the sighing of the losers. *Epistola*: they are so drunk they would not stop gaming to eat. *Sequentia sancti Evangeli*: you lose. *Gloria tibi domine*: I win. *Credo in unum deum*: to win, they strive to obtain the noose of the hanged man. The *offerta* is the paten and the amount you wager, and the *ostia* is a silver coin. The *calice* [chalice] is a glass of wine, the *Segreta* is the anger that gnaws at you in your irritation. The *prefazio* is when you lament that you have lost, saying "Alas!" *Consecrare* happens when your money become somebody else's. . . . *Dominus vobiscum*: you did evil when you were able. *Et cum spiritu tuo*: and further, you did it to those who played with you. *Ite missa est*: now you see how much wrong you have done, and you grow desperate. *Deo gratias*: you act out your desperation, sometimes even killing yourself. And the gospel confirms that if you did evil in this life you will have eternal punishment in the next.[4]

We do not know the exact origin of playing cards, though various hypotheses have been advanced. What we do know is that they were a real innovation, a new form of entertainment invented by medieval man, and that they appeared, quite certainly, in Europe in the last quarter of the fourteenth century. Very very few early playing cards have survived, because of their fragility and because by their nature they were meant to be used and thrown away. From the time playing cards first appeared, the kings of France took a keen interest in their production, which they saw as a fiscal resource. Monarchical control of this type of game is reflected in the vision of a strongly hierarchical society that the cards themselves project, where the sovereign is the dominant figure.[5]

The rare decks of cards that do survive are ones made for great aristocratic families like the Visconti, the Sforza, and the Este. And they are in fact decks of tarot cards: to the normal set of playing cards have been added a further twenty-two, called "*atout*" or "*arcani*," and representing diverse symbols or statuses in the world: the Pope, or Pope Joan; Death; the Last Judgment; Force; the Hanged Man (figure 51); and so on. The deck preserved at the Bibliothèque Nationale in Paris and known as the "tarot cards

of Charles VI" (1368–1422) were actually made toward the end of the fifteenth century, in Italy. Another deck, renowned for being almost complete and for the richness of its decoration (gold background, touches of silver for coats of arms and suits) is the "Visconti" deck, which is unfortunately divided between the Accademia Carrara of Bergamo and the Pierpont Morgan Library of New York. It was made sometime between 1441, the date of the marriage between Francesco Sforza and Bianca Visconti, the daughter of Filippo Maria, Duke of Milan, and 1447, the year of the duke's death.[6] Most playing cards and tarot cards were naturally much less luxurious, simple lithographs subsequently colored in.

Born as the courtly pastime of rich and favored individuals (legend says that they were given to Charles VI as an antidote for his madness), tarot cards found a different use beginning in the eighteenth century and continuing today: they engross and console poor people anxious to know their own destinies and hoping for a brighter future, who trust in the nature and divinatory power of the tarot cards, to the detriment of their own purses and the delight of the conjurers and fortune-tellers who receive them.

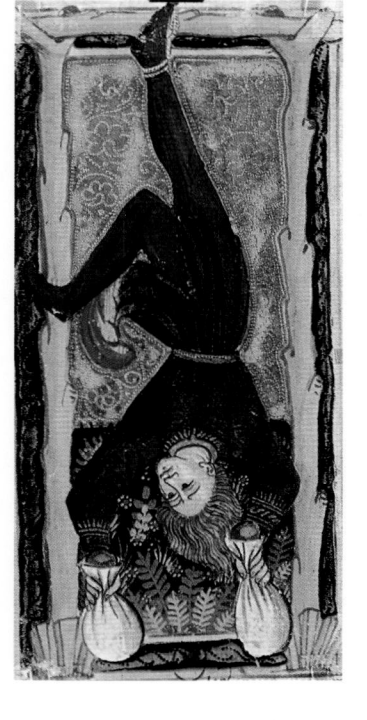

FIGURE 51 *The Hanged Man*, from the so-called deck of Charles VI.
End of the fifteenth century.
Paris, Bibliothèque Nationale

FIGURE 52 *Iacopo de Cessolis Preaches, Using a Chessboard as a Visual Aid*.
Miniature, 1486. Rome, Biblioteca Vatacana, Cod. Pal. Lat. 961, f. 1r

Chess, the Game of Kings

Unlike cards and dice, which were games of chance played in taverns and associated with drinking to excess and with quarreling and cursing, chess was not targeted for reproof by the preachers, since it was a game of intellect, the subtle and rarefied pastime of kings and nobles. The Dominican Iacopo de Cessolis even used chess as a metaphor for the whole of medieval society in his *Ludus scaccorum*, composed at the beginning of the fourteenth century as an outline for a sermon. The chessboard is the city, and the pieces that move about on it represent the different social classes, with their vices and virtues. In one manuscript of the *Ludus scaccorum*, dating from 1468 and preserved in the Vatican Library[7] (figure 52), the first miniature shows the Dominican in the pulpit; he points to a large chessboard as though he were preaching and moving the pieces around like marionettes.

Another priest, a character in a novel of Franco Sacchetti, was a "great chess-player" and always managed to checkmate a gentleman with whom he liked to pass the time. His house was burned to the ground, though, because he used to make the local folk come in to observe his victory every time he won by sounding the bell, and when he actually needed them to help put out the fire, no one came. His parishioners were tired of repeatedly interrupting their work in the fields and ignored the bell in the belief that it was sounding for another checkmate. The priest's rueful conclusion: "Henceforth I will know what to do, and will close the barn door, having lost the oxen."[8]

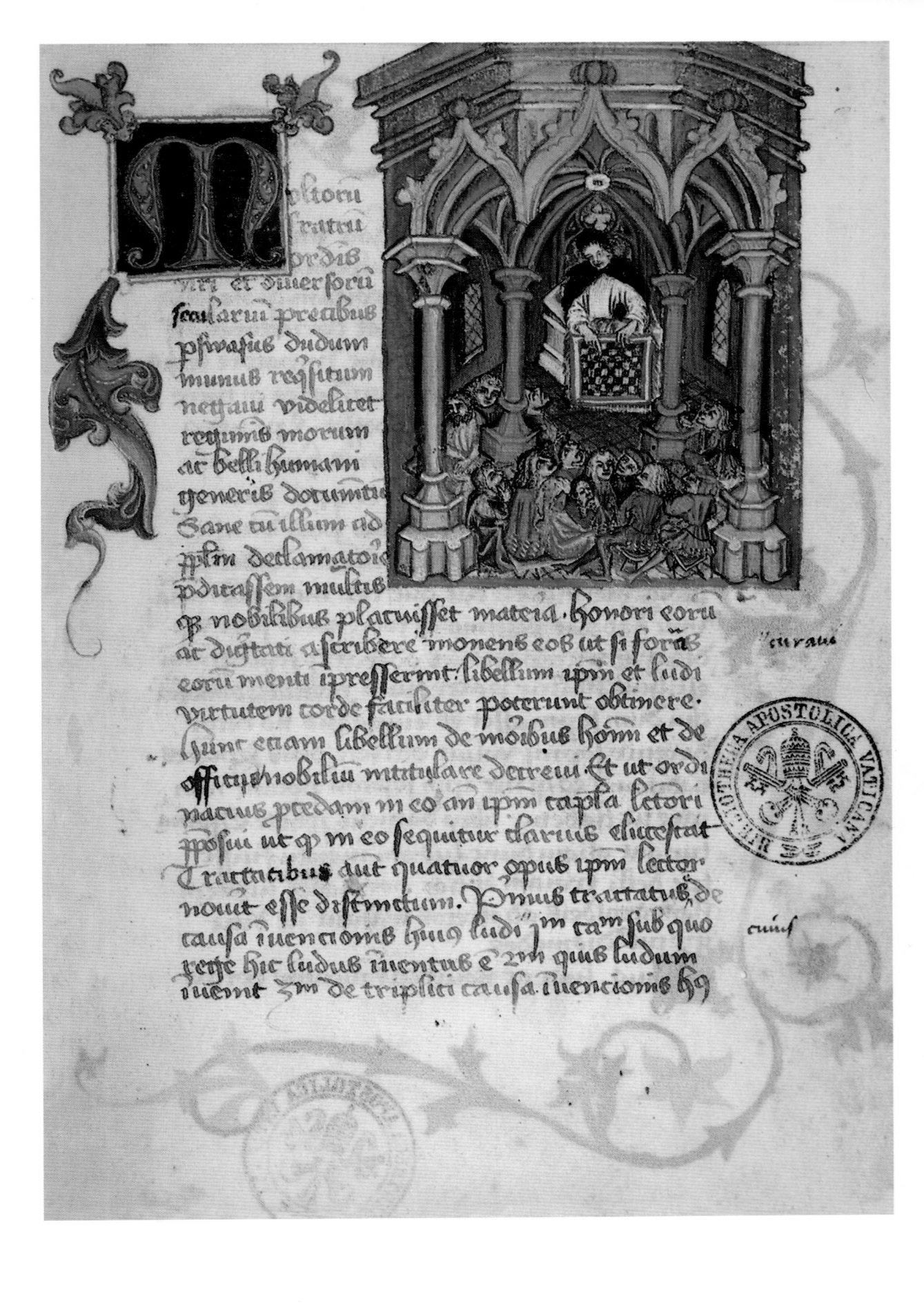

M oltoru
fratru
ordis
nri et diuersoru
secularui precibus
psuasus dudum
munus requisitum
negaui videlicet
regimis morum
ac belli humani
generis docuimentu
Sane tu illum ad
ipsum declamatoie
pditassem multis
qz nobilibus placuisset materia honori eoru
ac dictati ascribere monens eos ut si forã
eoru menti ipresserint libellum ipm et ludi
virtutem corde faciliter poterunt obtinere.
sunt etiam libellum de moibus hoim et de
officijs nobilium intitulare decreui et ut ordi
nacius predam in eo an ipm capla lectori
pposui ut qz in eo sequitur clarius elucescat
Tractatibus aut quatuor opus ipm lector
nouit esse distinctum. Pmus tractatus de
causa inuencionis huius ludi ·im· capm sub quo
rege hic ludus inuentus e ·2m· quibus ludum
inuenit ·3m· de triplici causa inuencionis hg

curaui

cuius

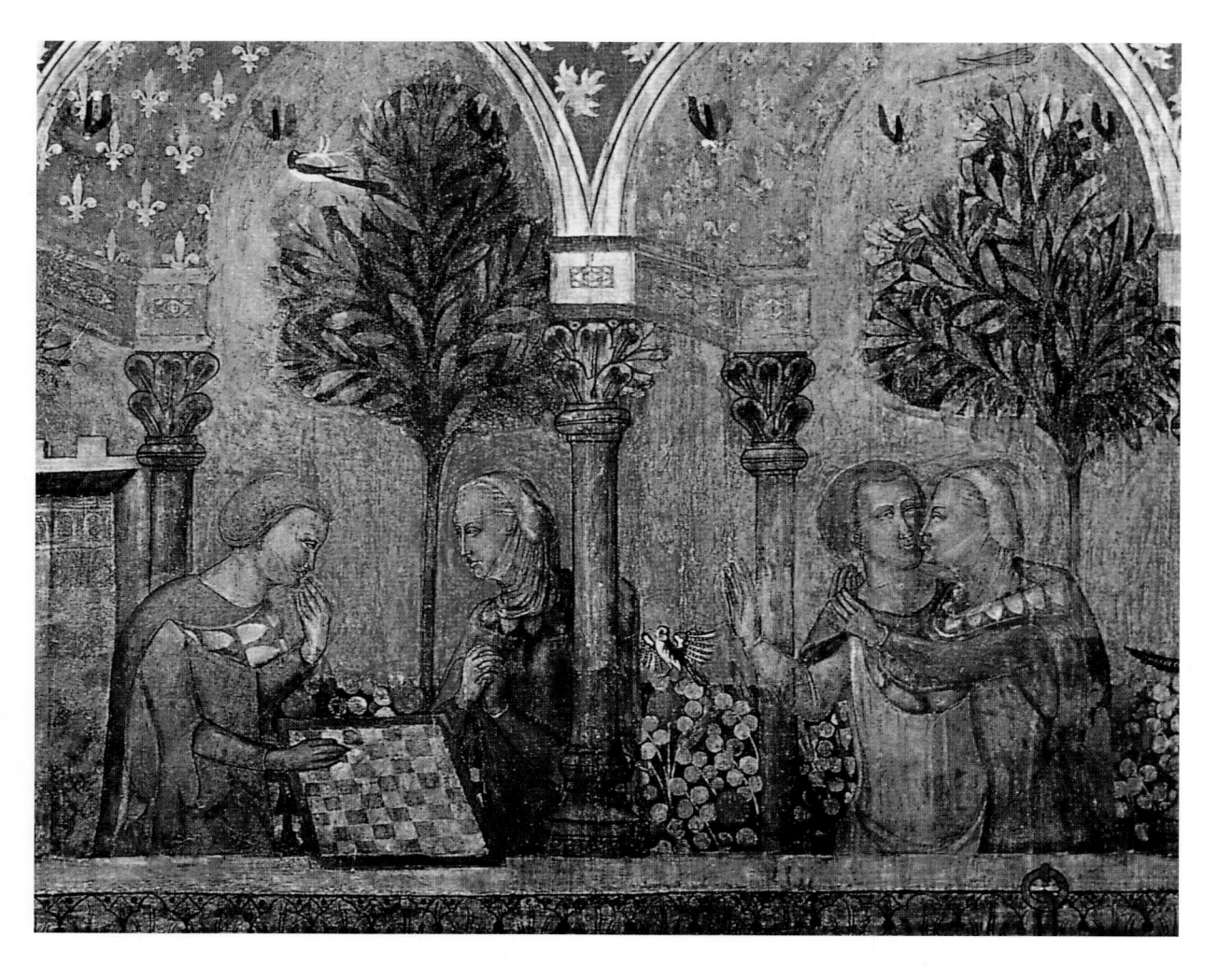

FIGURE 53 *The Wife of*
Duke Guernieri Plays Chess
with the Knight Guglielmo and
Attempts to Seduce Him.
Detail from the fresco cycle
La Chastelaine de Vergy, end of the
fourteenth century. Florence,
Museo di Palazzo Davanzati

The game of chess was displayed on countless small coffers and mirror covers made of ivory in the fourteenth and fifteenth centuries, and since those shown playing it were always kings, damsels, and knights, the game itself became a symbol of aristocracy. Hence it is understandable that a rich merchant in search of social status might want to have it painted in his own matrimonial bedchamber, as part of the tragic history of the *Chastelaine de Vergy*. Palazzo Davanzati in Florence is a case in point: the story of the unhappy lovers[9] was depicted in frescos on the occasion of the marriage of Tommaso Davizzi, who then owned the palazzo, to Caterina degli Alberti in 1395 (figure 53).[10]

According to Iacopo de Cessolis, chess was invented by a philosopher as a clever pedagogical method of correcting the cruel Evilmerodach, the son of Nebuchadnezzar, without risking his own life. This tale is represented in the fragmentary pavement mosaic of San Savino at Piacenza, dating from the end of the twelfth century (figure 54). And numerous chess pieces originating in central and southern Italy and datable to between the end of the eleventh and the end of the twelfth centuries prove that chess must have been widely played. At San Savino, a man on a throne holding

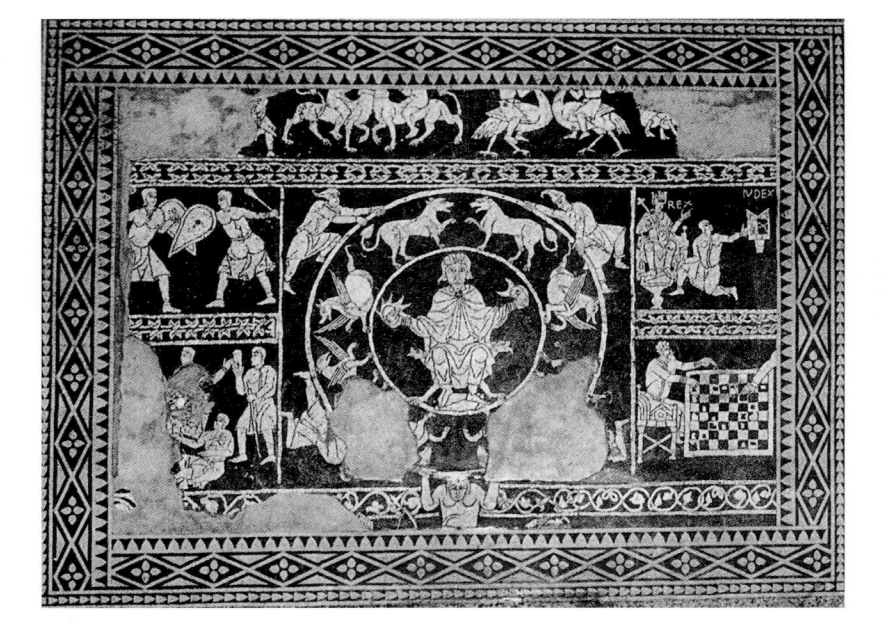

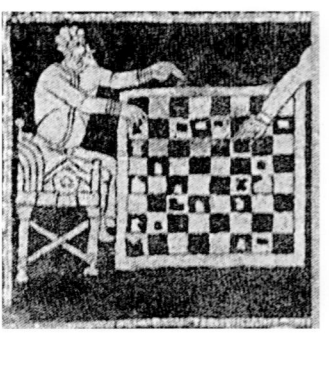

the sun and the moon in his hands in the central tondo recalls the standard iconography of *Annus* (the year). On either side of the tondo there are two panels; in the one on the upper right, a *Rex* (king) on a throne regards a book that a kneeling valet proffers to him, on which is written *Lex* (law). The word *Iudex* (judge) appears in the top right-hand corner; it must refer to a personified figure that has been lost. In the panel below, an aged man with beard and mustache is explaining the game of chess to someone who is unfortunately lost as well; the board is tilted so the viewer can see it. In the panel on the upper left, two warriors fight. In the one on the lower left, much of which has been lost, a seated figure, certainly a dice player, is accompanied by a drinker with cup in hand. William Tronzo elucidates this mosaic[11] with a series of convincing analogies: its message is that dicing, a game of chance, leads to violent quarreling, while chess, a game of intelligence and reflection, produces beneficial effects. The personage with the beard is in fact the philosopher who is using chess to teach Evilmero-dach to have respect for the law.

Chess originated in India in the sixth century A.D., and from there spread to the east and, through Persia, to the west. Sometime between June and December of 1058 San Pier Damiani, then the cardinal bishop of Ostia, wrote to Gherardo of Florence, who later became Pope Nicholas II, and to the archdeacon Hildebrand, the future Gregory VII, to complain that he had discovered the bishop of Florence[12] absorbed in a game of chess.[13] Damiani told them that he had severely reproved the "sinner" and warned him that according to canon law, a bishop who played at dice could be deposed ("Praesertim cum canonica decernat auctoritas, ut aleatores episcopi deponantur"). The accused bishop defended himself, saying that "dice were one thing and chess another. So if the authorities

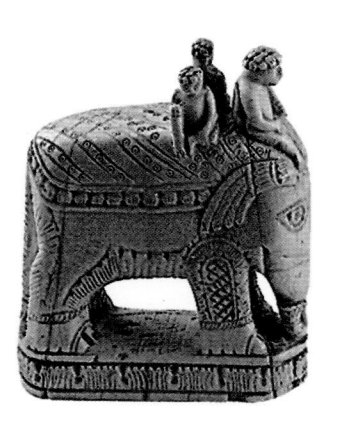

expressly prohibited dice, the very fact that they said nothing about chess meant that it was permitted." But Pier Damiani recorded his own emphatic response: "The reason the text does not mention chess is that the game of dice includes both types of game, dice and chess." And he concludes: "since this bishop was of gentle soul and discerning character" ("ille mitis est animi et perspicacis ingenii"), he gave in and accepted the penance imposed on him.[14] These personal qualities evidently led the bishop to weigh the power of his accuser and the probable consequences of defiance.[15]

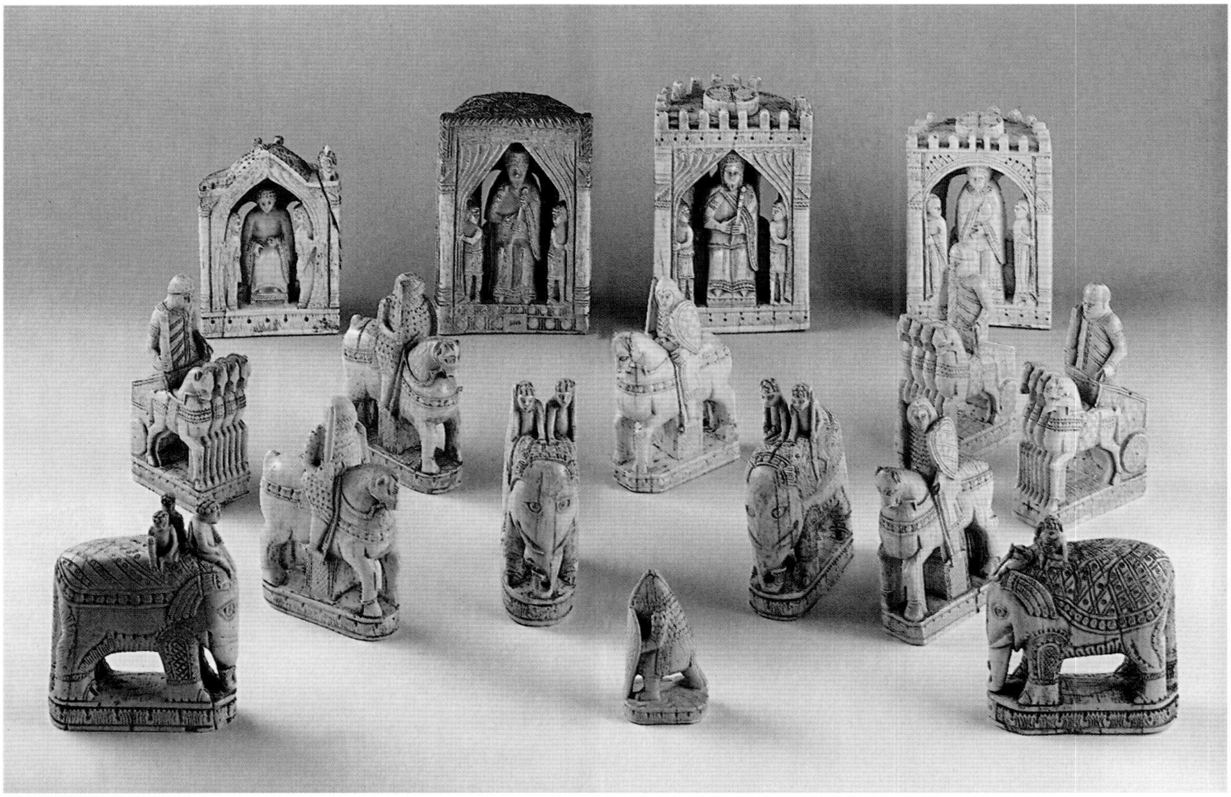

In the course of their long voyage from east to west, the chess pieces underwent a series of modifications, some substantial. The pieces that did not change were the ones corresponding to the king, the knights, and the pawns. The piece known in Arabic as the elephant (*ualfil*) was humanized as the bishop in English, the *alfiere* (standard-bearer) in Italian, and the *fou* (demented one) in French. The Arabic-Persian camel (*rukh*) was translated into Latin as *rochus* and is still called the rook in English, but *torre/tour* (tower) in Italian and French. The *Fers* or vizier, the commander in the east, actually changed sex, becoming *Fiers* (virgin, lady, queen)—a rather inappropriate piece in a game that simulates a war situation. Nevertheless, in the finest set of pieces, preserved until the French Revolution among the treasures at Saint-Denis and known as the "the chess set of Charlemagne" (actually it dates from the end of the eleventh century), we still find an ele-

FIGURE 55 Sixteen chess pieces, from the so-called "chess set of Charlemagne." Ivory, end of the eleventh century. Detail: The piece known in English as the bishop. Paris, Bibliothèque Nationale, Cabinet des Médailles

phant in place of the bishop—probably on account of the influence of Arab models, since these pieces were made in southern Italy (figure 55).[16]

The medieval pawns lacked freedom of movement, and could not attack from a distance; like the modern ones, they advanced one or two squares at a time, mirroring the style of fighting—essentially man-to-man combat—of the feudal era. The city communes of central and northern Italy also knew a game that took the form of violent combat between groups of armed men on foot. It was not chess, however, but a type of military training for urban defense, called a *battagliola* (miniature battle), in which the players, men of every social class, fought it out with fists, sticks, and stones in a sort of ritual combat. Normally *battagliole* were scheduled to take place during Carnival time, and they were very violent, leaving many wounded and on occasion a number of dead.[17] The *battagliole* survive to this day during Carnival in the town of Ivrea, but the players hurl oranges instead of stones. Despite this attentuation, by the time the fight is over someone always winds up in the hospital.

Carnival, or "Farewell to Meat"— A Thoroughly Profane Holiday

The Carnival at Ivrea is the only one that still maintains a link with the Middle Ages, the epoch in which this festival originated. Neither the one in Venice, which was brought back to life about thirty years ago, nor the one in Viareggio, instituted in 1873, with its allegorical floats and papier-mâché puppets, can claim to have an uninterrupted tradition. In fact, Carnival is virtually dead in the modern world because of the death of its great antagonist: Lent.

The higher standard of living in our society has erased the difference between ordinary life and festival—a time of ritual, involving better clothing and food than normal, and the collective celebration of an event that draws everyone in and makes them one. For us the fundamental distinction is the one between periods when we are busy and periods of free time, time free of work. But we dress and eat well every day and spend part of every day relaxing, generally alone rather than in a group or as a group. In addition, the religious sense is much diminished with respect to the Middle Ages, when the community came together in the sacred edifice to participate emotionally in the incarnation and await the sacrifice of Christ. Watching the appearances of the pope and cardinals on television is not the same thing.

It was at the Council of Nicea in 325 that a period of fasting for forty days as preparation for Easter was first prescribed, and by the time of Charlemagne this had become a common and respected practice. During Lent you were allowed to eat just one meal a day, in the evening, and it

FIGURE 56
The Month of January.
Miniature from Andrea de
Bartoli, *Officium Beatae Mariae
Virginis.* Forlì,Bbiblioteca
Comunale, ms. 853,
unnumbered leaf

was absolutely forbidden to eat meat. Throughout the Middle Ages other rigors went along with these lenten restrictions on diet: various forms of penance, and abstention from sexual relations between man and wife and from anything else that might conflict with the idea of purification, like shows, the theater, dancing, and the use of arms.[18]

The prohibition on eating meat, though, was always the rule most strongly connected to the idea of Lent. Meat in the Middle Ages was a symbol of force, of a sanguine and bold character. The rich and powerful were accustomed to hunting for large animals; for them the chase was a simulacrum of war in which they proved their courage and endurance, and their tables were always laden with venison and wild boar. The peasant, on the other hand, had to be content throughout the year with small animals, like the occasional bird, hare, or hen. Only from November to January, when the cold and the earth's slumber kept them indoors—the peasant in his kitchen, often huddled by the fire, and the lord in his hall or seated at table—did they eat the same food, though not in equal quantities, for that was the season of pork, which was eaten fresh, or salted, or prepared as sausages and salami (figure 56).

The Romans too ate pork, but very sparingly and with no particular relish or attention. It was the great migrations of the Germanic peoples that spread the consumption of the meat of suids. The Germans were expert at raising swine (which they allowed to run free in the forests where the acorns that fell from the oak trees provided plenty of fodder) and were great consumers of milk and butter, which they procured from herds that were pastured in vast communal terrains. It is no accident that the cuisine of northern Italy, where Germanic tribes settled in greatest density, is still based on butter, bacon fat, and a high consumption of sausages made of pork and meat in general. In central and southern Italy, which were much less affected by the migrations, the Mediterranean cuisine of Roman antiquity, based on olive oil and the high consumption of cereals and legumes, has survived.

The monks of the Middle Ages were entirely dedicated to the latter type of diet; vegetables and legumes held pride of place on their tables, and meat was absent, except for fish. The fact is, they believed that since fish did not copulate, they were immune from the sin of sexual indulgence that had caused the downfall of Adam and Eve, and hence were not to be regarded as meat at all: for meat of all kinds was contaminated by sexual generation. The vegetarian diet of the monks was also meant to suggest the refusal of worldly things and the choice of a nonviolent mode of life guided by the values of the soul rather than those of the body, as well as continence rather than sexual indulgence, and a life of simplicity rather than one of display and festivity. The powerful ate meat, the powerless ate greens. *The Battle between Lent and Carnival* is a thirteenth-century text from Picardy, and in it the first to rush to the aid of Carnival are the meats: grilled

meat, pork in parsley sauce, sausages great and small, "meat on spits, roasted pigeon, pigeon cooked in pastry, filet of venison with black pepper, and
of course beef." On the opposite side, among the partisans of Lent, the fish
of the sea, the pond, and the stream menace fiercely. Then the dairy products arrive: "Butter advances ahead of the rest, with sour milk following
right behind; hot pies and casseroles appear on great round plates. Cream

proceeds, brandishing a lance, against the backdrop of the deep gorge."[19] The clash of these opposing forces ends with a victory for Carnival, which not only gets to eat meat all year round but also gets to appropriate "lenten meat"—fish, in other words, which would not be out of place on the victor's table, since many kinds of fish were highly prized.

So in sum, meat had symbolic importance, and doing without it was a deprivation. The early form of the word *carnevale* (carnival in Italian) was *carnelevare*; it is attested from around the year 1000 and comes from the Latin "carnem levare," meaning to deprive oneself of meat on the last day before the onset of Lent. The derivation of *quaresima* (Italian for "Lent") is more specifically religious: the Latin expression is "quadragesima dies," or "fortieth day." The Council of Nicea, as noted above, had decided that a period of sobriety lasting forty days should precede Easter, and there the terms *quarantesima* or *quarantena* began to be used to designate it, by analogy to the forty days spent by Jesus in the desert.

Over the centuries the liturgical calendar succeeded in overriding all other festivities: the *Natalis solis*, the feast of the sun's birth, became the *Natalis Christi*, the birthday of Christ (*natalis*, or in Italian, *natale*, means birth; Christmas in Italian is still called *Natale*); the Jewish Passover became the Christian Easter; the search of Ceres for her daughter Proserpine, who had been stolen by Pluto, became the festival known as *Candelora*,[20] in celebration of the purification of Mary on February 2. The proverb "Candelora, candelora, de l'inverno semo fora" ("Candelora, candelora, we have got through winter") expresses the hope that the worst of winter is over and is directly connected to the significance of the pagan feast, for in the myth Proserpine disappears every winter and returns with the return of milder weather.

Carnival, on the other hand, is an annual event that has no religious content, even if it does serve to prepare for a period of penance imposed by the Church. Although it is a purely medieval festival, not the continuation of one of the pagan festivals of antiquity, it has many characteristics of the latter: travesty, the use of masks, and the display of attitudes with regard to food, sex, and behavior that were normally repressed, to the point of insult and violent brawling in the *battagliole*. We can get an idea of what the rowdy hordes of Carnival must have looked like from some of the miniatures (figures 57 and 58) that illuminate the *Roman de Fauvel* (a satirical work in verse composed between 1310 and 1314 by Gervais du Bus). Until not so long ago a similar hubbub, analogous to the *charivari* familiar elsewhere in Europe, would still arise in the rural parts of Italy when older people got married, or an elderly widower married a younger bride.[21]

In the Middle Ages the dating of the new year often began on March 25, the day of the incarnation of Christ; in any case the arrival of Carnival, the date of which varied with the date of Easter but always fell at a time when winter was ending and spring commencing, forcefully marked the

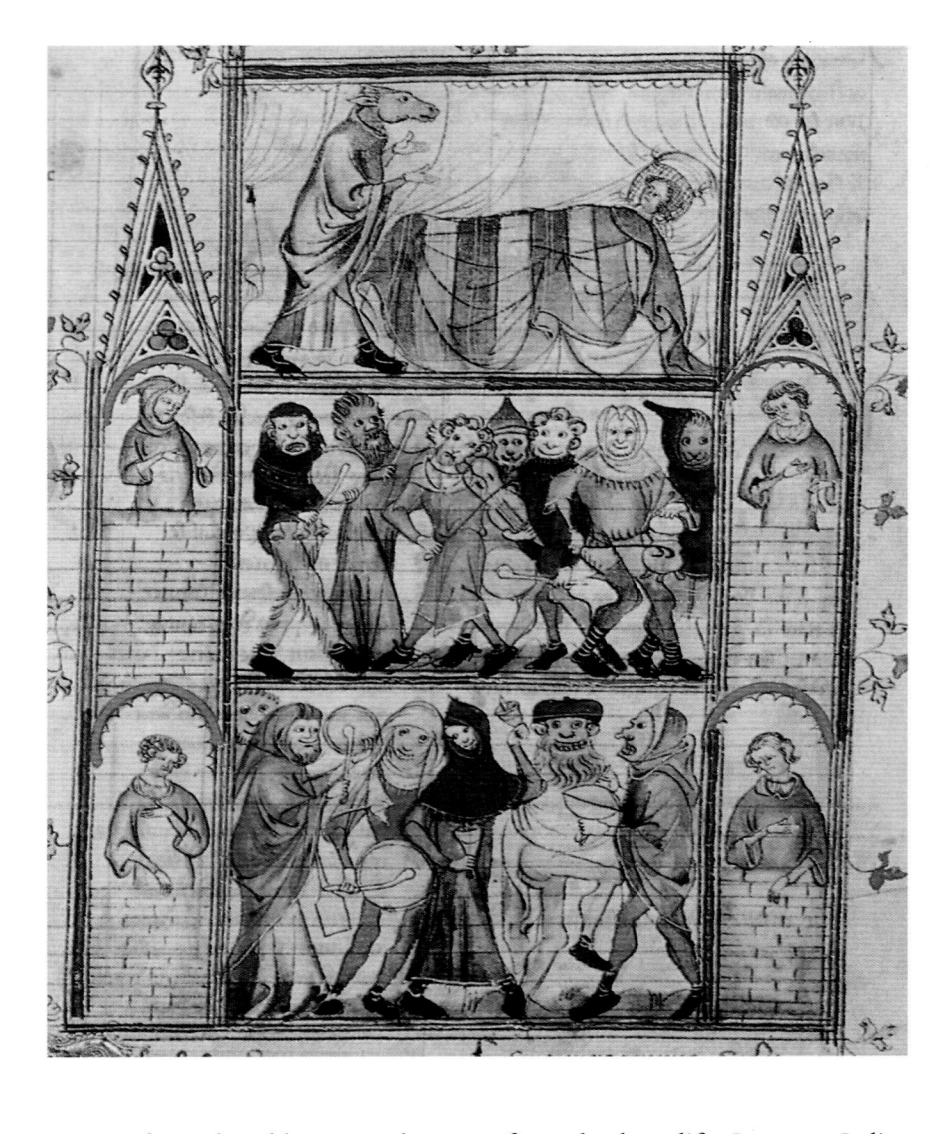

FIGURE 57 *Charivari*.
Miniature, 1316.
From the *Roman de Fauvel*.
Paris, Bibliothèque Nationale,
ms. Fr. 146, f. 34

passage from the old year to the new, from death to life. In many Italian cities *la vecchia* ("the old woman," a straw dummy) is still burned on the last day of Carnival to show that winter has reached the end of its life (*hiems*, the Latin word for winter, is feminine in gender): a way to exorcize the fear of the world of the dead, their powers, and their possible return, at the very moment at which nature resumes its cycle.

The Birth of Purgatory[22]

With the end of the period of "license" (it was compulsory for Carnival to end on Tuesday) the Church regained control, and (from the eighth century on, at any rate) immediately summoned all the faithful to penance through the rites of Ash Wednesday, which reminded everyone that they were descendants of the sinner Adam, who was made from dust and returned to dust.

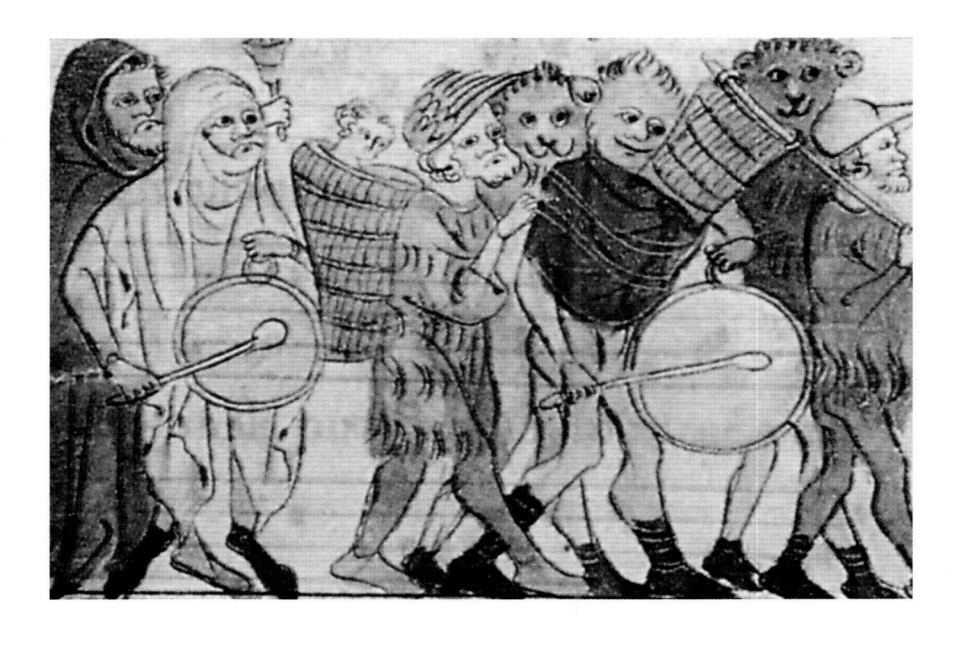

From the end of the twelfth century Christians had the chance to con-
template more than just the terrors of hell. Through a long evolution of
ideas there arose a new kingdom in the geography of the next world: purgatory, where it was firmly believed (despite the absence of any basis in
Scripture) that sins of a less serious kind could be compensated for, while
awaiting passage to paradise. To the living purgatory also offered, and offers, the consolation of believing that they can influence the fate of their
dear departed with masses and good works, and maintain their bond of af-
fection with them. From an iconographic perspective, purgatory had limited impact in terms of the imagery exposed to public view, because the
representation of it was too similar to the depiction of hell. Saint Lawrence
the martyr, who was burned alive on a grate, is one of the saintly protec-
tors of purgatory; in a fresco of 1330 at Orvieto (figure 59) we see him wel-
coming the souls as they are finally liberated from all suffering.

Even the "purgatory of Saint Patrick," the chasm that, according to
Jacopo da Varazze, served as a channel between our world and the kingdom
of purgatory, seems like the beginning of a journey to the underworld.

And since Saint Patrick was preaching in Ireland and having little
success, he prayed to God to show some portent by which men
would fear and repent. At God's command he drew a large circle
with his stick at a certain place, and there the earth opened up, and
a pit appeared, very wide and deep. The saint had a revelation that
this was a purgatory, into which any who should descend would
have no need to do any other penance, or suffer any other purgatory for their sins; nor would they even return, but would spend
the rest of their lives there. Those who did emerge from the pit
[because their sins were few] would have to stay in the pit from

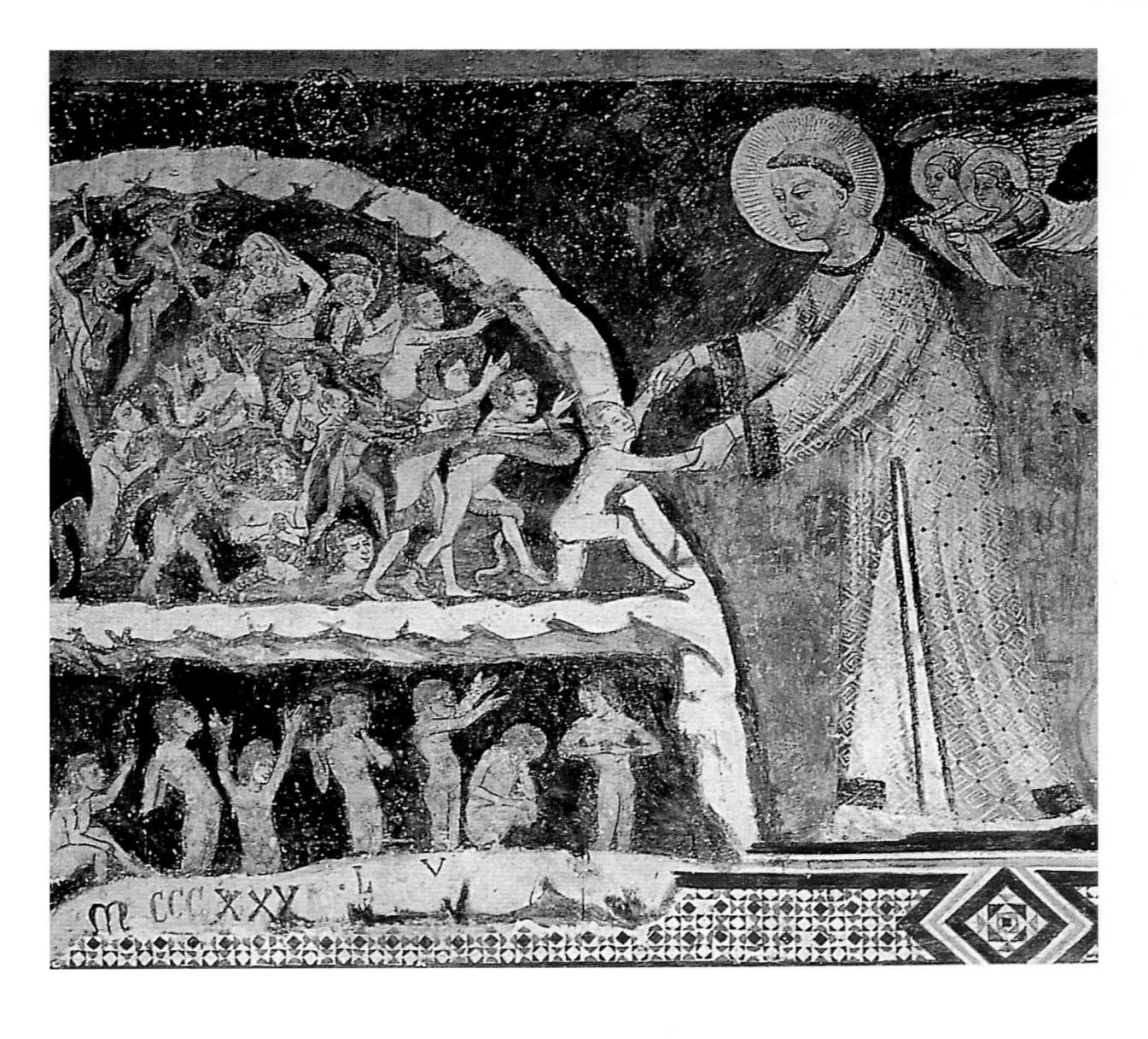

one day to the following day. And many who did enter the pit never emerged.[23]

FIGURE 59 *Purgatorio.* Fresco, 1330. Orvieto, San Lorenzo de Arari

City Time: The Invention of the Escapement Clock

The Church sought to keep its flock bunched together and urged them to come to church often, drawn by the strong peal of the bells. From the Latin system of counting the hours from sunrise, the Middle Ages adopted the terms *prime, tierce, sext,* and *nones* to denominate the hours corresponding roughly to our 6 A.M., 9 A.M., 12 noon, and 3 P.M. The Church added four more: *matins* at around midnight, *lauds* at dawn, *vespers* at evening, and *compline* before bedtime, when the day was "complete." Together, these eight constituted the canonical hours or the set times for

prayer and liturgical chant that structured the days and nights of monks[24] in abbeys that normally lay at a distance from the cities.

Beginning with the rebirth of the communes in the twelfth century, though, the role of the bells was increasingly to punctuate the working hours of urban laborers, inviting them to sanctify the entire day. The sounding of the bells was regulated by sundials that told local time. When the sun was not shining, the flow of time was measured by hourglasses filled with water (which used to freeze up in northern Europe in winter) or sand, or calibrated candles, or water clocks.

So the length of the hours varied according to the season: they were shorter in winter and longer in summer. But at the end of the thirteenth century the invention of the mechanical clock[25] ushered in a new kind of time, made of hours theoretically equal in length. The machinery of the clocks was also used to make little mechanical figures move about, and these *automi* or automatons (as they are called in Italian) delighted the population so much that they were a major reason for the mechanical clock's success, more so even than improved timekeeping. In Italy the first clock with automatons was set up at Orvieto in 1351, on a tower of the cathedral at the corner of Via del Duomo and the Piazza del Duomo. "Maurizio" is what the townspeople call it, and it still works (figure 60). The name is probably a corruption of the ancient phrase "ariologium de muriccio," or "worksite clock." It was the first mechanical timepiece that sounded the hours of the working day in a manner that was (in principle) uniform for those engaged in the construction of the cathedral. The automaton itself was cast in 1348 in an alloy from which the bells were also cast, and the clothing he wears would seem to connote him as an oblate servant of the works department of the cathedral (figure 61a). The dark hue of the metal may have helped him to keep the nickname "Maurizio," which is related to *moro* (moor). With a hammer the automaton strikes the large bell every hour, and on his belt is the following inscription (figure 61b): "Da te a me campana, fuoro pati / tu per gridar et io per fare i fati" ("O bell, this was the pact between you and me: you to sound forth, and I to do my business"[26]). And the bell itself replies, though the inscription has been damaged by the passage of time, "Se vuoi ch'attenga i pati dammi piano / se io cassirò e dara' invano" ("If you want me to respect the pact, don't strike too hard, otherwise I shall break and you will strike in vain").[27]

Clocks did not keep the kind of precise time to which we are accustomed. Because of wear on the mechanism, they generally accumulated a lag of at least an hour during the course of a day. As well, the minute hand was only introduced in 1577 by a German, Jost Burgi: the fact that no one had felt the lack of it previously suffices to give us an idea of both the broad tolerance that was accorded to the flow of time and the imprecision with which it was measured in a society where most things were approximate,[28] with a tranquil rhythm of existence and no hard deadlines, appointments,

or connections to catch. The statutes continually refer to the need to "regulate the clock" in an attempt to keep control of those hours that were always running too fast or too slow.

Around the middle of the fourteenth century, when large public clocks moved from the church bell tower to the tower of the palazzo of the commune (the "city hall"), time ceased to belong exclusively to God, and secular time was born. The first clocks had neither dials bearing the numbers from one to twelve nor hands: all they did was sound the hours, and they were thought of as being very similar to bells. In fact the word in English for a machine that keeps time, *clock*, originally meant bell (as the related words in German and French, *die Glocke* and *la cloche*, still do).

Dante in the *Divine Comedy* compares the harmonious procession of the circle of the blessed to a mechanical clock that rouses the bride of Christ, the Church, to recite matins in honor of Christ, so that he will continue to give it his love:

Then, as the tower-clock calls us to come
at the hour when God's Bride is roused from bed
to woo with matin song her Bridegroom's love,

with one part pulling thrusting in the other,
chiming, *ting-ting*, music so sweet the soul,
ready for love, swells with anticipation;

so I was witness to that glorious wheel
moving and playing voice on voice in concord
with sweetness, harmony unknown, save there

where joy becomes one with eternity

(*Paradiso* 10.139–148;
translation by Mark Musa)

What Dante describes is a clock furnished with toothed wheels, driven by weights and counterweights. The mechanism "pulls" and "thrusts" because as one wheel turns it triggers a second one that strikes the hours. In another passage from the *Paradiso*, the dancing rings of blessed spirits that move at different speeds bring to the poet's mind a clock in which the primary wheel, which turns once every twelve or twenty-four hours, seems to stand firm:

As wheels in clocks are synchronized to move
one slowly, looked at closely, almost still—
the other seems to fly compared to it,

just so those whirling wheels by differently
dancing, through their movement, fast or slow,

revealed to me the measure of their bliss.

(*Paradiso* 24.13–18;
translation by Mark Musa)

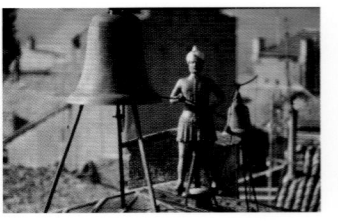

FIGURE 60
The automaton "Maurizio."
Metal alloy, 1351.
Orvieto, tower of the cathedral
at the corner of Via del Duomo
and the Piazza del Duomo

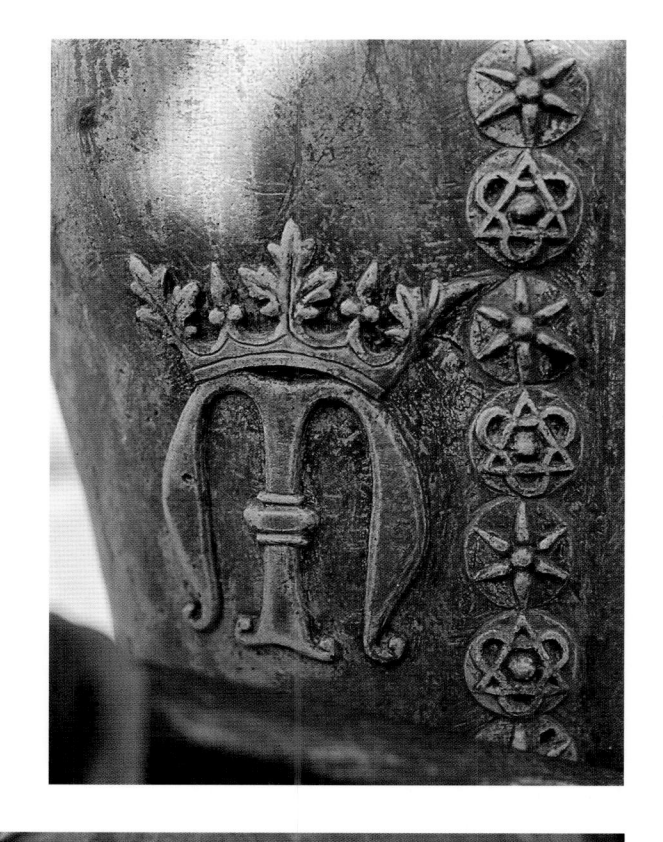

FIGURE 61A "M," the initial letter of "Maria"; detail from the inscription on the clothing of the automaton "Maurizio."

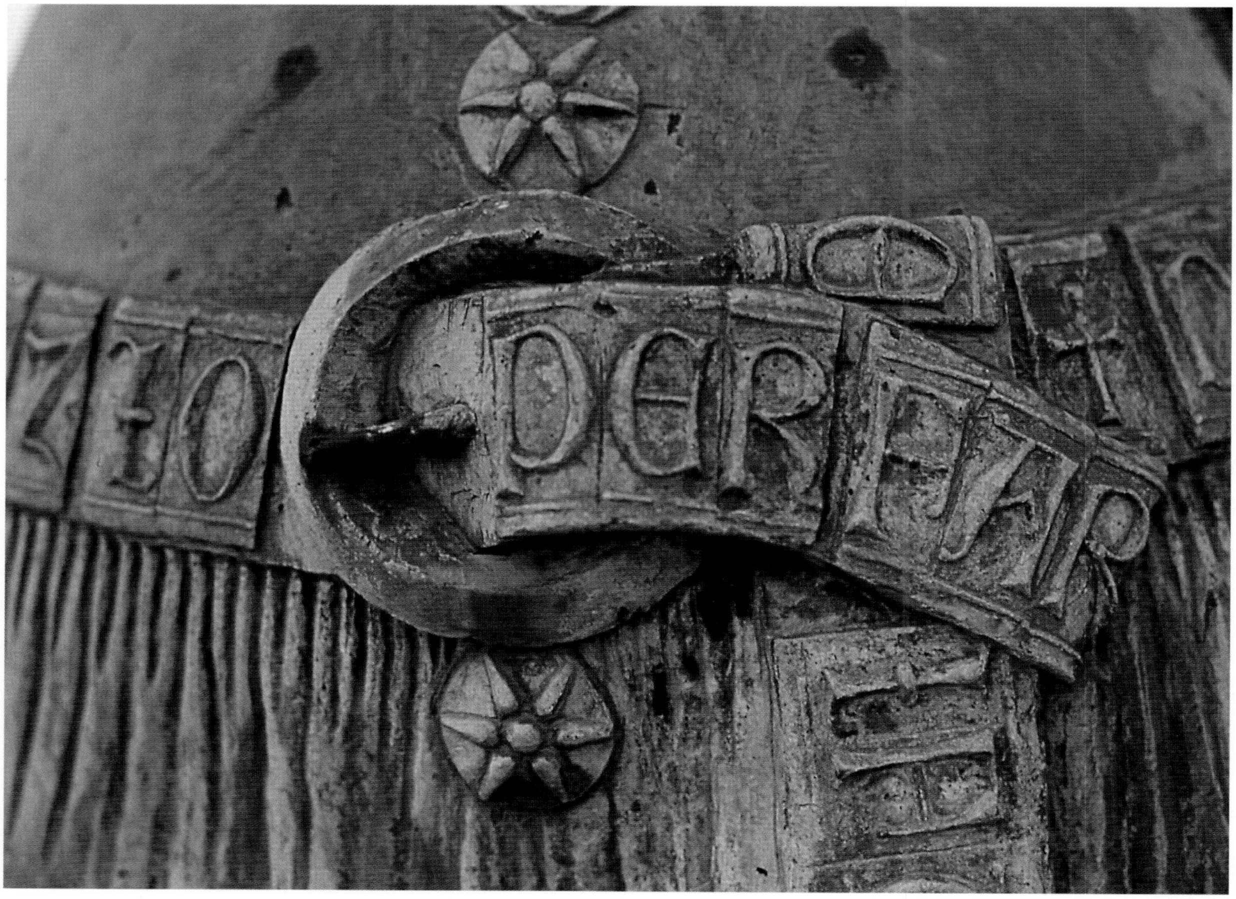

FIGURE 61B Detail of the inscription on the belt of the automaton "Maurizio."

When clocks did gain dials, these at first rotated around a fixed pointer. Often the clocks were astronomical devices as well, and showed the movement of the heavens. If the clock stopped because someone had forgotten to draw the weights, it could be started again at evening and adjusted by the position of the stars. Thanks to the work of Galileo, Christian Huygens of Holland (1629–1695) was able to make the first pendulum-driven clock in 1665. Finally the movement of the gear wheels was kept regular by the constant oscillation of the pendulum.

One of the oldest surviving clocks originally belonged to the cathedral of Strasbourg; built in 1354, it signaled the hours by activating a mechanical rooster that fluttered its wings and crowed at every stroke. This clock was kept in use until 1789, and today can be seen in the museum at Strasbourg. And there are at least two other mechanical clocks that still work perfectly, the ones at Wells (1392) and Salisbury (1386).[30]

The first mechanical clocks worked a little like the spring that turns a spit. A rope to which a weight had been attached was wrapped around a rod and unwound with a constant acceleration. A set of geared wheels was able to slow the movement in such a way as to keep the clock going, and for quite a long time, if the device was mounted high above the ground, in a tower or bell tower. But to keep it going day and night at a set rate, a different solution was needed: the real qualitative leap in the making of clocks was the introduction of the escapement.[31] The escapement

> is a device placed at the extremity of the mechanism, with the double function of interrupting its movement at the desired instant, and periodically distributing the energy into a regulating organ. This system in effect allows a small amount of the driving force generated by the weight to "escape" in regular quantities, in such a way as to keep the oscillator, which has the task of dividing time up into equal intervals, in motion.[32]

This ingenious system constantly halts the toothed wheel and then sets it back in motion, at regular intervals, and at the same time keeps the machinery running by itself for a long period. The identity of the inventor has been debated for a long time. Some thought that a primitive escapement mechanism was to be found among the sketches of Villard de Honnecourt, a celebrated architect of the thirteenth century who left a rich notebook containing some drawings of medieval machines, but on close inspection this proved not to be the case.[33]

In 1344, on the façade of the Palazzo del Capitano at Padua, Jacopo Dondi installed an astronomical clock of such perfection that he was given the honorific title "dall'Orologio," and his descendants from that time on bore it as part of their surname. His son Giovanni Dondi dall'Orologio (1318–1389) worked for fifteen years to complete a planetary clock, the *As-*

trarium, in 1364. It had an escapement mechanism and a wheeled balance and was equipped with seven dials, one for each of the planets then known, all of them rotating about the Earth in accordance with the Ptolemaic theory.[34] This clock was so complex that after the death of its maker no one was able to correct the weights and make the *Astrarium* run properly, until the rusty relic was given to the emperor Charles V in the sixteenth century. The monarch appealed to a proven clockmaker, Giannello Torriano of Cremona, who decided to rebuild the machine by copying exactly the original, which was beyond recovery. Famiano Strada wrote in the seventeenth century[35] that Charles V enjoyed constructing clocks himself under the guidance of Giannello Torriani, and that he "governed their wheels more easily than he did those of fortune."

Every day Giannello diverted the spirit of Charles V, who was passionately curious about such things, with new inventions. After lunch he would produce models of armed soldiers and horsemen, some beating on drums and others sounding trumpets, which would charge at each other and fight with lances. Sometimes Giannello released small wooden birds in his room that flew about everywhere. This was done with such marvelous artifice that the superior of the convent, who was present once, believed that these toys were made by magic.

Giovanni Dondi dall'Orologio had described his *Astrarium* in a treatise, and so precisely that on the basis of his drawings and explanations it has been possible in modern times to reconstruct it; an example can be seen at the Museum of Science and Technology in Milan (figures 62 and 63).

In the fifteenth century escapement clocks had become so widespread that they even influenced the representation of symbolic images. In the *Triumph of Time* attributed to Iacopo del Sellaio (figure 64), the god Cronus, hoary and tattered as befits his status, is shown above a clock, which is now the extent of his domain. Using an old sand clock, he adjusts the motion of the escapement mechanism that controls the weight-driven movements of the clock, which has a twenty-four-hour dial adorned with a radiant sun. The base of the clock is held in the bite of two dogs, one black and the other white: a summary reference to the legend of Barlaam from the celebrated medieval romance *Barlaam and Josaphat*.[36] The beginning of one of the fables contained in it tells of a man who, fleeing from a unicorn (death), falls into a pit (the world); he grasps a bush (life) and realizes that a white mouse (day) and a black one (night) are devouring its roots.

Botticelli has imagined Saint Augustine in a study that reveals the strong interest in science of its inhabitant (figure 65). A large armillary sphere sits atop the reading stand, and a book lies open on the shelf behind the saint (with the theorems of Pythagoras accompanied by drawings). In front of it stands a large timepiece, with the escapement mechanism carefully reproduced (figure 66). The hand points to midnight, suggesting the intensity of

Saint Augustine's meditation as he neglects sleep, gripped by thoughts of God and his own sins.

Names for the Notes

The sweet chiming of the clock was the detail that Dante chose to emphasize. The passing hours would bring back the identical sound at regular intervals, because it came from the wheels and gears of the mechanism. But how to make the complexity of sound exactly reproducible with a musical instrument? By placing the notes on a musical staff. The answer, seemingly obvious, actually rests on yet another medieval invention, which we owe to the great Guido d'Arezzo.

Guido was a Benedictine monk and a musician, who may have been born at Talla near Arezzo, or perhaps in the zone of Ferrara-Pomposa, between 992 and 1000, and who died at Ravenna in perhaps 1080. An extraordinary teacher of music, he was able to give singers the ability to sight-read any new song and sing it immediately and correctly without the help of the monochord, an ancient single-string instrument, and without assistance from the instructor.[37] A miniature from 1050 that illustrates the prologue to the *Regulae Rhythmicae* (the rules of rhythm) of his most famous work, the *Micrologus*, shows him as he writes on the codex placed on a stand: "Gliscunt corda meis hominum mollita Camenis" ("the hearts of men swell as they are softened by my muse"), a hexameter that poetically acknowledges the power of the Camenae, that is, of the Muses, to rouse us and stir our emotions (figure 67).

Guido placed great importance on the musical staff, which he designed with four lines instead of our five, giving equal value to the spaces and the lines; he used key letters and the colors red and yellow to indicate the semitones, yellow or green for "do," red for "fa." Using the method of analogy he adopted the sounds and intervals contained in the hymn to Saint John (from the eighth century) in order to locate the intonation of other sounds and intervals contained in other melodies.

On his four-line staff he placed the marks for the notes, which were uniform but which took on a different meaning according to their placement on the lines or the spaces between the lines—a series of sounds that rose progressively in pitch, laid out in a scale and distinguished by the first syllable of each verse of the hymn to Saint John, "Ut queant laxis." Guido very probably adapted the melody of the hymn for pedagogical purposes, that is, to make the ascending notes coincide with the beginnings of the "verses," which go as follows: "UT queant laxis REsonare fibris MIra gestorum FAmuli tuorum SOLve polluti LAbii reatum Sancte Johannes!" ("So that your servants may sing the marvel of your actions with free strings, remove the sin from their polluted lips, o Saint John!"). The re-

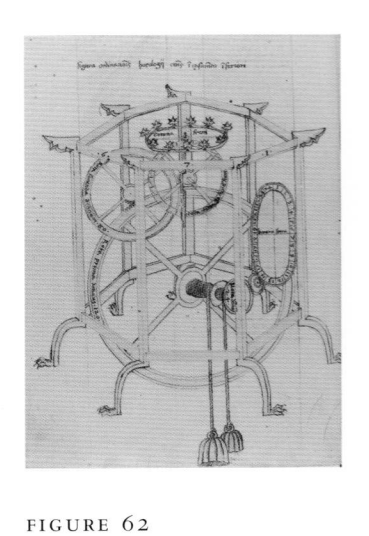

FIGURE 62
Giovanni Dondi
dall'Orologio. *Astrarium.*
Drawing, 1461.
Oxford, Bodleian Library,
ms. Laud. Misc. 620, f. 10v

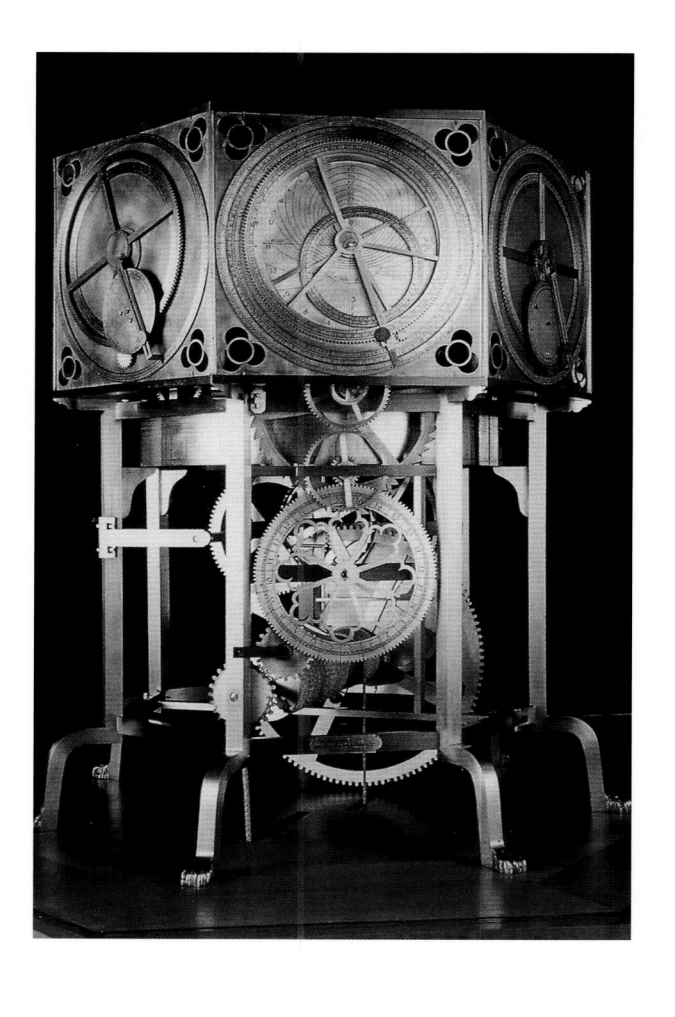

FIGURE 63   The *Astrarium* of Giovanni Dondi
dall'Orologio as reconstructed by Luigi Pippa.
Milan, Museo della Scienza e della Tecnica

FIGURE 64
Iacopo del Sellaio, *The Triumph of Time*.
Panel, 1480–1490.
Fiesole, Museo Bandini

sulting sequence of notes is "ut, re, mi, fa, sol, la." Only in 1635 did "do"
became the first note in Italy; "ut," however, remained first in France. At
the end of the fifteenth century "si" was added (from *Sancte Johannes*).

Uncertainty about the interpretation and meaning of the notes had
been abolished at last, and the exact intonation established. Before Guido
d'Arezzo the signs corresponding to the notes ("*neumi*") were marked on
the blank page "in the open," above the text, without the slightest indication of their pitch. With the reforms that he introduced, a new way of
writing music made its appearance; in evolved form, it is still in use.

Using the hexacordal scale, Guido created a form of solfeggio and gave
it practical application with the system of the harmonic hand or "guidonic hand," which he did not directly invent but did utilize and make widely known (figure 68). In this system, the notes and scales were indicated on
the tips and the joints of the fingers of the left hand in the correct order.
More precisely, seven hexachords (scales of six sounds) are laid out starting
from the extremity of the thumb (gamma = ut), and continuing counter-
clockwise in a spiral until the nineteenth sound dd-la-sol. The twentieth
sound of the seventh hexachord was located above the middle finger in this
scheme (figure 69).

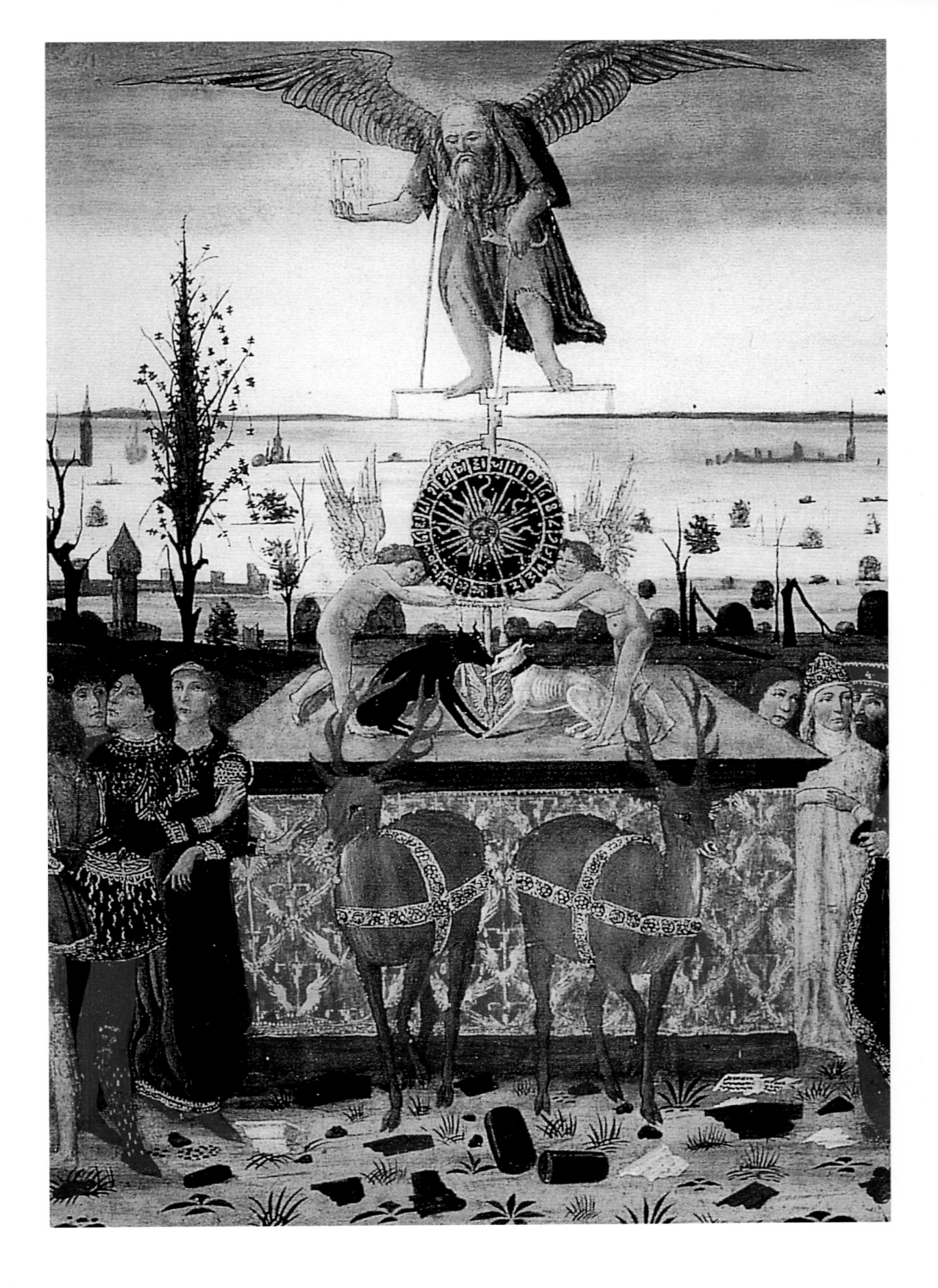

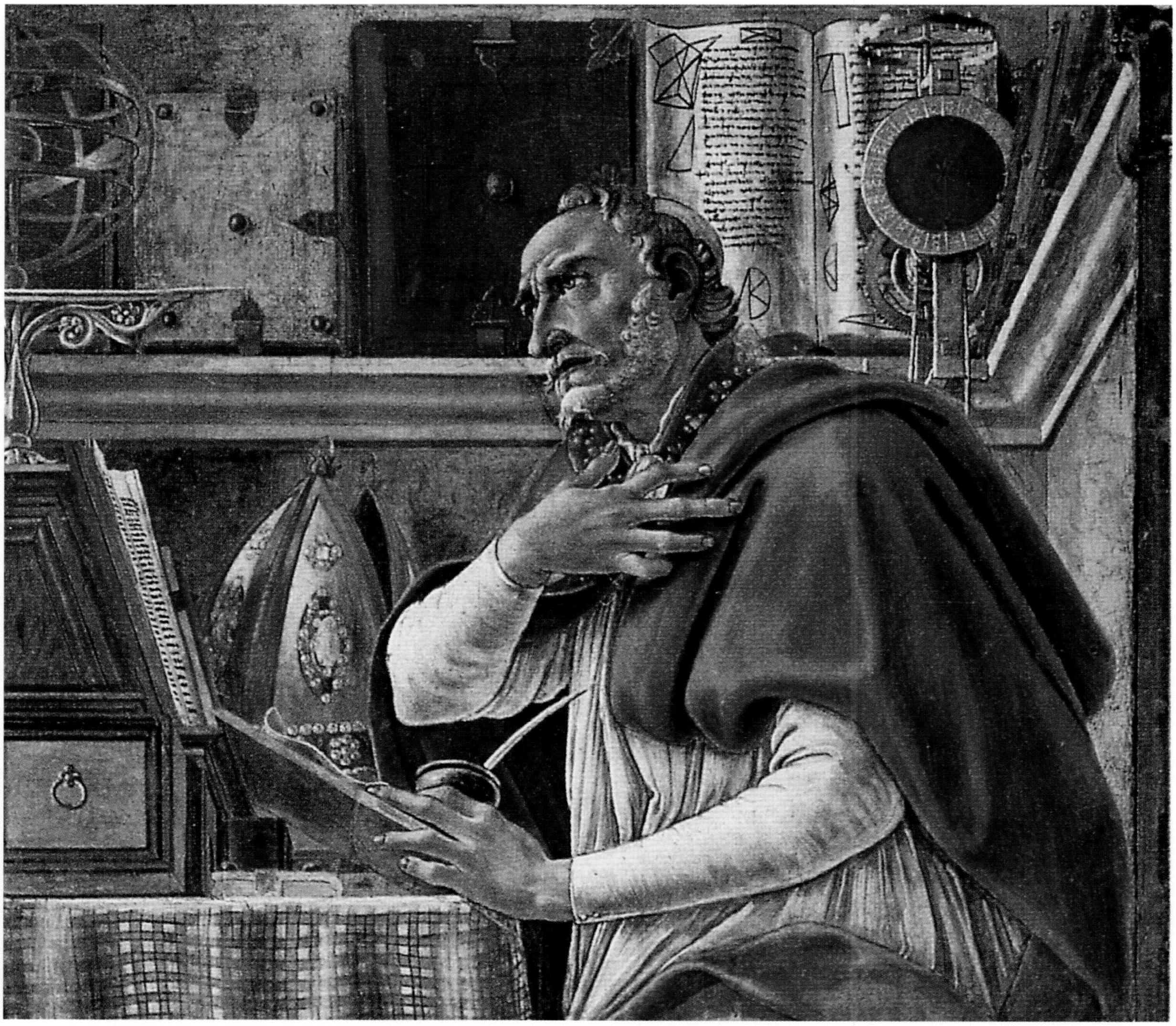

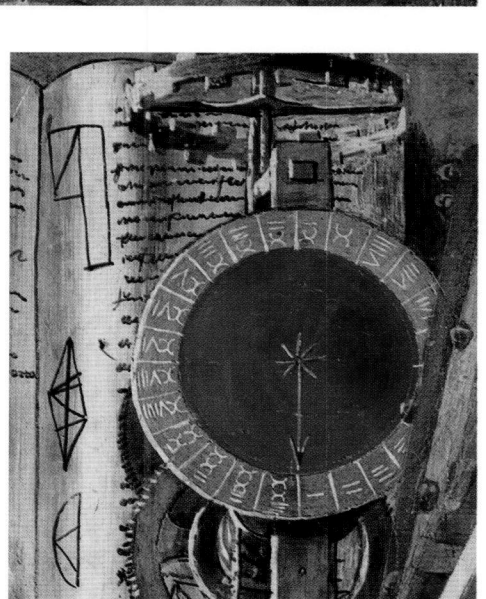

FIGURES 65 & 66 Sandro Botticelli, *Saint Augustine in His Study*.
Fresco, c. 1480.
Florence, Ognissanti Church

FIGURE 67 *Guido d'Arezzo*
Pen drawing with color added, 1050, from *Micrologus*.
Wolfenbüttel, Herzog August Bibliothek, cod. Guelf. 334,
Gud. Lat. 8°, f. 4r

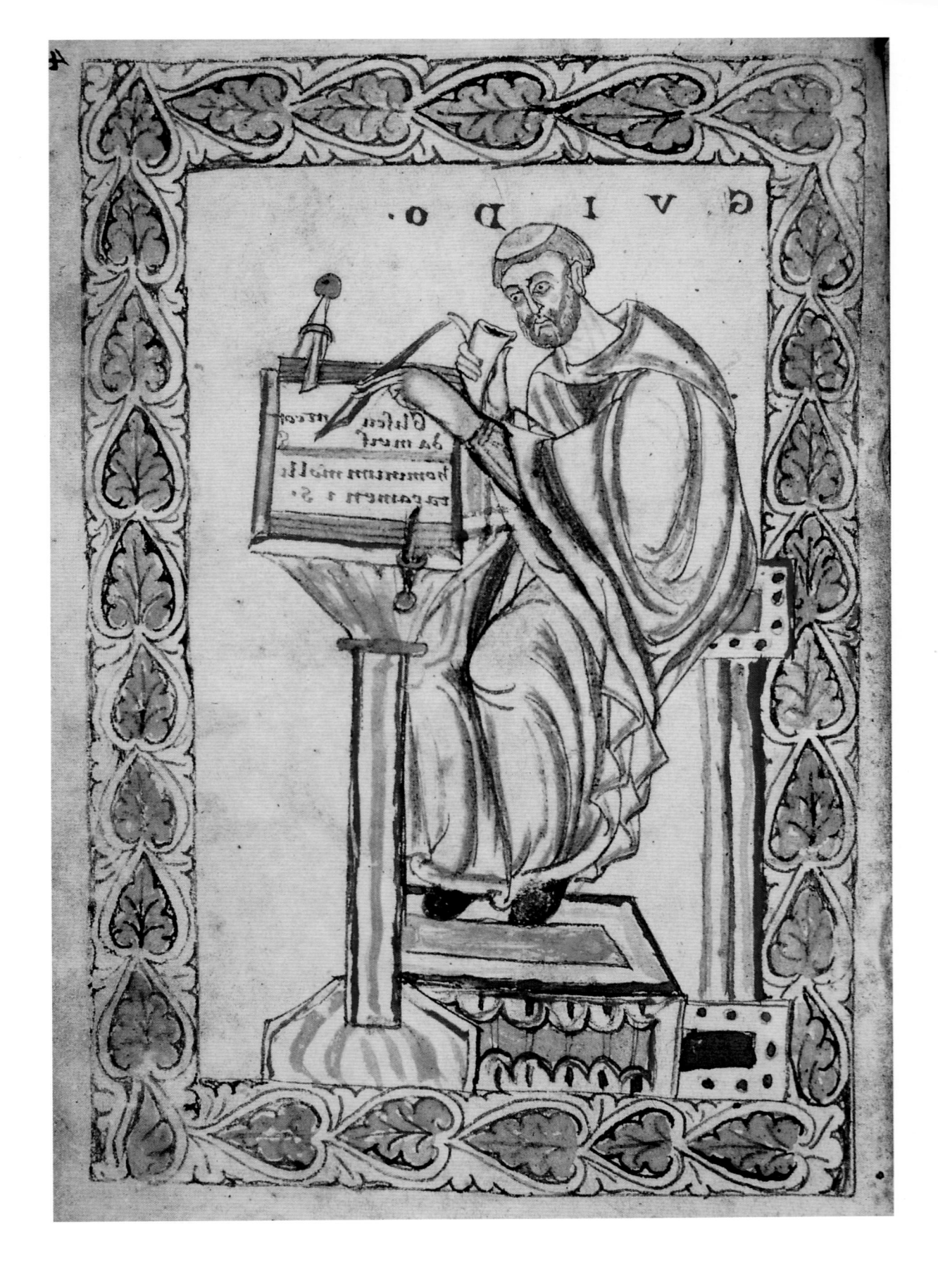

The harmonic hand was a device that singers greatly appreciated; Hollandinus of Leuven wrote in the fourteenth century, "Disce manum tantum bene qui vis discere cantum. Absque manu frustra disces per plurima lustra" ("Learn the hand if you want to learn to sing well. Without the hand you will struggle in vain for years and years to learn").[38]

"I know no more useful or better stone": The Powers of Coral

To this point we have been wandering about in the rooms of men of learning and examining their discoveries. Let us now go into an average house of the Middle Ages: in it we will discover the origin of many of our customs, and of a few objects and foodstuffs that we still use as well. We can start with the fears that many people today still hold at bay through the use of coral, for amulets of this substance were believed to be of great efficacy in the past.

In the fourteenth century Fazio degli Uberti dedicated several tercets to this mysterious marine growth and its marvelous power:

The Ligurian sea generates coral
at its bottom, like a shrub,
pale, with a color between clear and yellow.
A branch breaks off like glass
when it is grasped, and the bigger it is
and the more branches it has, the more beautiful it appears.
As soon as it emerges into the air, it becomes red
and not only does it change color
but becomes so strong and hard that it is like bone.
Having it with you when lightning strikes
gives your vision and your heart the strengh to gaze forth;
I know no more useful or better stone.[39]

Coral not only gave protection against bad weather; it was thought highly useful in curing all the diseases that were such a danger to the health of children. Giordano da Pisa certainly believed in it, as we see from a gloss, in one of his sermons, on the resurrection of a girl whom Christ touched with his hand:

Nothing can transmit its power to anything else, nor can anything receive the beneficial influence of any other thing, without direct contact between them. Hence we see that in order for precious stones to work their influence, men wear them. For they would have no effect without direct contact. Likewise you see that one

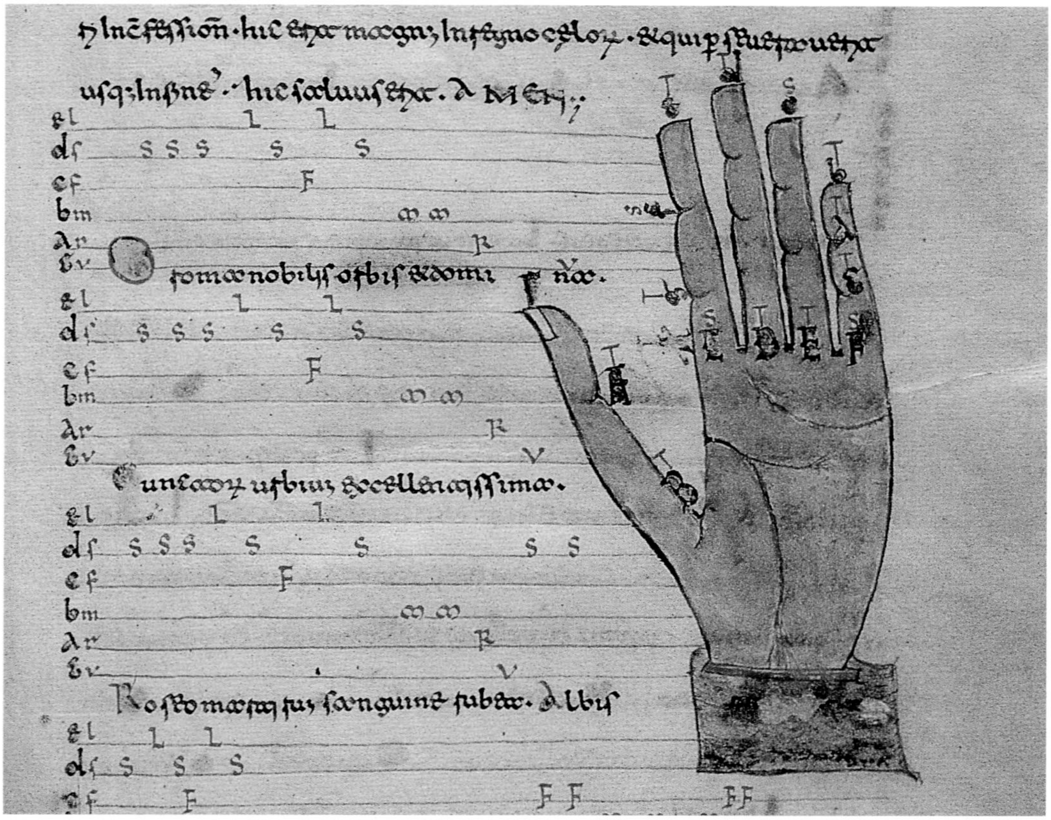

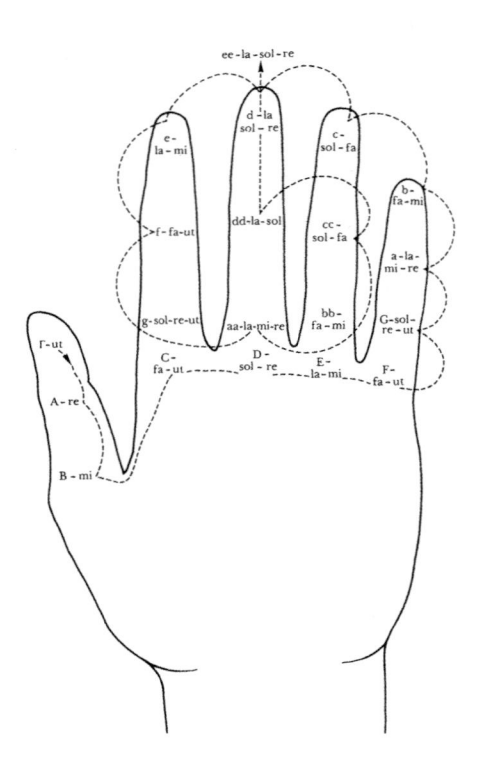

FIGURE 68 "Guidonic" hand.
Miniature, end of the eleventh century. abbey of Montecassino, Biblioteca, ms. 318, f. 291

FIGURE 69 The layout of the "Guidonic" hand.

FIGURE 70
Barnaba da Modena (active between 1361 and 1383), *Madonna and Babe with a Coral Amulet Around His Neck.*
Panel, c. 1367(?).
Boston, Museum of Fine Arts, Gift of Mrs. W. Scott Fitz

FIGURE 71 School of Lorenzo da Viterbo, *Saint Egidius Suckled by a Doe.*
Altarpiece, beginning of the fifteenth century.
Orte, Museo Diocesano

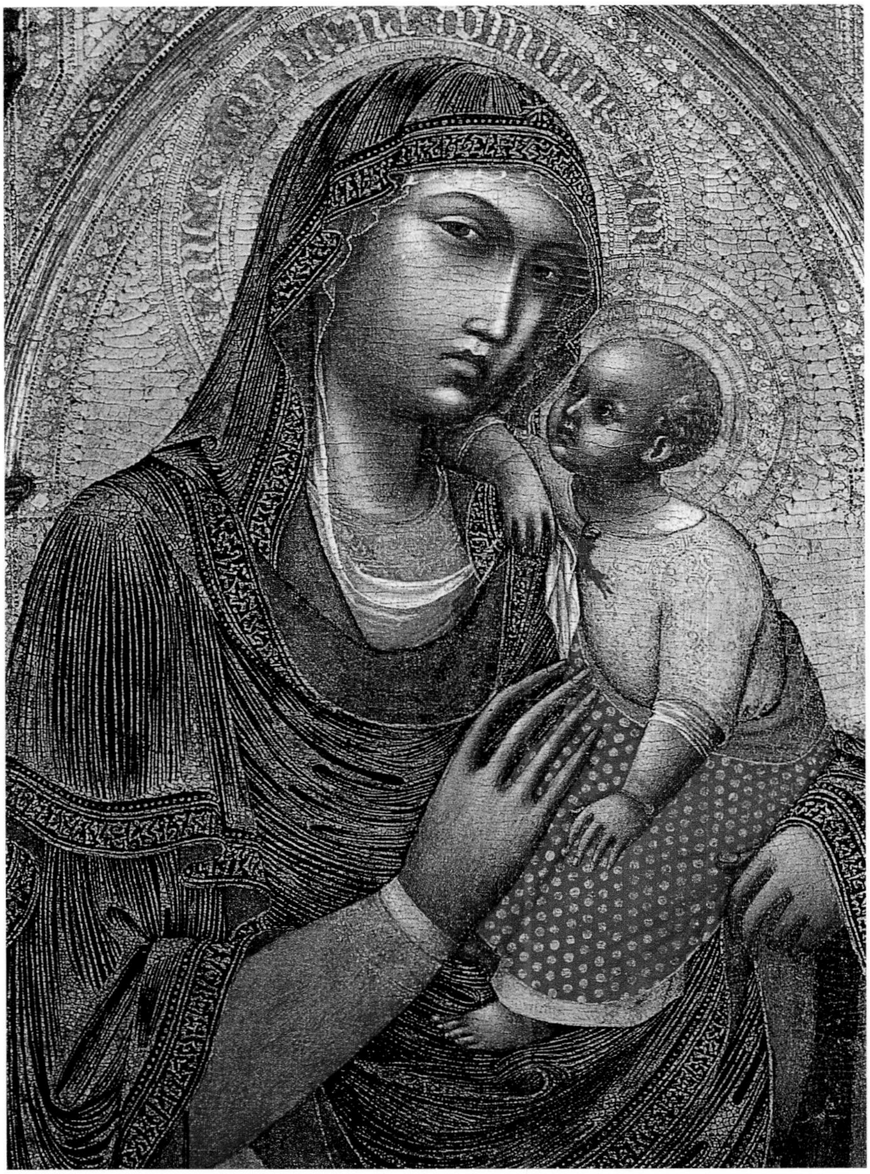

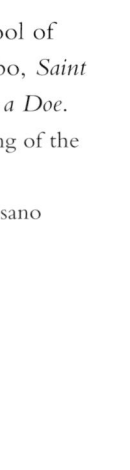

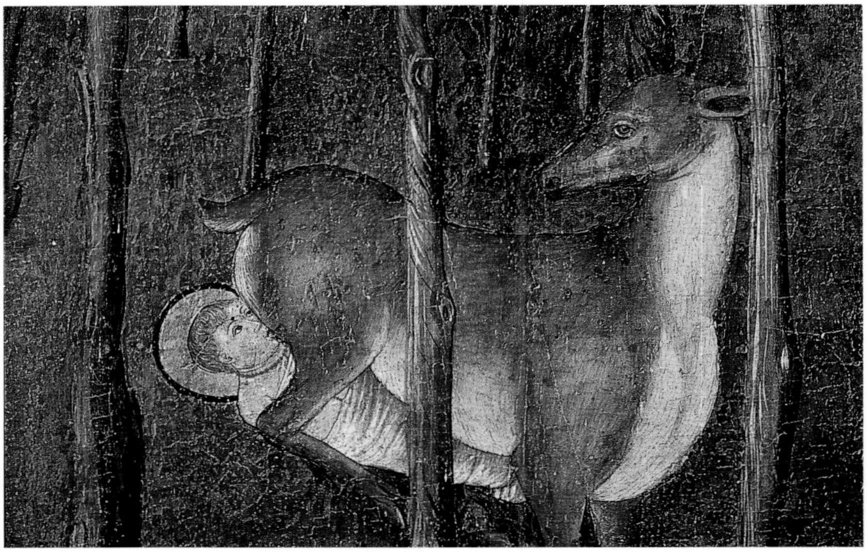

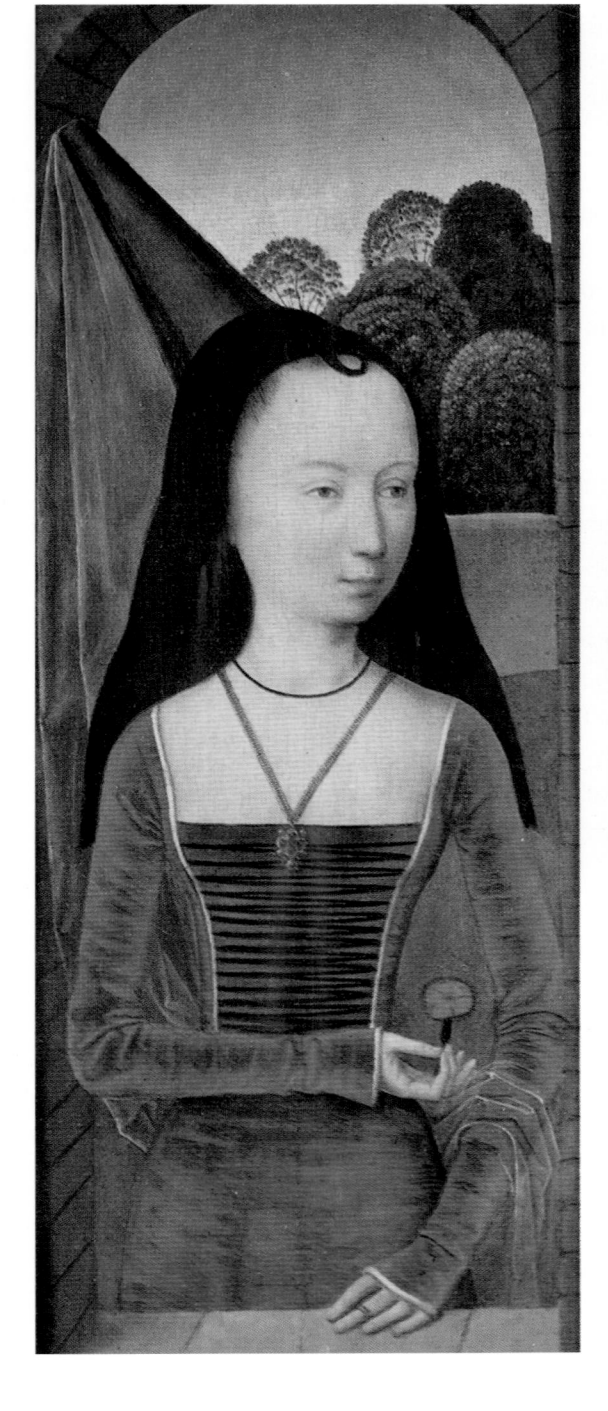

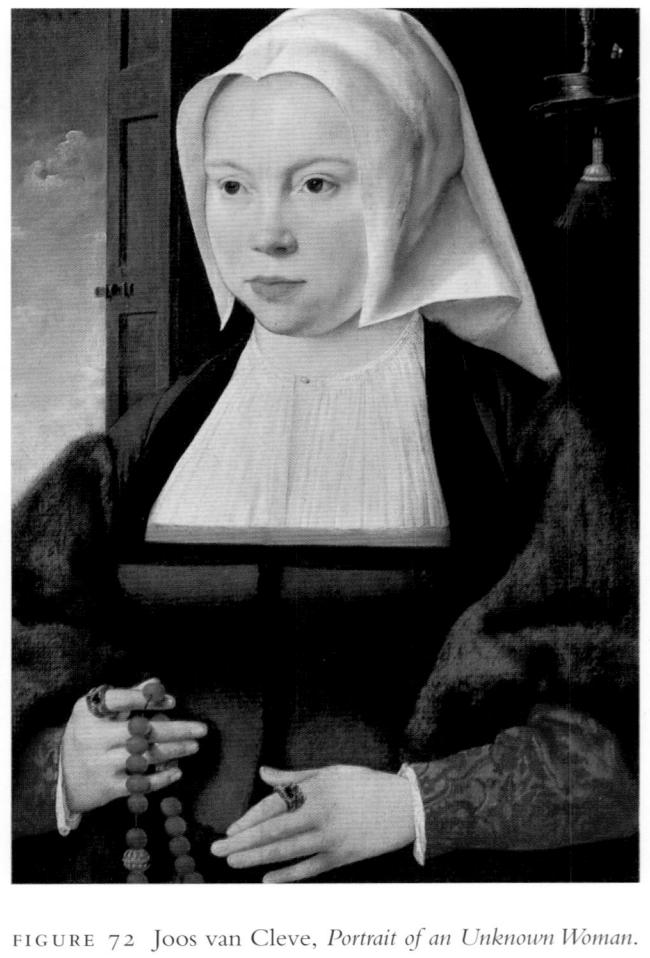

FIGURE 72 Joos van Cleve, *Portrait of an Unknown Woman.*
Panel, sixteenth century. Florence, Uffizi

FIGURE 73 Hans Memling, *Portrait of a Fiancée.*
Panel, c. 1480. New York, Metropolitan Museum of Art

puts a ring on the finger of another. And children put coral round their necks so that the power from outside may work upon them. Without direct contact it would not do any good.[40]

Often the baby Jesus himself wears coral, as for example in a panel (figure 70) by Barnaba di Modena, in which a beautiful red branch of the stuff hangs from his slender neck. Poor Saint Egidius would certainly have died in the forest soon after childbirth, if a provident doe had not suckled him. The fifteenth-century painter who illustrated this miraculous nourishment was careful to give him a beautiful necklace of red coral, perhaps to confirm the extraordinary luck of the babe in finding such an exceptional wet nurse (figure 71).

Coral, gems, pearls, and crystals were used to make strings of rosary beads, which were particularly popular in the fourteenth century and were often used simply as jewelry rather than for religious ends. The institution of a mystic diadem of prayers, like a rosebush around the Virgin (a tenfold *Ave Maria* repeated fifteen times, with a *Pater Noster* and a *Gloria* inserted between each repetition),[41] was attributed by the Dominican Alain de la Roche in the fifteenth century to Saint Dominic himself, but the recitation was already in use among the Cistercians in the thirteenth century. To keep track of the repetitions, Christians in the Middle Ages used a circlet called a paternoster, because ten beads of equal size that corresponded to the recitation of the *Ave Maria* were followed by a single larger one to signify the recitation of the *Pater Noster.* Boccaccio uses such an object ironically to sharpen his portrait of a hypocritical go-between: "always with paternoster in hand, she attended whenever indulgence was given."[42] And an irritated servant, who evidently used them frequently, defends herself against the accusations of her master in a novel of Franco Sacchetti, crying, "Don't imagine I don't know beans from the beads on a paternoster!"[43]

There is no doubt, however, that a young woman depicted by Joos van Cleve wearing an austere and immaculate bonnet that completely covers her hair was of a devout and serious character; the rosary beads she is fingering confirm it (figure 72). Thoughts of quite a different kind must be filling the head of another young woman, a fiancée, portrayed by Hans Memling wearing a low neckline and plenty of jewelry, and holding a red carnation, the symbol of love, in her hand (figure 73).[44] The long cone-shaped hat adorned with a veil that she is wearing is a prototype of the ones that popular illustrations, from the nineteenth century down to the present, have shown being worn by fairies—a case of genuine late-medieval attire being freely transformed and assigned to the world of imaginary things.

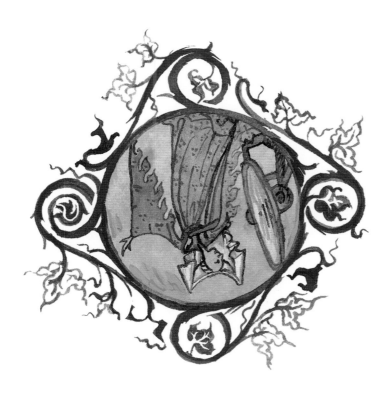

THREE Dressing and Undressing

Buttons, a Revolution in Fashion

Not only was coral made into jewels and rosary beads, it was used to make buttons as well—a novelty that first appeared in Italy in the thirteenth century, and came into widespread use in the fourteenth. At first buttons were regarded as ornaments, and were made and sold by jewelers. Women were prepared to spend, and to induce their family members to spend, so much money on buttons that they sometimes got into trouble, for there were laws against luxury consumption, aimed at limiting ostentatious display by the non-noble classes and preventing too much capital from being tied up unproductively.[1]

Franco Sacchetti amuses himself and the reader in one of his novellas by recounting the efforts of a magistrate, Amerigo degli Amerighi da Pesaro, to curb feminine embellishment; he has to confess that it is unstoppable:

> My lords, I have studied all my life to gain mastery of law, and now, when I thought I knew a thing or two, I find that I know nothing; for when I went about in search of the ornaments forbidden to your women, as you ordered me to do, I found that the things they are up to are not covered by any legislation. Let me tell you about a few.
>
> One woman was found wearing a *becchetto*[2] decorated with slashes above her hood. My notary said to her: "Tell me your name, be-

erat genuflis patriarca. et idola adorabat hic unicã filiam
habebat ĩ cĩ spm suũ ponebat. Illa uero repleta spũ sċo iner
ut natã de sua matre. i q̃da ciuitate aĩctẽ. xv. ab ãnocha
ciuitate. Que nutrita fuit alera susceperat eam nutrice nu
tures quãdo aut mortua emater. Beata margarita ampli
ori de sideno tenebat a sua martrice. quia uere formosa eãt
q x̃pm ĩ uocabat. ac oĩ timebar et adorabat. Ciosa eãt
patri suo et dilecta eãt adñ ihu x̃po. eãt aut anorũ duodeci
et delectabat in domo nutricis sue. Et audiuit certami
na omniũ martirũ. quia sanguis multas iustorũ. effunde
bar iullis tẽporibz p nõie ihu x̃pe. Illa uero repleta spũ
sċo tota se tradidit deo. qui eã saluã fecit et castã redidit. tũ
aĩa quã corpore. Et ipsa pascebat oues nutricis sue cõ
cetis puellis coetaneis suis.

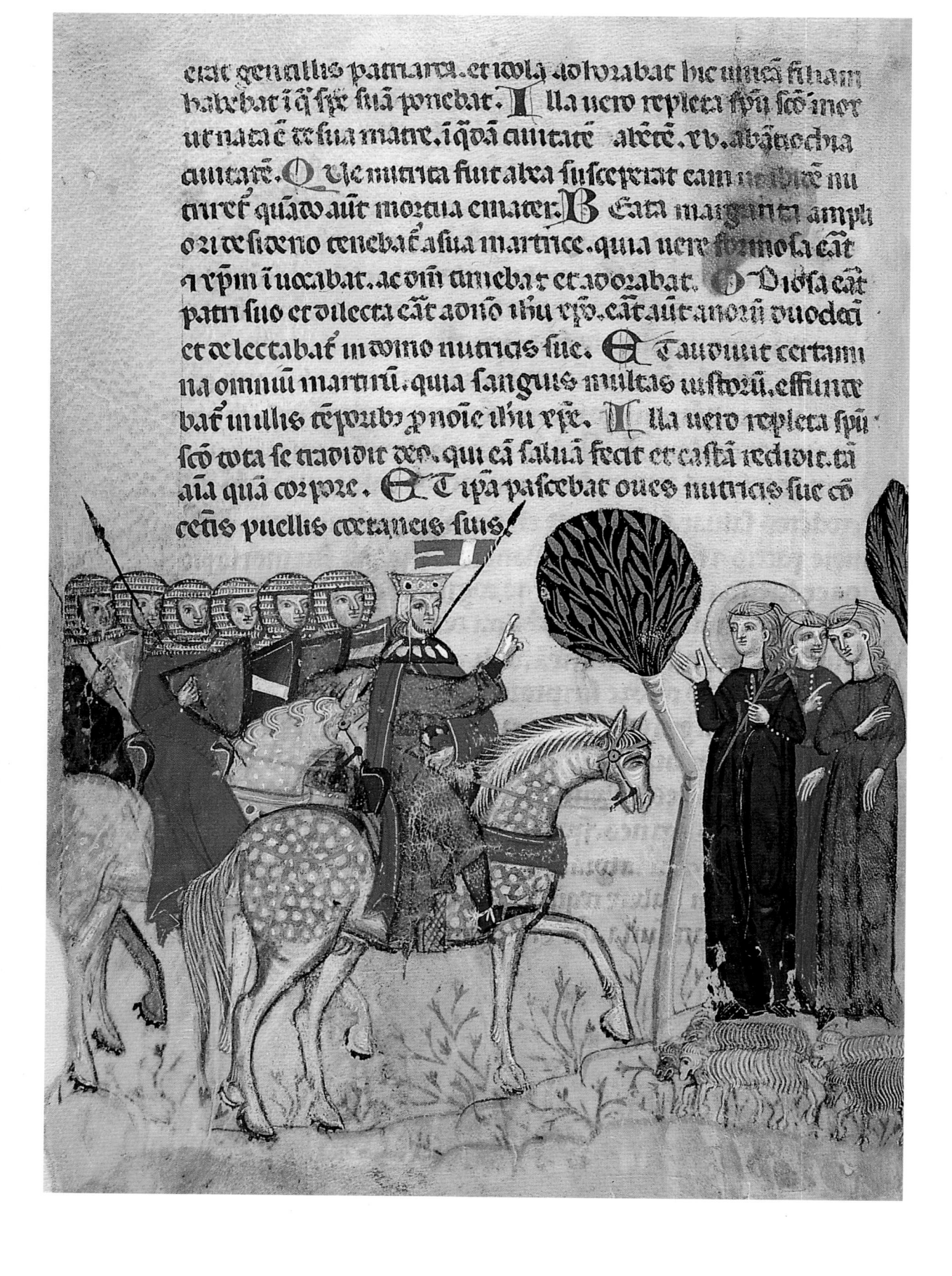

cause your *becchetto* has been cut." The good woman took off the *becchetto*, which was attached to the hood with a pin, and held it out in her hands, and declared that it was a garland. He inspected her further, and found that she was wearing numerous buttons on her front; so he said to her: "You can't wear these buttons." But the woman answered: "Yes sir, I can, for these are not buttons but *coppelle* [concave buttons]; look if you don't believe me: they have no knob, and there is no buttonhole either."[3]

FIGURE 74
The Encounter Between the King and Santa Margherita. Miniature, thirteenth century. Verona, Biblioteca Comunale, ms. 1853, f. 27v

Gradually the practical function of buttons came to the fore, and they were produced from brass or copper or glass (though as we saw, there were those who tried to pass the latter off as crystal[4]). Thanks to buttons, women in the thirteenth century were able for the first time to wear clinging dresses that accentuated their figures, with tight sleeves that displayed the shape of the arm (figure 74). They still wanted to wear clothing made of ample amounts of material, for that was a token of wealth; but with buttons, less cloth was needed for individual garments. So they wore dresses with long trains, and developed the "layered look" by adding garments on top of other garments, so as to use plenty of fabric. Buttons not only made it possible to adjust the neckline and the sleeves, they also made it possible to produce sleeves that were completely detachable.

That's Another Pair of Sleeves!

The common Italian expression "That's another pair of sleeves!" ("That is something quite different!") comes to us from the Middle Ages, when sleeves might be placed, out of practical necessity or perhaps for decorative reasons, in a clothes chest apart from the suit to which they belonged.

Normally people wore sleeves of a simple kind when they were in the house and more elaborate and elegant ones when they went out. There was another reason as well for having detachable sleeves: they were the part of one's clothing most likely to get dirty. For that matter, employees in shops were called "mezze maniche" (half sleeves) long after the Middle Ages, for as long as ink was used, in fact, because they used to cover the elbows and cuffs of their shirt sleeves with a second pair of black half-sleeves.

Yet another factor played a part: doing the laundry was a major chore in the Middle Ages, one that people preferred to put off as long as possible. Soap did exist; Madama Iancofiore, a courtesan in a tale of Boccaccio, used "musk-scented soap" as an instrument of seduction.[5] But dirty clothes were washed with ash and quantities of hot water (which took a lot of time and trouble to get hot). The protagonist of another novella by Franco Sacchetti, a certain Riccio Cederni, happened to put on a small helmet in which a cat had deposited "a lot of stinking filth." Let's listen to how difficult it was

to get his head, and the padded lining of the helmet, clean again. First he summoned his servant girl to get the excrement out of his hair:

> The servant, without thinking, wanted to wash him with cold water; but Riccio began to shout at her to light the fire and heat some lye [water infused with wood ash]. This she did, while Riccio stood waiting bareheaded for the lye to become hot. When it was hot he went into a tiny courtyard where there was a sewer to drain off the dirty water. And there he worked at washing his head for about four hours. When his head was washed, though not so clean that it didn't still give off an odor, he told the servant to bring him the helmet, but it was so besmirched all over that neither she, nor he, dared touch it. There was a bucket in the court, so he decided to fill it with water, and when it was full, he immersed the helmet in it, saying, "Let it soak as long as necessary." Riccio then put on the warmest hood he had, but he still got a toothache on account of not being able to wear his helmet, and had to stay inside for a number of days. As for the servant, you would have thought she was washing out a stomach [of a calf or a pig], as she had to unsew the lining and spend two days washing it.[6]

Detachable sleeves were worn by rich women and queens for style, of course, not necessity. Women used to present a sleeve to the knight they favored, and he would wear it as a fluttering banner attached to his cuirass. In the romance *Érec et Énide*, Chrétien de Troyes (c. 1130–c. 1185) describes the beginning of a tourney: "What a spectacle of vermilion banners, of veils and sleeves, turquoise or white, given as tokens of love! What an assembly of lances tinted blue or ochre-red, gold, silver, and other colors, striped or spotted!"[7]

In 1297 Violante of Sicily, the wife of King Robert of Anjou, was robbed by a most nimble thief, who succeeded in slipping off one of her precious sleeves while she was absorbed in watching a spectacle.[8] By the beginning of the thirteenth century sleeves were simply fastened to the rest of the clothing with ribbons or buttons, a custom that lasted for many centuries and enjoyed special favor in the fifteenth century. In a splendid painting by Georges de la Tour, *Le Tricheur à l'as de carreau* (*The Cheat with the Ace of Diamonds*; figures 75 and 76), examples of all the different types of fastening are to be found: on the left, the cheat has allowed the ends of the ribbons to dangle; the wary player opposite him has her sleeves attached with buttons; and the young man about to be swindled on the right has used ribbons tied in bows to attach his sleeves, which are made of a plain white fabric, to a contrasting luxurious corset with designs in silk worked into it.

During the Middle Ages, improved methods of weaving and the high volume of trade led to the production and circulation of luxury fabrics of

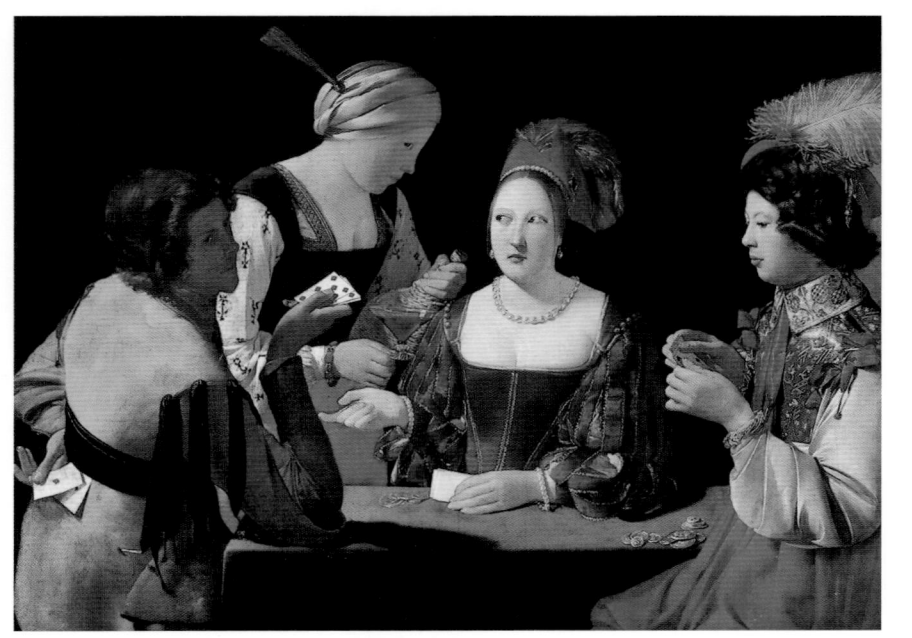

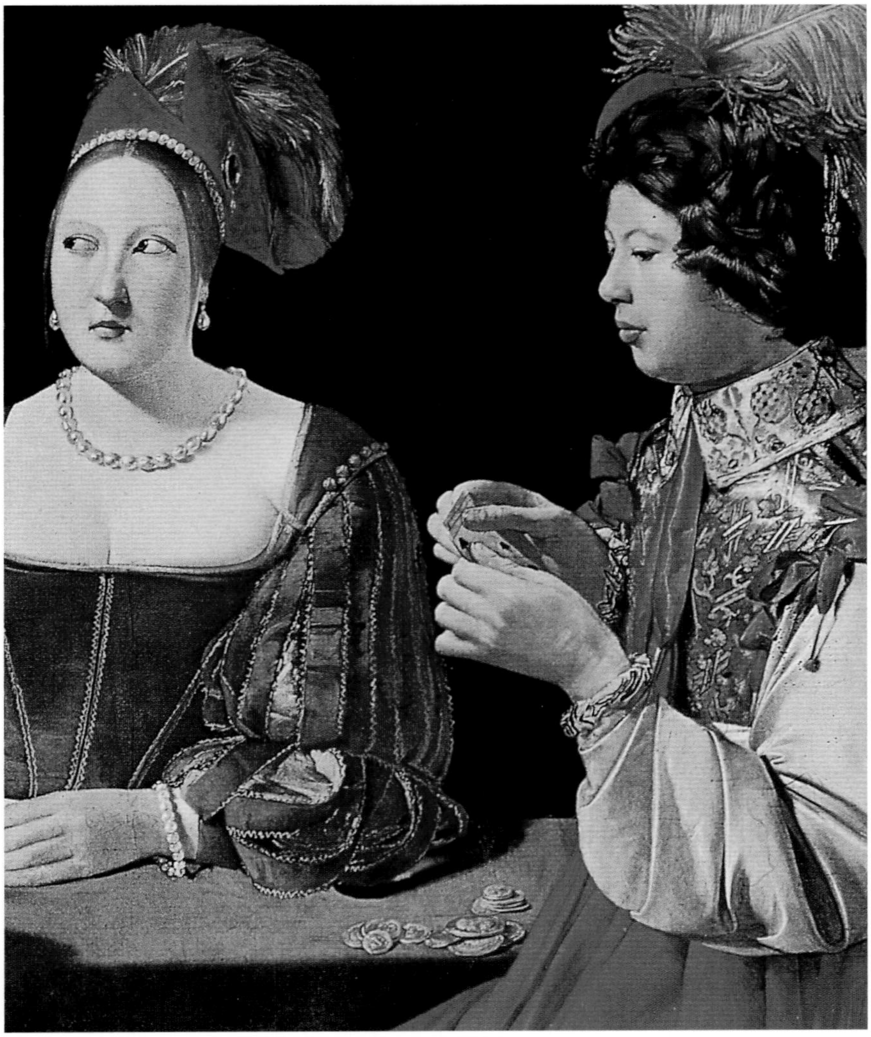

FIGURES 75 & 76
Georges de la Tour, *The Cheat with the Ace of Diamonds*. Oil, c. 1625. DETAIL: The lady card player and the young victim of the cheat.
Paris, Musée du Louvre

many different kinds. A text from the time of Charles d'Anjou informs us about the regal dress required for his coronation at Rome on January 6, 1266, and lists a series of individual garments, among them a silk shirt, a dalmatic (a special ceremonial garment) of golden cloth, a tunic of red velvet, a stole with broad damascene trim, and slippers of red velvet.[9]

How important a part of a person's wardrobe the sleeves were considered is revealed by one of the many charitable acts of Saint Catherine of Siena (1347–1380), narrated with admiration by her biographer, Raymond of Capua. Catherine had given her own sleeveless woolen tunic, which she wore beneath another that did have sleeves, to a young man who was barely clothed; in reality he was neither a beggar nor a ragged pilgrim but Christ himself, in disguise. Acceding to his repeated requests to be given something made of cloth to wear too, she led him to her parents' home.

> Catherine went directly to where the undergarments of her father and her brothers were kept; she took a shirt and tights, and, filled with joy, handed them to the mendicant. But he, having received these things, did not cease to pester her: "Tell me, madame, what am I supposed to do with this tunic that has no sleeves? Give me the sleeves for it as well so that I can leave the house properly dressed." The saint, not at all annoyed, indeed seized by greater fervor, began rummaging through the house looking for a sleeve of some sort. She came upon the new tunic belonging to the domestic servant, which had never been worn, hanging from a pole. Immediately she took it, quickly detached the sleeves, and willingly offered them to the poor man.[10]

But the young man was still not satisfied, and demanded clothing as well for a friend of his who was lying quite unclothed in the hospital. This time the saint found herself in difficulty because

> everyone in the house except for her father barely tolerated the way she gave things away; and the servants locked up everything they owned for fear that the saint would take it to give to the poor. Catherine for her part had already deprived the servant of enough; she could not deprive her of her whole tunic, because the woman was very poor.[11]

She would willingly have given up her own tunic if shame had permitted it, but failing that was willing to exchange the suit for whatever else the supplicant might desire. Finally he ceased to importune her; but that night he appeared in sleep to the saint, revealed his identity, and offered her a dress adorned with pearls and other gems. I confess that one detail of this story sticks in my mind: the surprise the servant must have felt when

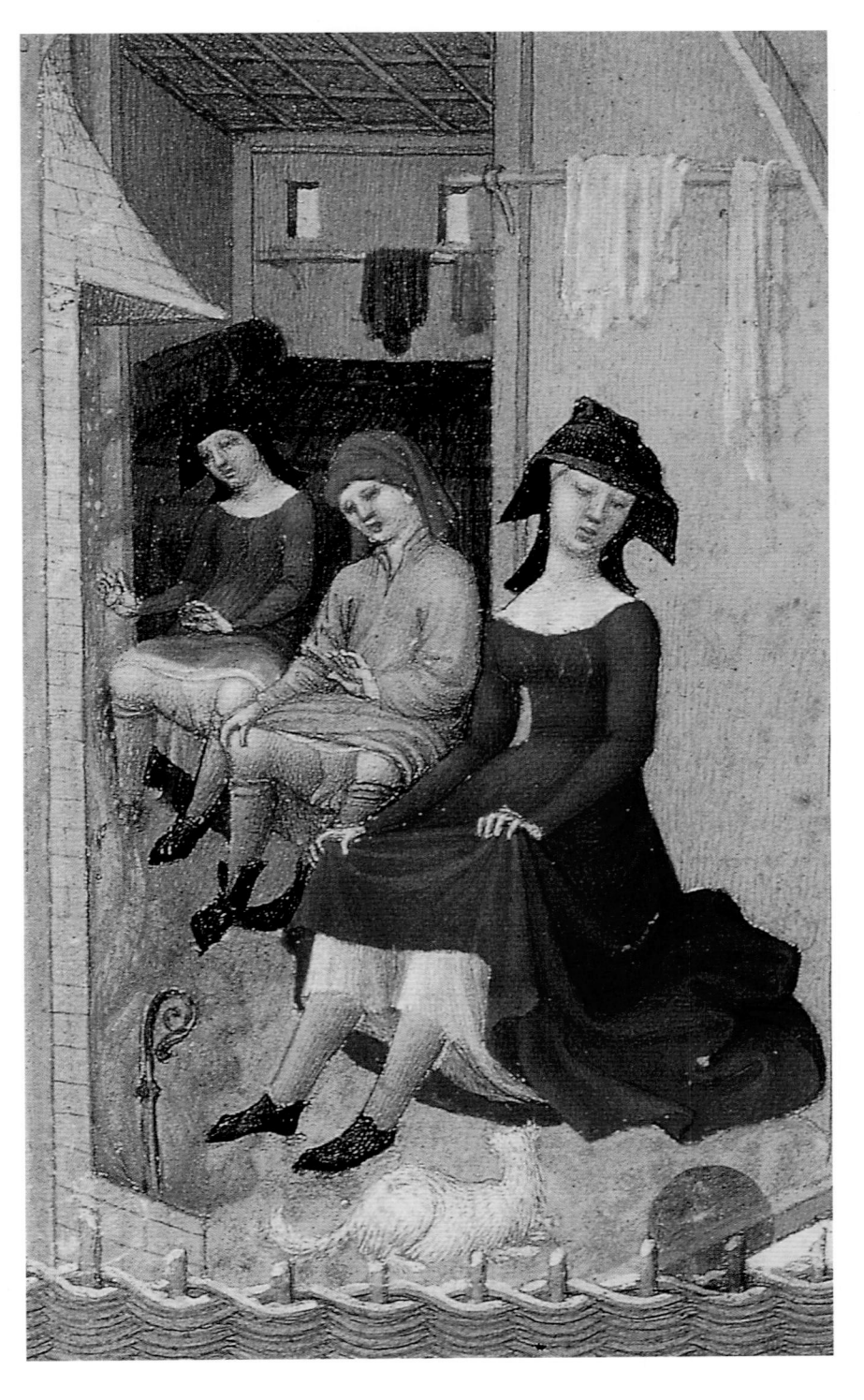

FIGURE 77
The Month of February.
Miniature from *Les Très riches
heures du duc de Berry*, c. 1413.
Chantilly, Musée Condé, f. 2v

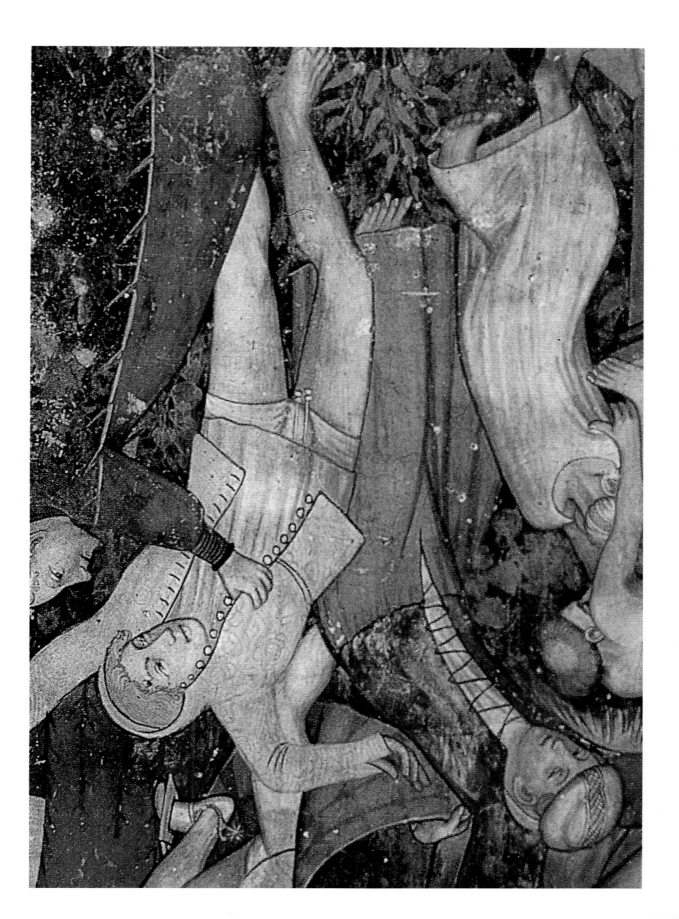

she saw that the sleeves of her new dress had flown away, like the wings of a butterfly.

FIGURE 78 *The Effects of the Fountain of Youth.* Fresco, detail, middle of the fifteenth century. Cuneo, Castello della Manta

Underwear and Trousers, Tights and Cobblers

Catherine of Siena, carried away by a rush of generosity, donated something to the mendicant that only her own idea of decency made her think absolutely necessary even for a poor man: underwear. Actually, people of low status, both men and women, were quite used to doing without it, as we see for example in a miniature illustrating the month of February from the *Très riches Heures du duc de Berry* of 1413, in which the peasants raise their clothing to expose their genitals to the warmth of the fire (figure 77). Underwear, called *mutande* (literally, "articles to be changed") in modern Italian, were also called *panni da gamba* (leg cloths) in the Middle Ages. The Romans knew of underwear, but had always despised and resisted adopting it, regarding it as barbaric. One of the first items of historical testimony from the time of the Longobards comes to us from Paulus Diaconus, who tells how Alahis, the Longobard Duke of Trento, greeted a deacon who came to him on an embassy from the Bishop of Pavia, Damianus, in a very contemptuous manner. The duke had an underling tell the deacon that he would be admitted "si munda femoralia habet" ("if he had clean underwear"). To this the postulant replied that he was wearing very clean underwear, having put it on that very morning fresh from the laundry. The duke countered that he cared not a whit whether the man's underwear was clean; he wanted to know whether or not the person wearing it was clean. To this the deacon promptly replied that the only judge of that was God.[12]

The word *mutande* for underwear is actually used in a Venetian inventory of 1335,[13] but the object itself varied in name and shape over the course of the centuries. At the time of Franco Sacchetti the stylish kind was so small that, says the writer crudely, men "have stuffed their asses into a little sock."[14] The word he uses, *calcetto* (*calzetto* in modern Italian) actually means a sheath or liner that men might wear on their feet underneath their tights, or *calze*. Underwear of a quite modern kind is displayed by a group of people who are eager to test the effect of the "fountain of youth" in a lively fresco from the middle of the fifteenth century in the hall of the Castle of Manta (near Cuneo). Some are still undressing, white-haired and haggard; some have already taken the plunge; and some, their youth regained, are getting dressed again. One of the latter, having recovered his youthful charm, is being helped by a friend to slip on a tight doublet that has a long matching row of buttons and buttonholes (figure 78).

This young man will need the laces that are dangling from his underwear in order to get completely dressed: he will use them to draw the clinging tights that style demanded snugly up to his haunches. The eyelets

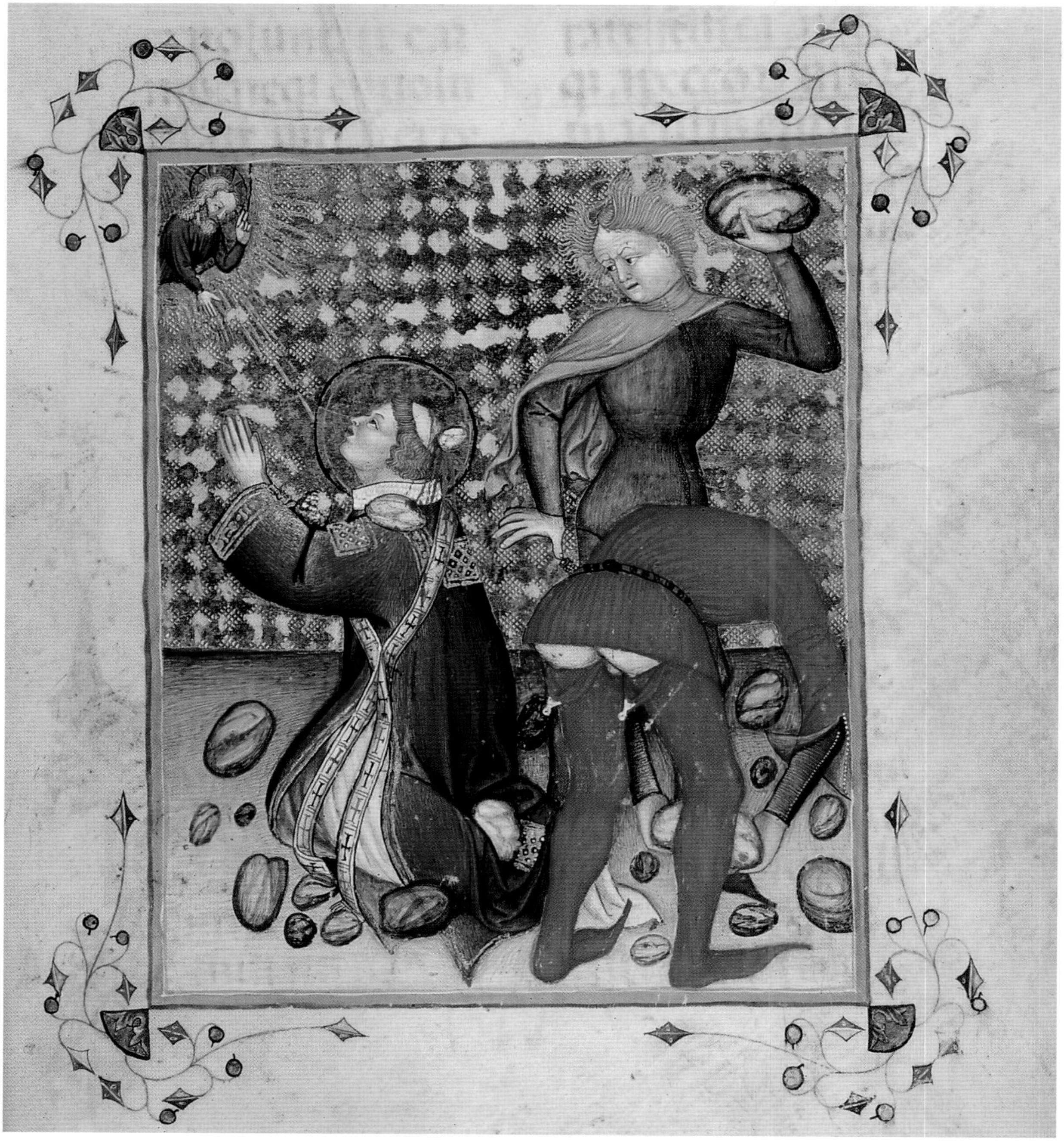

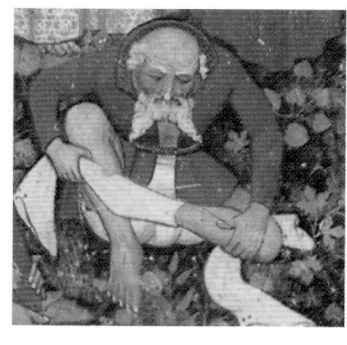

FIGURE 79 *An Elderly Man Undresses Before Entering the Fountain of Youth.*
Fresco, detail, middle of the fifteenth century. Cuneo, Castello della Manta

FIGURE 80 *The Martyrdom of Saint Stephen.*
Miniature, between 1350 and 1378. Paris, Bibliothèque Nationale,
ms. Lat. 757, f. 286

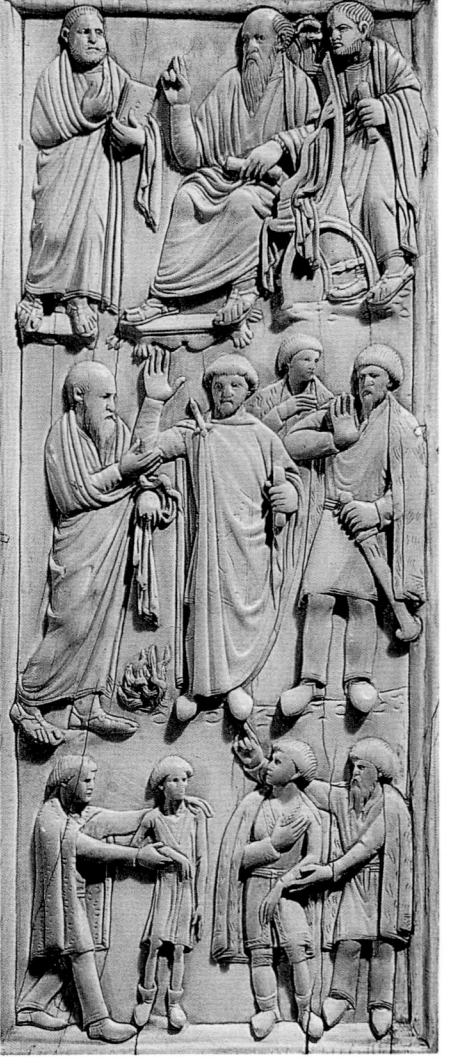

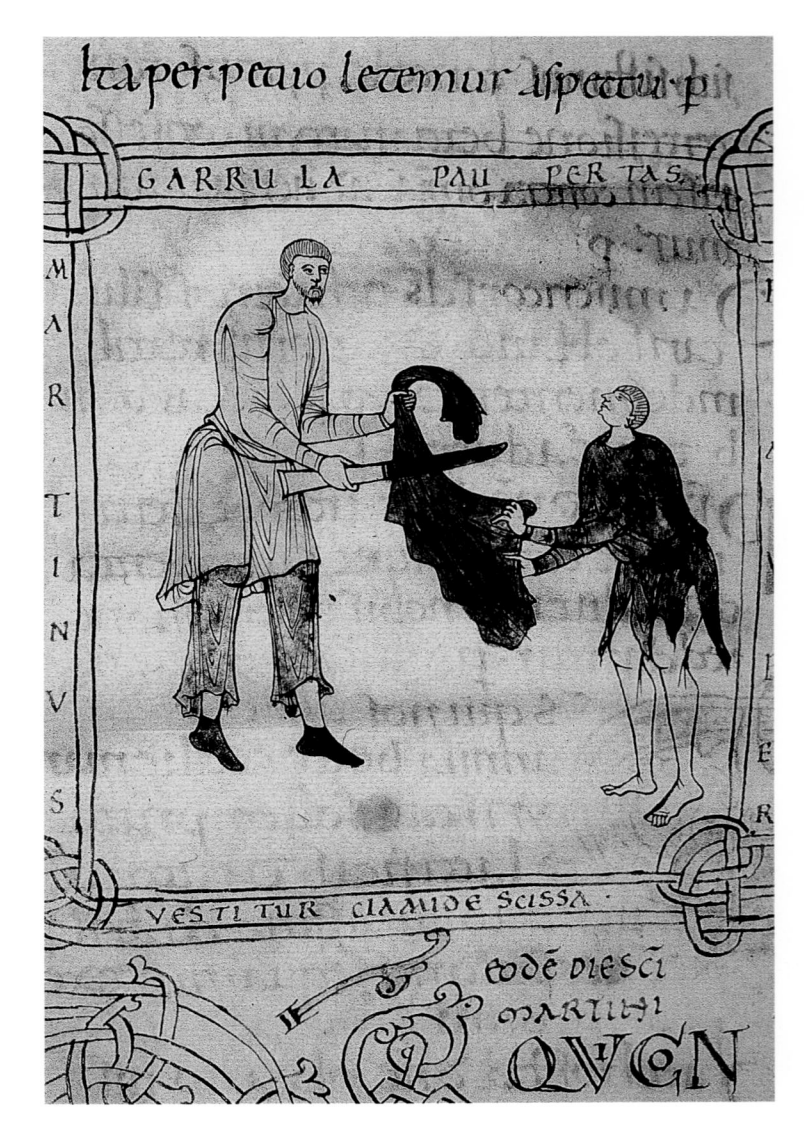

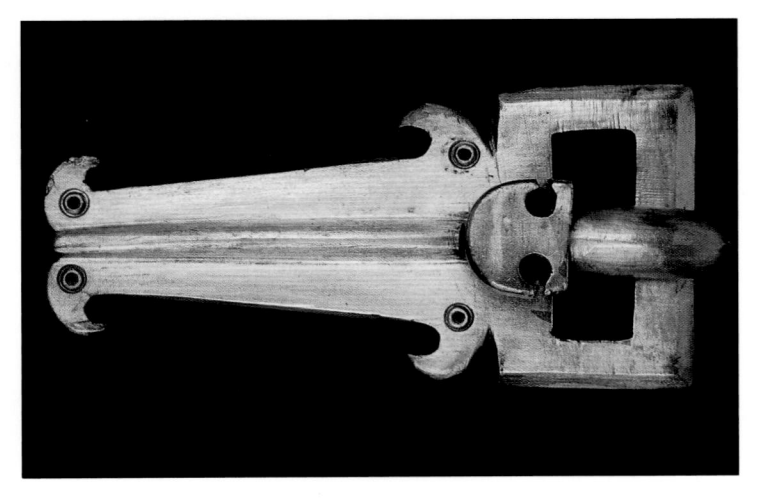

FIGURE 81 Stories of Saint Paul.
Wing of a diptych, ivory, sixth century.
Florence, Museo del Bargello

FIGURE 82 *Saint Martin Donates His Cloak.*
Miniature from the Missal of Warmondo,
969–1002. Ivrea, Biblioteca Capitolare,
ms. LXXXVI (31), f. 114r

FIGURE 83
Silver Longobard buckle with tongue.
Seventh century.
Cividale del Friuli, Museo Archeologico
Nazionale, inv. 1520-R.A. 163

used for that purpose are clearly visible on the tights that an elderly man is removing, sitting cross-legged beside the fountain (figure 79), as they are on those of an elegant cavalier about to mount his horse. Beside him, the gloved hand of a companion bears a whip—which reminds me: gloves too were an invention of the Middle Ages.

To bend over you had to unlace your tights, at least partly, since the fabric was not elastic. One of the men wearing late thirteenth-century clothing who are using stones to put Saint Stephen to death displays himself quite unself-consciously as he stoops to the ground to pick up a large rock with which to finish off the martyr (figure 80). Tights like these, furnished with soles, functioned as footwear too, and that is the reason why, even today, to get our shoes repaired in Italy, we go to the shop of a tradesman called, not a cobbler, as in English, but a *calzolaio*.

The new fashion for tights drove out the earlier type of loose breeches (*brache*), which sometimes reached down to the knee or even the ankle (like our pants), that the Germans habitually wore below a short tunic, a costume to be seen on several of the characters involved in the episodes concerning Saint Paul on one wing of an ivory diptych of the sixth century (figure 81),[15] or on Saint Martin, who is giving half of his cloak to a poor man, in a miniature from the end of the tenth century (figure 82).

We have the "barbarians" to thank as well for the buckles with tongues that we use to fasten our belts: a fine Longobard one in silver from the seventh century can be admired in the museum at Cividale del Friuli (figure 83).

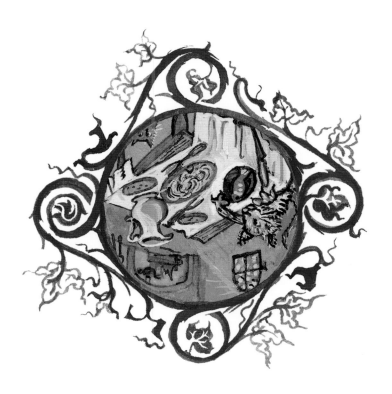

FOUR And Then came the Fork

Good Manners at Table: The Use of the Fork

The fork was another metal object that appeared at some point in the Middle Ages, but it is hard to say exactly when. Normally we would look for visual evidence of its appearance in scenes of people dining, and the scene of that kind most frequently depicted was the Last Supper of Christ and his disciples. But the Last Supper has an iconographic tradition so packed with symbolic significance that it only accepts minimal variations itself (which are almost always charged with precise messages), and it also exerts great influence on the iconography of profane banquet scenes. So although the texts may tell us that the fork was known, we see it represented only very rarely. Also, most people continued to eat in common, with a few platters of food, a few drinking vessels, and a few knives to cut the meat with: one more clue to the nature of medieval society, to which individualism was foreign, which tended to think and act collectively (there is the concept of the Last Judgment, but very rarely are we shown the judgment of a single person), and which was indifferent to the distinctiveness of each individual (until the end of the fourteenth century there are no realistic portraits, only verisimilar depictions of types).

Churchmen held that the use of the fork would make people soft, that it was an instrument of diabolical perversion. San Pier Damiani (1007–1072) had no pity at all for the poor Byzantine princess Theodora, who was

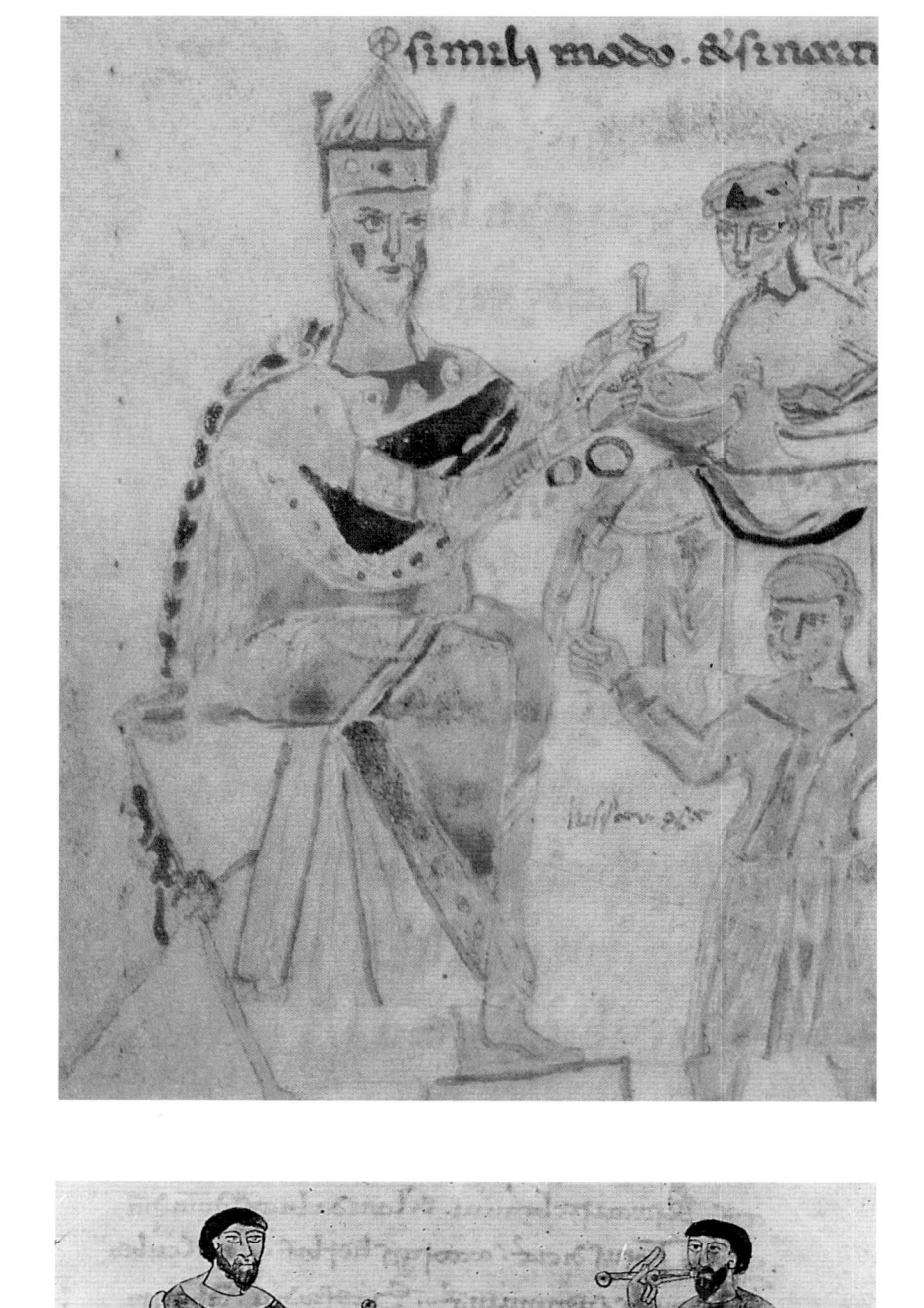

FIGURE 84

King Rotari at Table.
Miniature, beginning of the
eleventh century. From the
Codex legum Langobardorum.
Cava de' Tirreni (Salerno),
Biblioteca della Badia,
ms. 4, f. 69v

FIGURE 85

Dining with Knife and Fork.
Colored drawing, beginning
of the eleventh century (but
the codex very probably derives
from an illustrated one of the
Carolingian epoch), of Rabanus
(or Hrabanus) Maurus,
De Universo.
Abbey of Montecassino,
ms. Casin. 132, f. 515

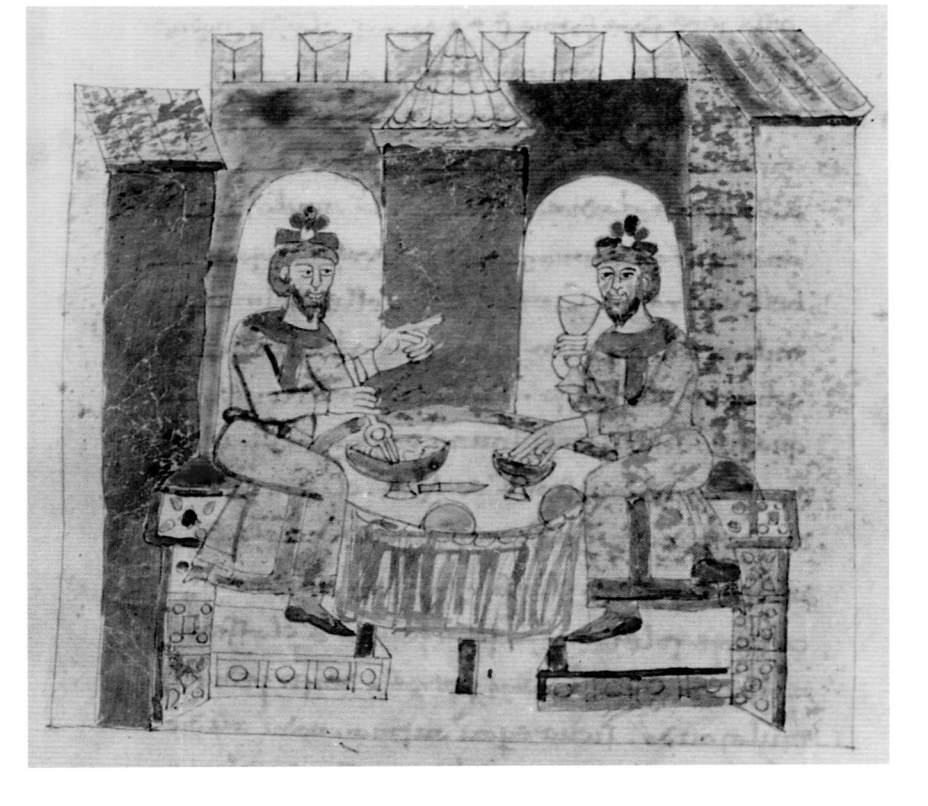

FIGURE 86 *A Rich Banquet.* Colored drawing, beginning of the eleventh century (but the codex very probably derives from an illustrated one of the Carolingian epoch), of Rabanus (or Hrabanus) Maurus, *De Universo.* Abbey of Montecassino, ms. Casin. 132, f. 408

sent to Venice as the bride of Doge Domenico Selvo, and who used a fork and surrounded herself with other refinements, trying to bring some gentility to the manners of the westerners: "She did not touch the food with her hands, but had each dish cut into tiny pieces by her eunuchs, which she then advanced to her mouth using a sort of miniature golden spear with two prongs, and barely tasted." The young woman died a terrible death as her flesh was slowly eaten away by gangrene ("corpus eius computruit"), which the saint interpreted as the just punishment divinely ordained for this enormous sin.[1]

Innocent III, when he was still Lotario dei Conti di Segni (1160–1216), in his *De miseria humanae condicionis* (*On the Misery of the Human Condition*) casts the dark shadow of death over a long list of pleasures: "What is more vain than to adorn the table with decorated tablecloths, knives with handles of ivory, golden drinking vessels, silver platters, with cups and beakers, bowls and basins, with soup plates and spoons, with forks and saltshakers, with water bowls and pitchers, with boxes and fans? . . . For it is written: 'When a man dies, he takes none of all that, nor does his glory go down with him.'"[2]

The earliest iconographic attestations of the presence of the fork appear at around the time of San Pier Damiani's invective: in a miniature from the beginning of the eleventh century in the *Code of Longobardic Law,* King Rotari grasps a fork at table (figure 84); and it is also being used by the decorous diners in a pair of other, more or less contemporary, miniatures

(figures 85 and 86) taken from a manuscript of *De Universo* by Rabanus Maurus, which launch his long catalogue of the various types of tables, foods, and beverages and illustrate his chapter on citizens. "Citizens," the author explains, "are called by that name so that they may come together to live as one, and so that their common life may be better furnished, and safer."[3] The illuminator wished to emphasize that the social rite of dining is an element of civility, and that table implements, including the fork, exemplify the pleasures of urban existence.

From the twelfth century, I know of only one depiction of the meal taken by Christ and the eleven apostles after his resurrection (Luke 24:42) in which a solitary fork can be seen lying on a white tablecloth; it is found in one of the miniatures of the *Hortus deliciarum* (*Garden of Delights*) of the abbess Herrad of Hohenbourg (figure 87).[4] We do not know if the donor herself personally directed that it be included on account of her own acquaintance with good manners; in any case, it very much resembles the real medieval forks that survived goodness knows what adventures before arriving safely at the Horne Museum in Florence (figure 88).

The spreading use of the fork was closely connected with the expanding consumption of a typically medieval foodstuff that has remained a pillar of Italian cuisine, pasta, because it was the utensil best suited to impaling that hot and slippery foodstuff.

"Macaroni and lasagne made with bran"

The dinner table is a theater, at which character is expressed through codes of behavior. In the Middle Ages each diner had a slice of bread instead of a plate, and the food might be served directly onto that. Otherwise it was served on a *tagliere*, a combination of platter and cutting board used by two diners at the same time. When food had to be shared in this way, differences of character and temperament were quick to surface.

Franco Sacchetti tells, with his usual brio, a tale of two table companions, one an intolerable glutton and the other witty enough to find a way to let him know it. The one renowned for bolting down his food no matter what its temperature was a certain Noddo d'Andrea, who

> prayed to God that the food should arrive burning hot when he was eating with someone else, so that he could eat his companion's share. If they were served steaming hot pears baked with wine and sugar, all Noddo's companion could count on getting was the bare platter. Once it happened that Noddo and others were eating together, and Noddo was sharing a platter with a pleasant man named Giovanni Cascio. When boiling hot maccheroni were served, Giovanni, who had been told repeatedly about Noddo's habits and now

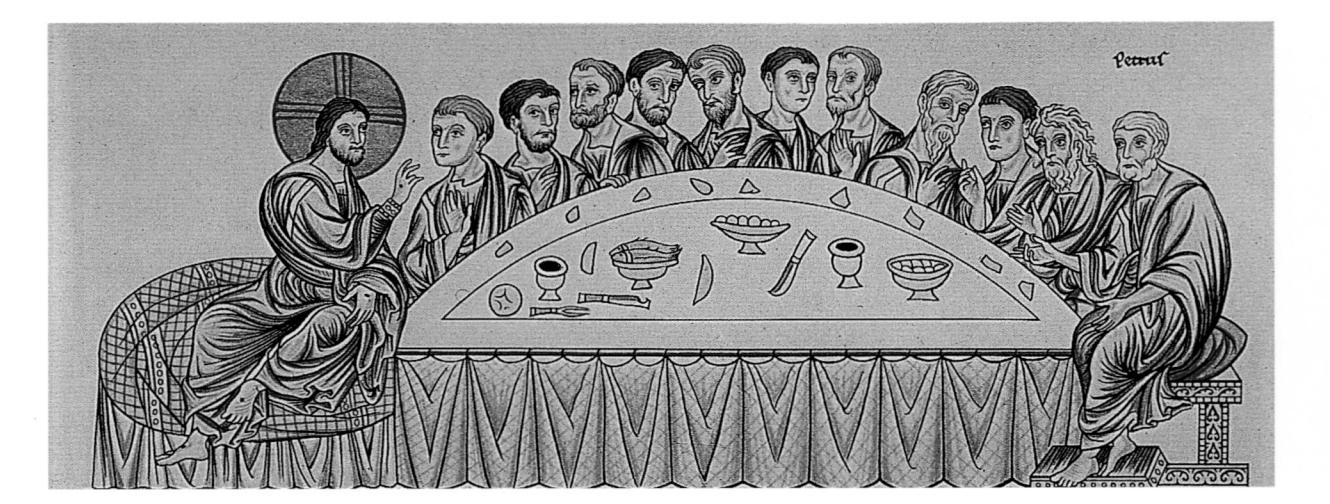

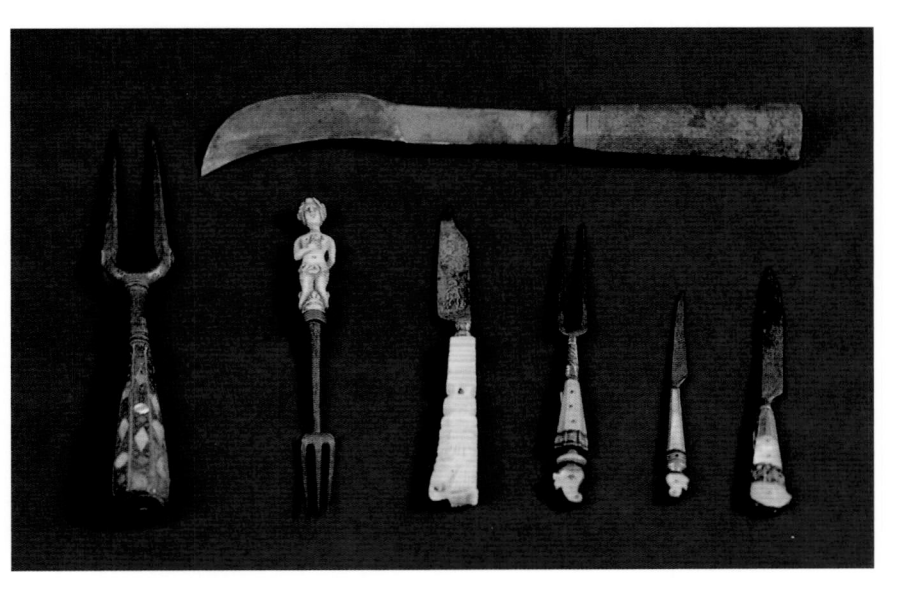

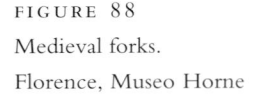

found himself sharing a platter with him, said to himself: "Isn't this great? I thought I was coming to dine, but instead I've come to sit and watch while Noddo gobbles all the food, and to top things off, they are serving maccheroni. I will be lucky to get out of here without him eating me too." Noddo started to mix the maccheroni in the sauce, gather bunches of them, and gobble them down. He had already swallowed six mouthfuls while Giovanni still had the first one on his fork, not daring to put it in his mouth because he could see that it was still steaming. Giovanni realized that the whole serving of maccheroni would "go to Capernaum"[5] unless he did something, and said to himself: "He can't be allowed to devour my whole portion."[6]

So every time Noddo swallowed a mouthful, Cascio tossed one to the dogs that were nosing around the table, until Noddo stopped, unable to bear the

sight of so much food going to waste; in fact, he even let his companion have a double portion, to make up for what he had missed.

By Boccaccio's time, pasta was considered an authentic treat, a symbol of abundance and pleasure. A character named Calandrino was led to believe that there existed

> a region named Bengodi ["you revel"], where the vines were tied with sausages, and there was a money goose, and a young goose at that. And there was a mountain made of grated parmesan cheese, and above it were people who did nothing else but make maccheroni and ravioli and cook them in chicken broth, and then toss them down; and everyone could have as much as they could eat.[7]

The ingredients of pasta (the word literally means paste or dough) are simple: flour made from hard wheat, and water. The Romans had these things, but pasta was unknown to them. They used mixtures of flour and water to make bread, which they baked with dry heat; or they mixed ground meal with water to make paps and porridges cooked with wet heat, by boiling or steaming. Within their frame of reference, pasta was "unthinkable," according to two experts in culinary history, Silvano Serventi and Françoise Sabban, because the two stages of its preparation cut across their categories: the dough is like that of (unleavened) bread, but is cooked with wet heat like a porridge.[8]

The Romans had a food they called *laganum*, the evident source of our word *lasagna* and its plural, *lasagne*, but it was a thin sheet of pasta cooked in the oven or fried in hot oil—methods of cooking that do not correspond to our conception of pasta, which has to be boiled in water. Only in the thirteenth century are *lasagne* cited in the medieval sources; at around the same time, pasta in thin strands makes its appearance, called by the unmistakable name *vermicelli* ("little worms").[9] Isidore of Seville, an encyclopedic author of the sixth and seventh centuries, appears at first glance to bridge the gap between antiquity and the Middle Ages with respect to pasta, because the text of his *Etymologiae* printed in the nineteenth-century *Patrologia Latina* of Migne defines *laganum* this way: "laganum est latus et tenuis panis, qui primo in aqua postea in oleo frigitur" (literally: "laganum is a flat thin bread, which is fried, first in water, then in oil"). But since this passage is entirely omitted from the critical edition of the text of Isidore by Lindsay, I fear that the bridge is only a mirage. Who knows what interpolated manuscript Migne found this passage in?[10]

Pasta as we know it came about slowly and laboriously, and touched many different cultures of the Mediterranean. At first it was served in the broth in which it had been cooked (it often still is), while at a later stage, it was drained and served as a dish in its own right—what in Italy we call *pastasciutta* (drained pasta) and what the rest of the world simply calls pasta.

Sicily was a major producer of dried pasta from the twelfth century on, and Sardinia was another center of production, especially in the thirteenth and fourteenth centuries, but we find pasta registered in many ports, such as Pisa and Genoa, and in Provence as well. It became an important commodity, traded and exported along routes that touched North Africa and Andalusia.[11]

At Palermo in 1371 a list of fixed prices was posted for "maccaruni blanki di symula e lasagni di simula" (white macaroni of bran and lasagne of bran) and for "maccaruni blanki di farina e lasagni di farina" (white macaroni of flour and lasagne of flour). The two types of pasta, one made from hard wheat, the second from soft, were sold at different prices. In the document, a further distinction is made between *pasta axutta* (dried pasta) and *pasta bagnata* (fresh pasta). Since goods considered basic necessities are always the ones subjected to price controls, this testifies to the importance that pasta had attained as a source of nourishment.[12]

The Florentine Marchionne di Coppo Stefani, to illustrate how rapidly the heaps of corpses rose in the common graves during the terrible plague of 1348, wrote that it was like seeing the preparation of a dish of lasagne with cheese ("come si minestrasse lasagne a fornire di formaggio").[13] The sheets of pasta were the corpses, and the cheese placed between each layer was the bit of earth thrown on top of the dead: a bit of earth because that is all there was time for. The crude realism of this comparison, taken from the everyday world of familiar things, confirms the habitual role that pasta played in the Italian diet.

Two miniatures from two different manuscripts of the *Tacuinum sanitatis* (*Notebook of Health*) from the late fourteenth and early fifteenth centuries portray, respectively, the manufacture of pasta in a home kitchen and in industrial quantities, probably for trade.[14] In the first (figure 89), two women are conscientiously going about their job. They have not removed their fine clothing or their stylish pointed shoes, but they have unbuttoned the cuffs of their tight sleeves and rolled them up, and tied long aprons around their waists. The one working the dough has also covered her head to protect her hair. The workspace is bare, as the small rooms of medieval houses usually were, for there was little room for furniture within their narrow confines. The two have divided the labor between them, so we can see the beginning and end of the process. The woman at the table adds water to the flour and kneads the mixture into dough, while her companion lays the long strands on a sort of rack or ladder, and with precise movements lifts them up to let them air and make sure they dry without sticking together.[15] In a niche with two shelves at the back of the room there is a pitcher, and beside it a glass full of red wine, perhaps a pick-me-up for the two workers.

In the second miniature (figure 90) the pasta is being made with the same division of labor and the same rhythm. But the racks for drying the

pasta are bigger and more numerous, and the women (one of them bare-foot) are not wearing the fine dresses of the ones in the previous miniature, but worn and ripped clothing: no doubt a more realistic portrayal of working conditions and the recruitment of labor. In the same manuscript is depicted[16] a harvest of apricots (called "*Armeniaca*," because they came from Armenia)—the only "fruit," as Jacques Le Goff ironically remarks, that the West gained from the Crusades.

The Power of Water and Wind: The Mills

The spread of pasta went along with a fundamental change of diet. In the early Middle Ages the population was sparse, and herding and hunting in the great tracts of forest supplied people with enough food for a diet built around meat and meat products. In the late Middle Ages, on the other hand, the extraordinary growth of the population meant that, if people were to eat, more fields had to be brought under the plow, with cereals increasingly forming the bulk of their diet; and this made them vulnerable to dearth.[17] A "provisionato" (stipendiary) of Guglielmo V, Lord of Avio (1307–1358) was thrown into prison and fined a large sum for having dared "to eat macaroni with bread, at a time of dearth." Sacchetti relates this tale in one of his novellas, and it doesn't matter whether or not the episode actually occurred; what does matter is that he and his readers would have thought it entirely realistic.[18]

So much flour was needed that the mills were always turning. They were water-driven, since water was the principal driver of machinery in the Middle Ages. The mills were such a constant feature of the landscape that they became proverbial. Our friend Sacchetti begins a novella by comparing a mill wheel to the wheel of fortune (which at the time of the story had carried Mastino della Scala, Lord of Verona from 1329 to 1351, to its highest point): "When messer Mastino was at the high point of the wheel in the city of Verona, he gave a feast, and all the buffoons of Italy rushed to it, as they always do, to make money and draw water to their mill."[19] The same writer once again uses the expression "to draw water to one's mill," which is still used in Italian with the meaning "to seek one's own advantage," in connection with the impulse to find new saints and forget about the safe and familiar ones:

> And this idolatry goes to such lengths that genuine saints are abandoned for others that, very often, have more candles placed in front of their painted images, and more waxen models dedicated to them, than Our Lord. And so the old way is often abandoned for the new. Often the religious are the cause, proclaiming that some body buried under their church has performed a miracle. They have a painting

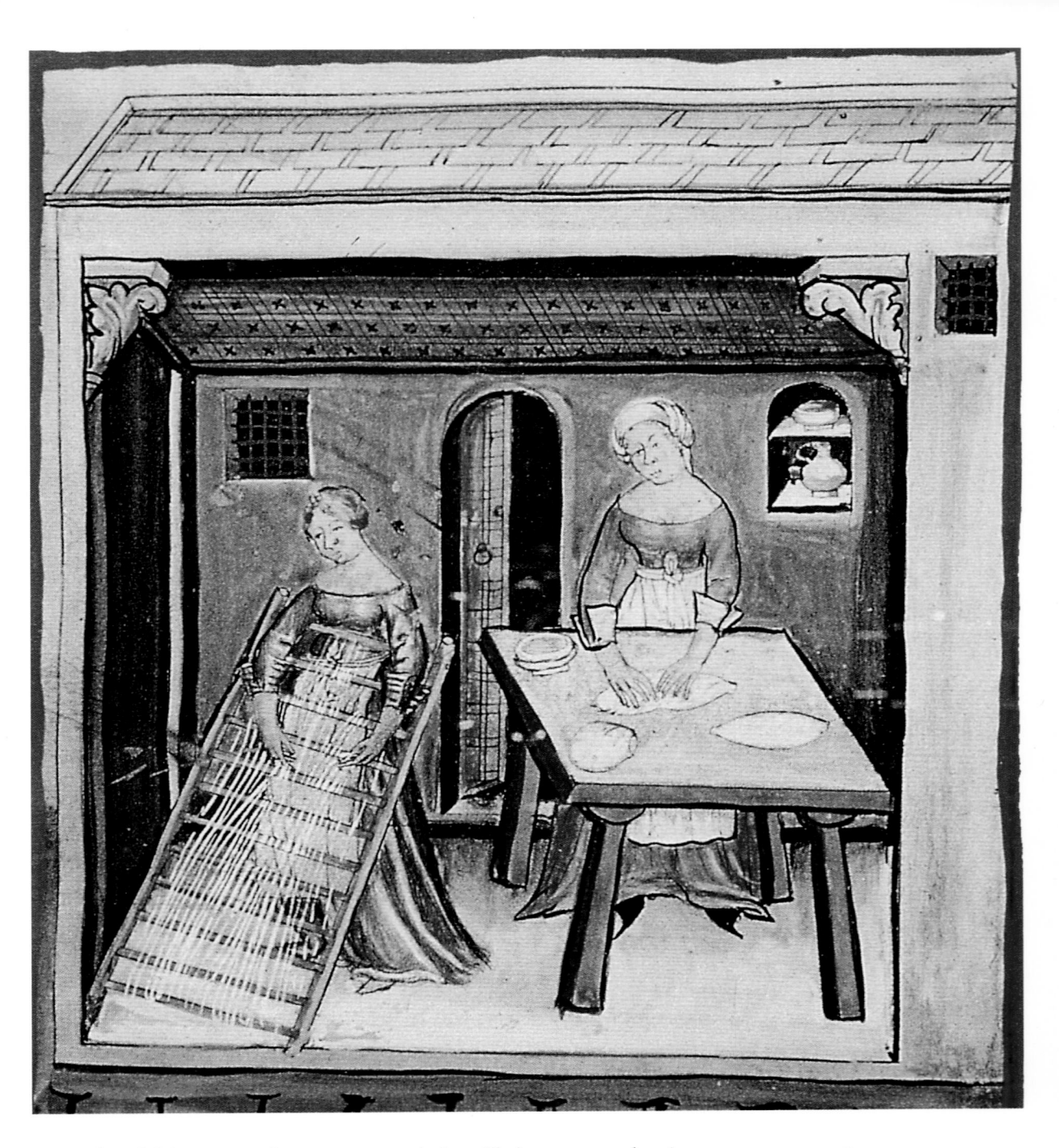

made of this, not to draw water to their mill, but wax and coins; while faith is entirely neglected.[20]

Saint Bernard, writing long before Sacchetti, had described with heartfelt emotion the beneficial effects of the water of a river and its multiple uses:

The river enters the abbey as much as the wall acting as a check allows. It gushes first into the corn mill where it is very actively employed in grinding the grain under the weight of the wheels and in

FIGURE 89
Making Pasta at Home.
Minature, from a manuscript commissioned by George of Lichtenstein, bishop of Trento, between 1390 and 1419. Vienna, Österreichische National-bibliothek, ms. Series Nova, 2644, Tacuinum Sanitatis, f. 45v

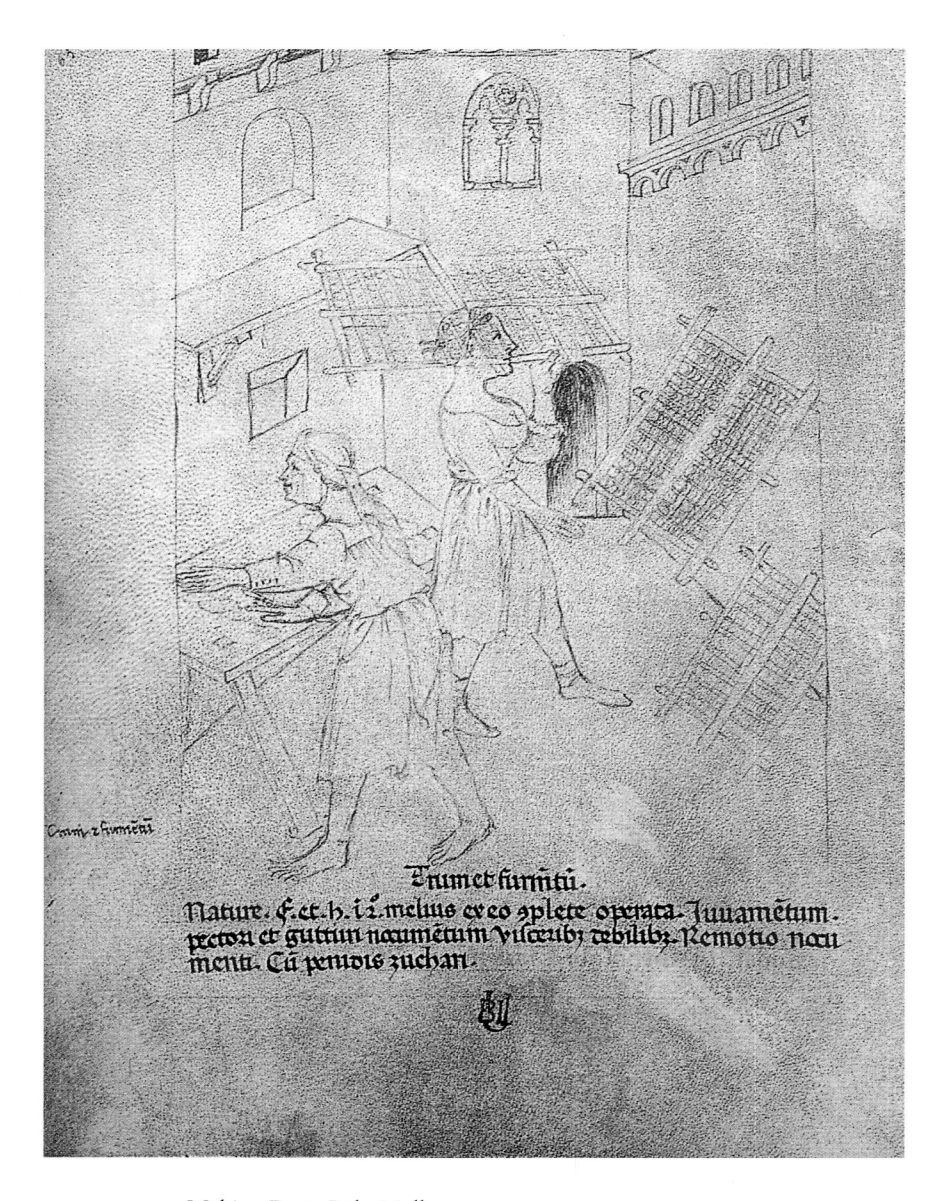

FIGURE 90 *Making Pasta Industrially.*
Miniature, end of the fourteenth century.
Liège, Bibliothèque Universitaire, Tacuinum Sanitatis,
ms. 1041, f. 32v

FIGURE 91 Pieter Brueghel the Elder, *A Windmill.*
Detail from *Procession to Calvary.* Panel, 1564.
Vienna, Kunsthistorisches Museum

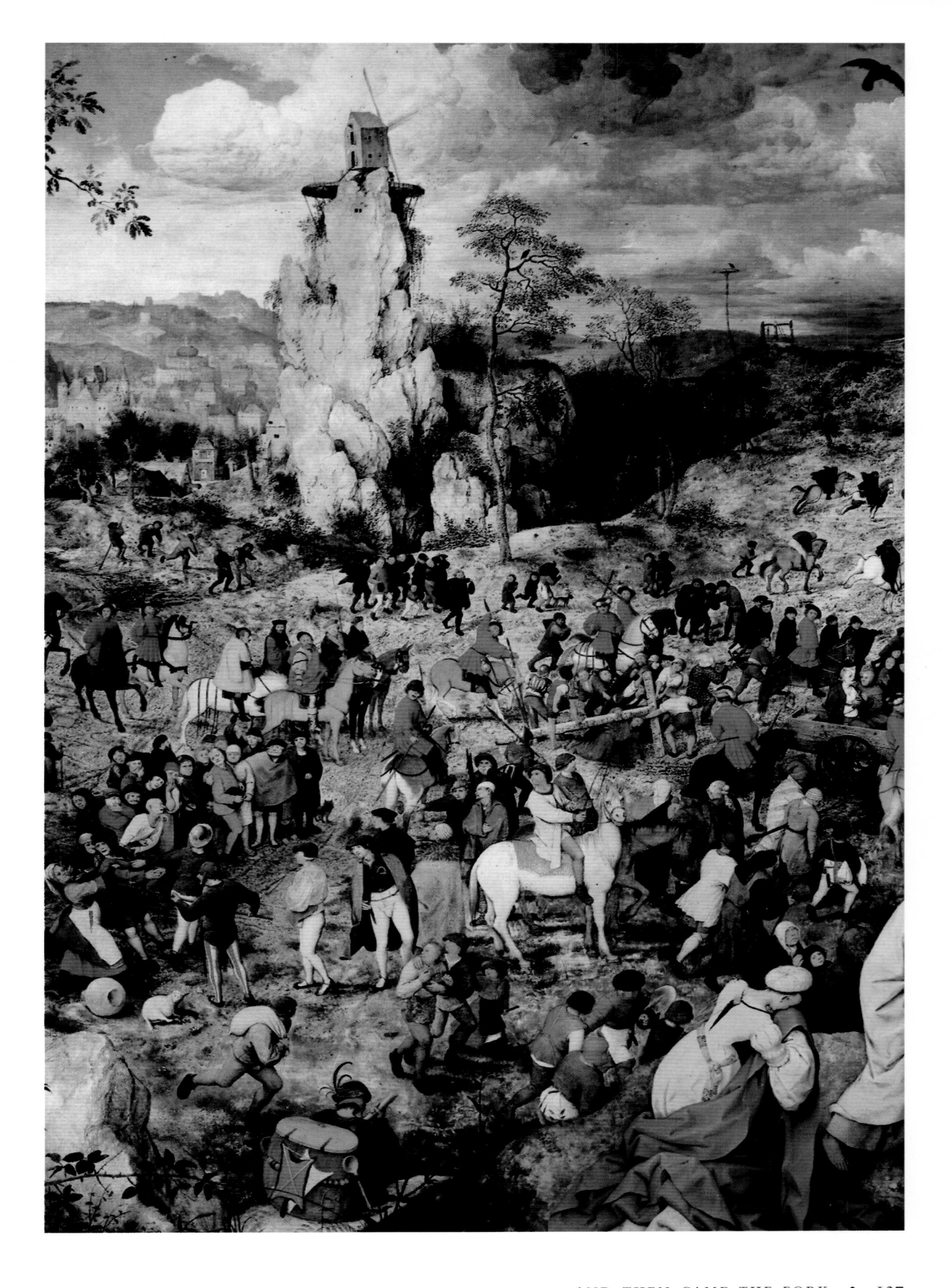

shaking the fine sieve which separates flour from bran. Thence it flows into the next building, and fills the boiler in which it is heated to prepare beer for the monks' drinking, should the vine's fruitfulness not reward the vintner's labor. But the river has not yet finished its work, for it is now drawn into the fulling machines following the corn mill. In the mill it has prepared the brothers' food, and its duty is now to serve in making their clothing. This the river does not withhold, nor does it refuse any task asked of it. Thus it raises and lowers alternately the heavy hammers and mallets, or to be more exact, the wooden feet of the fulling machines. When by swirling at great speed it has made all these wheels revolve swiftly, it issues foaming and looking as if it had ground itself. Now the river enters the tannery, where it devotes much care and labor to preparing the necessary materials for the monks' footwear; then it divides into many small branches and, in its busy course, passes through the various departments, seeking everywhere for those who require its services for any purpose whatsoever, whether for cooking, rotating, crushing, watering, washing, or grinding, always offering its help and never refusing. At last, to earn full thanks and to leave nothing undone, it carries away the refuse and leaves all clean.[21]

Machines for crushing olives, sawmills, fulling mills for cloth, paper mills, and flour mills were all busy at the edges of the cities lucky enough to be located near a watercourse in the thirteenth and fourteenth centuries. The Romans knew of water mills but did not exploit them, partly because slave labor made it pointless to search for alternate sources of energy, but mainly because the ancient mentality despised manual labor as servile. For this reason, the ancients never systematically applied their inventions to practical reality.[22] The Greeks, for example, had discovered the driving power of steam (the same power that drove the first locomotives), but they only used it for tricks to amaze the people. But in the Middle Ages the altered historical and cultural circumstances—however gradually, artistic works, for example, came to be seen as the products of individual talent, not just as output resulting from simple manual input—made it possible fully to grasp the utility and the broad range of applications of the mill. Where there were prevalent strong winds, air was substituted for water to drive machinery: the first windmills appeared in the twelfth century, with the central apparatus being rotatable to capture winds blowing from different quarters, and they still add a picturesque touch to the landscape of the Netherlands, even if the huge blades now whirl only for the pleasure of tourists (figure 91).

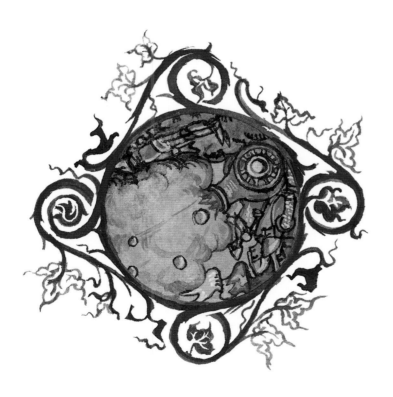

FIVE Making War

With Lances Aimed and Ready

The mills represented an important economic resource for those who controlled them, and for that very reason gave rise to endless disputes over things like the payment of rent, which was not always in money. From a document of 1249 preserved in the state archive in Siena we learn that a certain Pietro Ingilese leased one sixth of a mill belonging to the Abbey of San Salvatore del Monte Amiata for more than ten years without paying the agreed rent of "two horseshoes."[1] Throughout the Middle Ages iron was always a precious metal that had to be used with care. Spades and plowshares were usually made of wood, with iron used only to reinforce the cutting edge.

A famous passage describes the consternation of King Desiderius and the Longobards who were besieged at Pavia in 773 when they unexpectedly saw "the fields bristling with a crop of iron" ("segetem campis inhorrescere ferream") as the army of Charlemagne advanced.

> Then came in sight that man of iron, Charlemagne, topped with his iron helm, his fists in iron gloves, his iron chest and his Platonic shoulders clad in an iron cuirass. An iron spear raised high against the sky he gripped in his left hand, while in his right he held his still unconquered sword. For greater ease of riding other men kept their

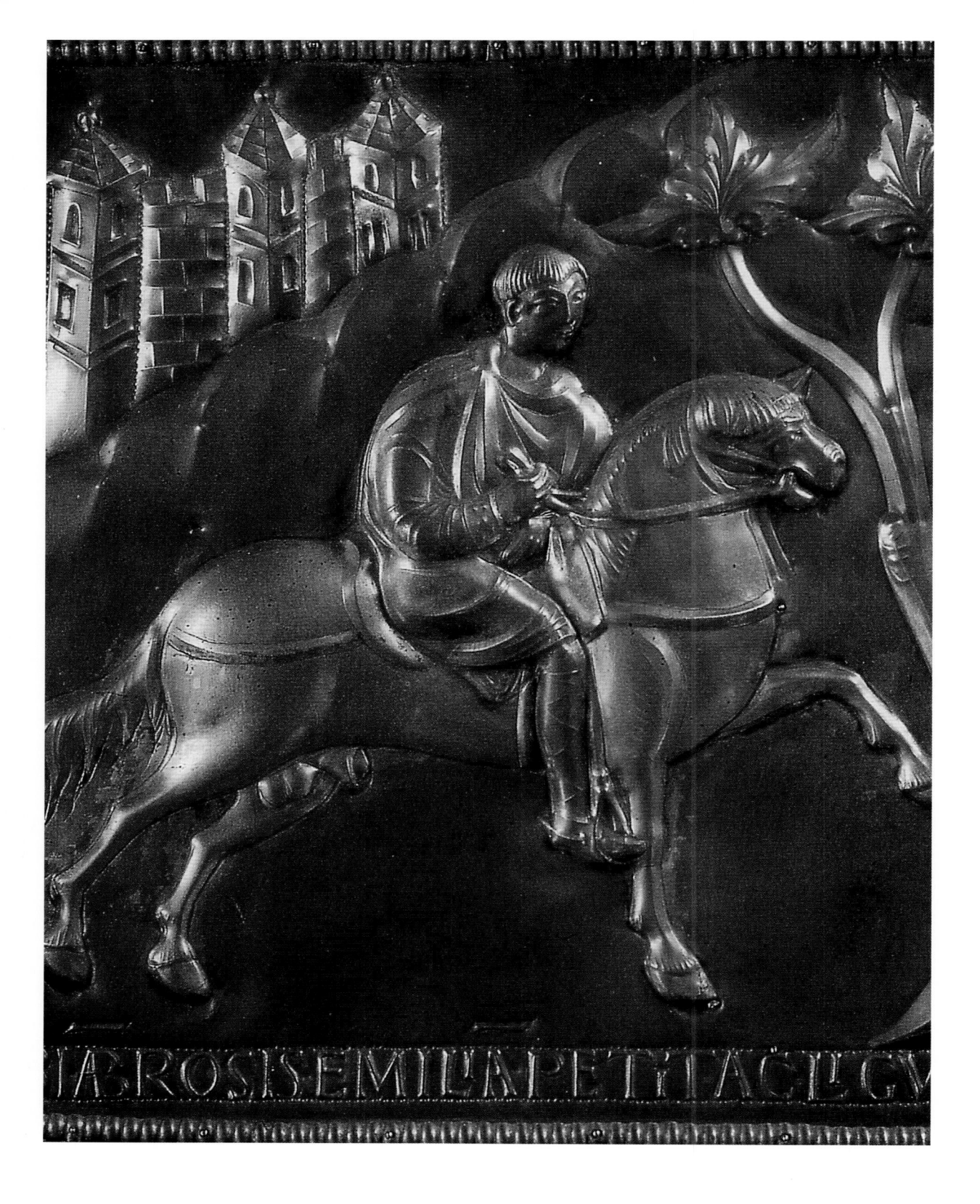

thighs bare of armor; Charlemagne's were bound in plates of iron. As for his greaves, like those of all his army, they too were made of iron. His shield was all of iron. His horse gleamed iron-colored and its very mettle was as if of iron. All those who rode before him, those who kept him company on either flank, those who followed after him, wore the same armor, and their gear was as close a copy of his own as it is possible to imagine. Iron filled the fields and all the open spaces. The rays of the sun were thrown back by this battle line of iron. This race of men harder than iron did homage to the very hardness of iron. . . . "Oh! the iron! Alas for the iron!" Such was the confused clamor of the citizens of Pavia.[2]

FIGURE 92
Saint Ambrose Rides in the Direction of Liguria and Emilia.
Bas relief, silver, from the "altar of Vuolvinius," between 842 and 847.
Milan, Sant'Ambrogio

A horseman armed with a sword and a lance, his feet lodged firmly in a set of stirrups that allowed him and his horse to function as a single unit, was invincible against an enemy on foot because of the overpowering impact he could deliver. Stirrups were an important technical innovation that came to Europe from the east and were widespread by the time of Charlemagne; they changed methods of fighting and made the horse essential. Because the stirrup was unknown to the Romans, cavalry played a relatively unimportant role in their warfare. The Avars did use stirrups, which were adopted in the Byzantine Empire and then farther west as a result of contact with the peoples of the steppe.[3] In classical Latin the word for horse is *equus*, but in the early Middle Ages it was replaced by the word *caballus*. The edict of the Longobard King Rotari in 643 gave a lot of space to the *caballus*, specifying numerous particulars in minute detail, down to the trappings of the animal. For a nomadic people there were few things more precious than the war horse.[4]

On the famous gold and silver altar in Sant'Ambrogio in Milan, which was commissioned from the great Vuolvinius by Angilberto II, bishop of the city from 824 to 859, Saint Ambrose is shown twice on horseback with his feet firmly planted in the stirrups, the first time as imperial prefect of Emilia and Liguria and the second time in flight from Milan, as he attempted (but in vain, for the hand of God summoned him back) to escape from the populace who wanted to acclaim him bishop. In the first of these two scenes the artist also takes great care to show the spurs (figure 92).[5]

The horse became an even more stable and useful platform with a further innovation: its feet were shod with iron shoes nailed directly into its thick hooves. From the eleventh century on horses were always protected by iron horseshoes that gave them much greater traction over broken and uneven terrain. When Richard I was planning to take part in the Crusades, he requested that 50,000 iron horseshoes be forged.[6]

As we saw, Charlemagne gripped "an iron spear raised high against the sky . . . in his left hand," ready to hurl it like a javelin. It was the Normans who adopted a new technique in the eleventh century; the Norman war-

FIGURE 93

Horsemen Charge with Lances Under Their Armpits in the Battle Between Britons and Vikings. Miniature, c. 1130. From the *Life and Miracles of Saint Edmond, King and Martyr.* New York, The Pierpont Morgan Library, ms. 736, f. 7v

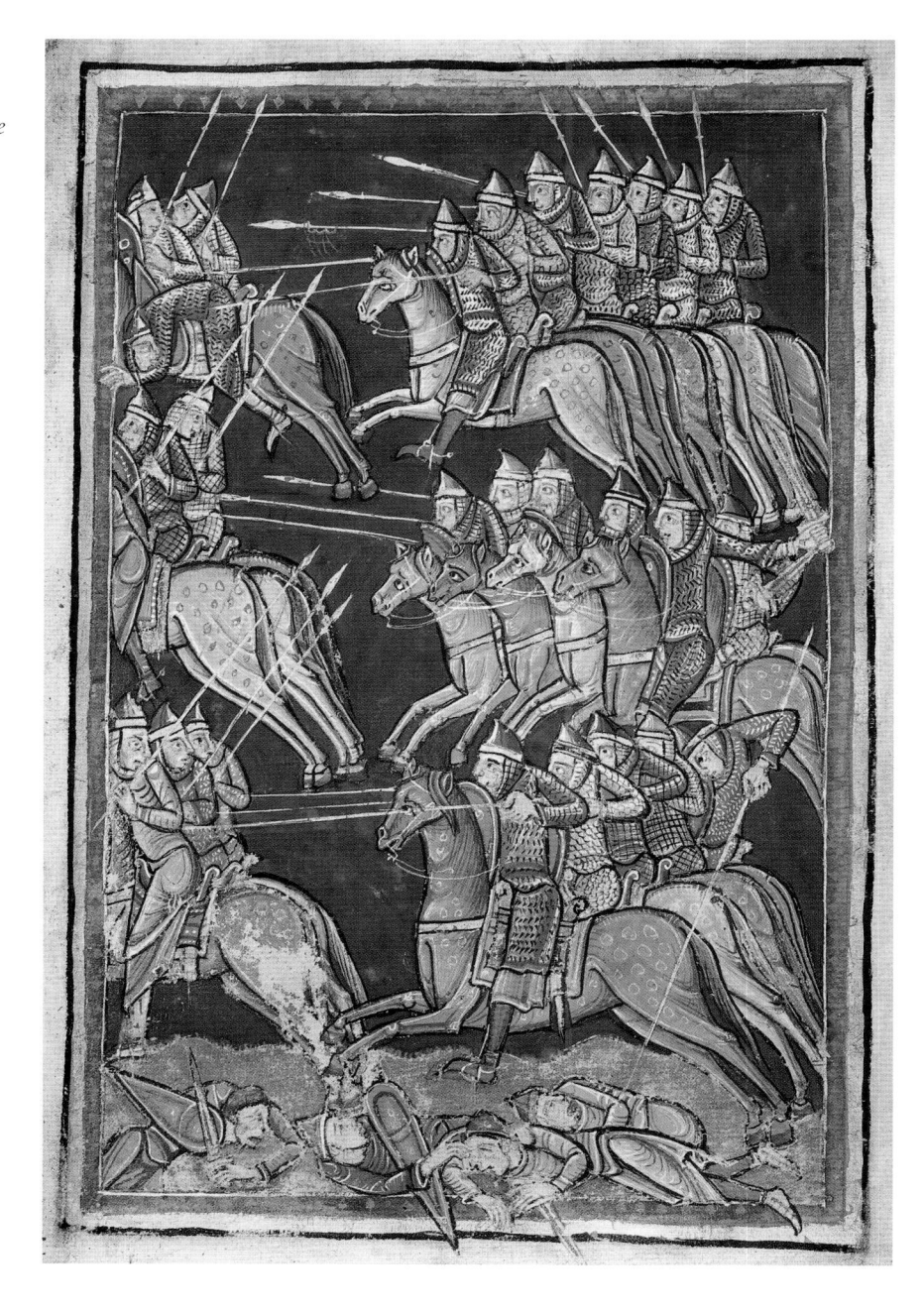

rior held the lance tightly under his armpit, with his arm bent to hold it steady, and launched a frontal charge, exploiting to the full the stability his stirrups gave him on the horse and the momentum that horse and rider together attained as they reached full gallop (figure 93). A further refinement was developed in later centuries: the butt of the lance was fitted into a "rest," an iron attachment on the right side of the breast of the cuirass. Expressions derived from this medieval weapon system still crop up in modern Italian: we say that someone has "the lance in the rest" ("lancia in resta") when they are getting ready for a confrontation, or that they are going "di spron battuto" ("with spurs dug in") when they are at full tilt; "ironshod" still means "toughened up," and it's an embarrassment when you "lose the stirrups" ("perdere le staffe"), in other words, when you lose your self-control.

Draped in Colors

The combatants clashed amid flapping banners adorned with symbolic figures. These banners came into use as a way to tell opposing bands apart at a distance, and to indicate where fighters who became disoriented or separated from their group should go. "As a sign to others we put names on banners, on coats of arms, on shields; that's why many coats of arms are abbreviations, like SPQR for Senatus Populusque Romanus, which is a coat of arms and a symbol widely known," said our friend Giordano da Pisa in a sermon; in this passage he is thinking mainly of crucifixion scenes.[7] The Church used banners too, in processions, for example, in which beautiful colored fabrics bearing images of Jesus Christ or the saints fluttered.

The word *bandiera* (Italian for banner, standard) comes from the Latin word *banda*, meaning a strip of colored cloth. Paulus Diaconus mentions the use of banners in the ninth century.[8] The Longobard Tatus, to seal his victory over the Heruli, took possession of the banner ("vexillum quod bandum appellant") of their king, Rudolfus, who had died in battle. In the world of the Italian communal cities too, the ensign of the *podestà* (the official in charge of public order) was borne on a banner, and the whole commune had its own standard or *vessillo*. In later generations the *capitano del popolo* ("captain of the people," a popular magistracy) had his own *gonfalone*. In intercity wars, a cluster of banners, among them the banner of the commune, fluttered on the *carroccio*, a large four-wheeled wagon used in battle and drawn by oxen who were also arrayed in the insignia of the commune (figure 94). On the wagon there was a bell (the *martinella*[9]) that sounded as the battle began, as well as the city's flags, the trumpeters who signaled the troops to advance or to halt, and an altar at which to say Mass. The wagon served as a visual reference during the fighting and gave temporary shelter to the wounded. It was defended by picked squads, since the

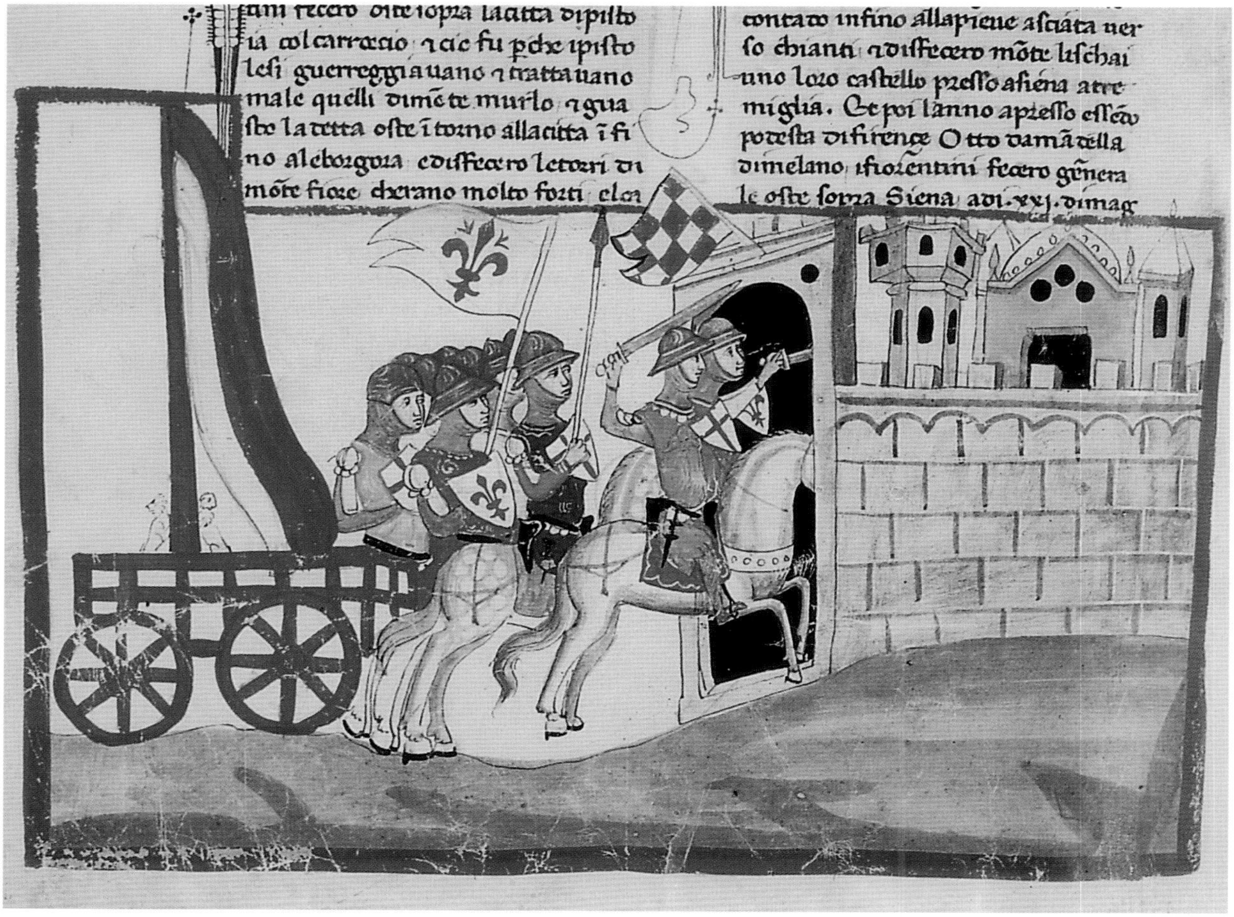

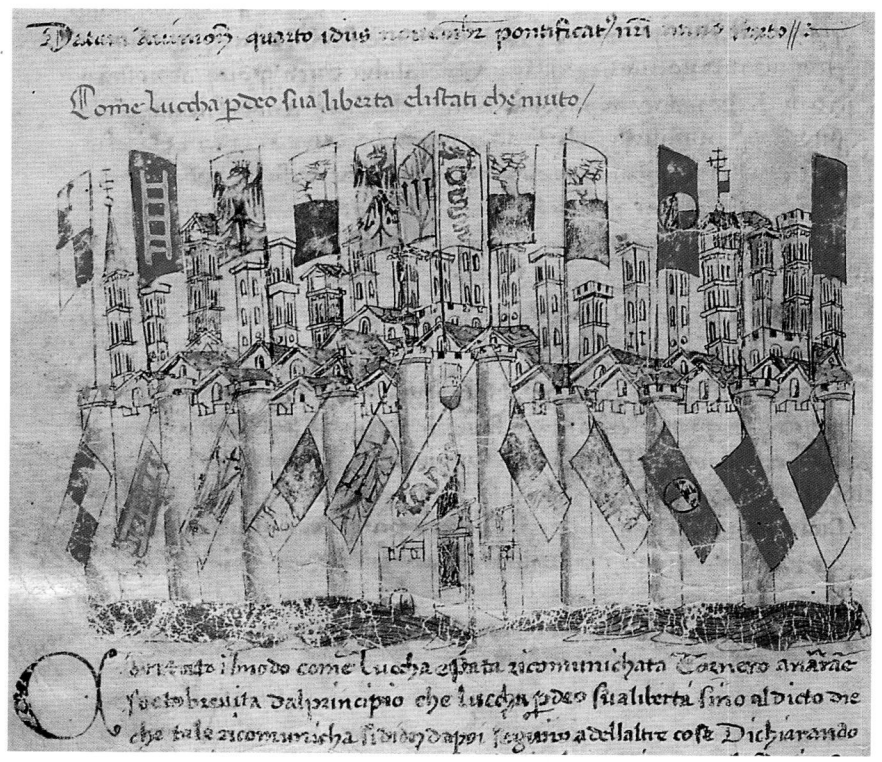

FIGURE 94
How the Florentines Attacked Pistoia with a Large Force and Took Carmignano.
Miniature, probably from between 1350 and 1375. From Giovanni Villani, *Nuova cronica.* Rome, Biblioteca Vaticana, ms. chigiano LVIII 296, f. 72v

FIGURE 95
How Lucca Lost Its Liberty, and the Regimes That It Exchanged.
Miniature, from Giovanni Sercambi, *Croniche.*
Lucca, Archivio di Stato, ms. Bibl. 107, f. 44v (vignetta CXXIII)

loss of the *carroccio* was considered a serious setback, and often meant that the tide of battle had turned. Frederick II captured the *carroccio* of Milan in the battle of Cortenuova in 1237, a crushing defeat for the city, and sent it off to Rome to be shown on the Capitol. We still have the proud epigraph that accompanied it:

> O Rome, behold the wagon of the august Caesar, Frederick II, a perpetual ornament of the city of Rome. Captured during the defeat of Milan, it arrives here as a resplendent booty to tell of the triumphs of your Caesar. Here it will stay, to the dishonor of the enemy. It has been sent here for the glory of Rome: love for Rome convinced us to send it here.[10]

A miniature from the *Croniche* (Chronicles) of Giovanni Sercambi shows the political shifts that occurred in the city of Lucca from 1313 to 1333 in the language of banners (figure 95). The caption reads: "Come Luccha perdeo sua libertà e li stati che mutò" ("How Lucca lost its liberty, and the regimes that it exchanged").[11] Above serried ranks of towers flutter the standards of the winners, a forest of colored drapes bearing symbols that tell of the succession of various "lords" of Lucca, while a ring of the same banners hung upside down along the turreted walls relates the defeats of those same lords in a series of rapid coups.[12] Reading from the left, the arms of the victors belong to: Piero Rossi of Parma, Mastino della Scala, Giovanni of Bohemia and his son Carlo, Castruccio Castracani, Carlo the son of Giovanni of Bohemia, Gherardino Spinola, Marco Visconti of Milan, the sons of Castruccio Castracani, and Ranieri di Donoratico; on a distant bell tower flies the small red-and-white flag of Lucca itself. The final, victorious banner—for the moment—is that of the commune of Pisa, the only one not reflected upside down in the bottom row.[13]

"Earth itself thunders now": Gunpowder

Into the turbulent life of the fourteenth-century cities, ever ready to go to war against one another, came a new and terrible invention: gunpowder, a mixture of carbon, saltpeter, and sulphur. Francesco Petrarch reflected disconsolately:

> I would be surprised if you did not also have those balls of iron which are ejected by fire with terrifying thunder. For little men like you the wrath of immortal God thundering from the sky is not enough: O cruelty wedded to pride! The earth itself thunders now and the *flash that cannot be imitated*, as Virgil said, is now being imitated by human frenzy. What used to be thrust forth by the clouds

FIGURE 96
Giacomo Busca da Clusone(?),
A Skeleton with a Harquebus.
Detail from *The Triumph of Death.*
Fresco, 1485.
Clusone (Bergamo), Chiesa
dei Disciplini

of heaven is now being thrust forth by a machine conceived in hell. Some think it was invented by Archimedes at the time Marcellus besieged Syracuse. Yet Archimedes designed the weapon to defend the liberty of his fellow citizens and to avoid or put off the destruction of his city, whereas you employ it to enslave and kill free men. Until recently this fiendish tool was rare and viewed with great amazement. Now artillery of all kinds is as common as any other weapon because our minds are quick to learn the very worst.[14]

The noble and courageous knight who had dedicated years of his life to practicing the use of the lance and the sword, and to horsemanship, suddenly found that he could be finished off not by one of his peers, but by a man of base extraction and modest physical prowess, ignorant of the tactics of war and untouched by the knightly ethos, provided he had a harquebus in his hands. With this primitive long-barreled gun, he could strike at a distance, deceitfully, not in an honest hand-to-hand fight! The shift in mentality that resulted was still hard to accept at the beginning of the seventeenth century, when Miguel Cervantes put the following words in the mouth of Don Quixote:

A blessing on those happy ages, strangers to the dreadful fury of those devilish instruments of artillery, whose inventor, I verily believe, is now in hell receiving the reward of his diabolical invention; by means of which it is in the power of a cowardly and base hand to take away the life of the bravest cavalier, and to which is owing, that without knowing how, or from whence, in the midst of that resolution and bravery, which inflames and animates gallant spirits, comes a chance ball, shot off by one, who, perhaps, fled and was frighted at the very flash in the pan, and in an instant cuts short and puts an end to the thoughts and life of him who deserved to have lived for many ages. And, therefore, when I consider this, I could almost say, I repent of having undertaken this profession of knight-errantry, in so detestable an age as this in which we live; for though no danger can daunt me, still it gives me some concern, to think that powder and lead may chance to deprive me of the opportunity of becoming famous and renowned, by the valor of my arm and edge of my sword, over the face of the whole earth.[15]

Artillery was also used, ranging in size from quite small to very large cannon, wheel-mounted for mobility. Like the harquebus, it was dangerous to handle, slow to reload (the large "bombard" required two hours between shots), and difficult to transport, given the often defective state of the roads. Cannon did not last long either, because they frequently burst or deformed, becoming unusable. Each cannon also needed balls of a diameter adjusted

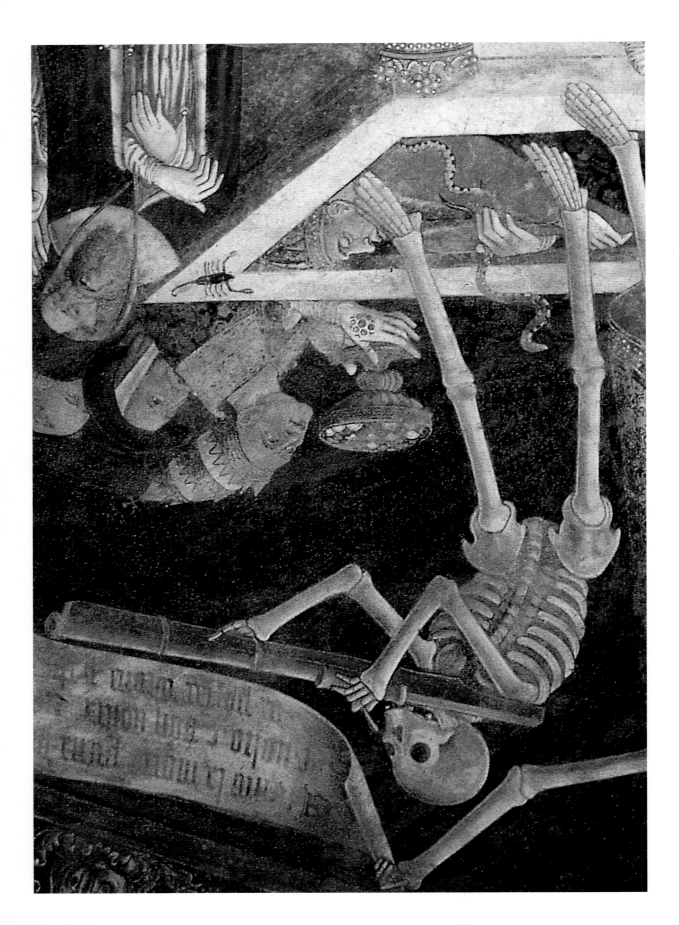

to its bore, because every maker produced cannon to the specifications that he considered best.[16] Yet despite all these difficulties the flash of fire and the crash of sound sowed terror among the enemy. Here is Giovanni Villani describing the English artillery at Crecy during the first battle of the Hundred Years' War between England and France in 1346: the bombards "made such a crash and burst of noise that it seemed as though God was thundering, with many killed and numerous horses toppled."[17]

The iconography of the "Triumph of Death" had to be brought up to date with the appearance of gunpowder, as we see in a fresco of 1485 in the Church of the Disciplini at Clusone, in the province of Bergamo. At the center, sovereign Death unfurls two scrolls, with texts taken from a widely known "laud" (praise). The one on the left says:

E' sonto per nome chiamata Morte / Ferischo a chi tocharà la sorte; /
Non è homo chosì forte / che da mi non pò schapare

I am called Death by name / I strike down those whose hour has come /
There is no man so strong / That he can escape from me

And the one on the right:

E' sonto la Morte piena de equaleza, / Sole voi ve volio e non vostra richeza /
e digna sonto da portar corona / Perché signorezi ognia persona

And I am Death, full of equality / I only want you, not your wealth /
And worthy I am to wear a crown / Because I am lord over every person

Death is flanked by two skeleton-servants, much smaller than their queen. The one on the left has just fired three arrows and is notching another three into his bow, while the one on the right is resting a much more modern weapon on his shoulder, "a short matchlock harquebus, or *schioppo manesco* as it was then called, made of a long barrel attached to a frame or stock by three circular bands" (figure 96).[18] The idea that the hour of our death is unforeseeable, and that neither individual ability nor courage nor noble blood can alter it, is effectively conveyed by the harquebus, which strikes its victims down without regard for age or rank, and much more quickly than the "pale horse," the apocalyptic steed on which Death rides.

The Horse, a Formidable Energy Resource

In the Middle Ages the horse was not just a bearer of grief and instrument of war. It had an important peacetime role too, so much so that it takes its place along with flowing water as one of the principal sources of drive:

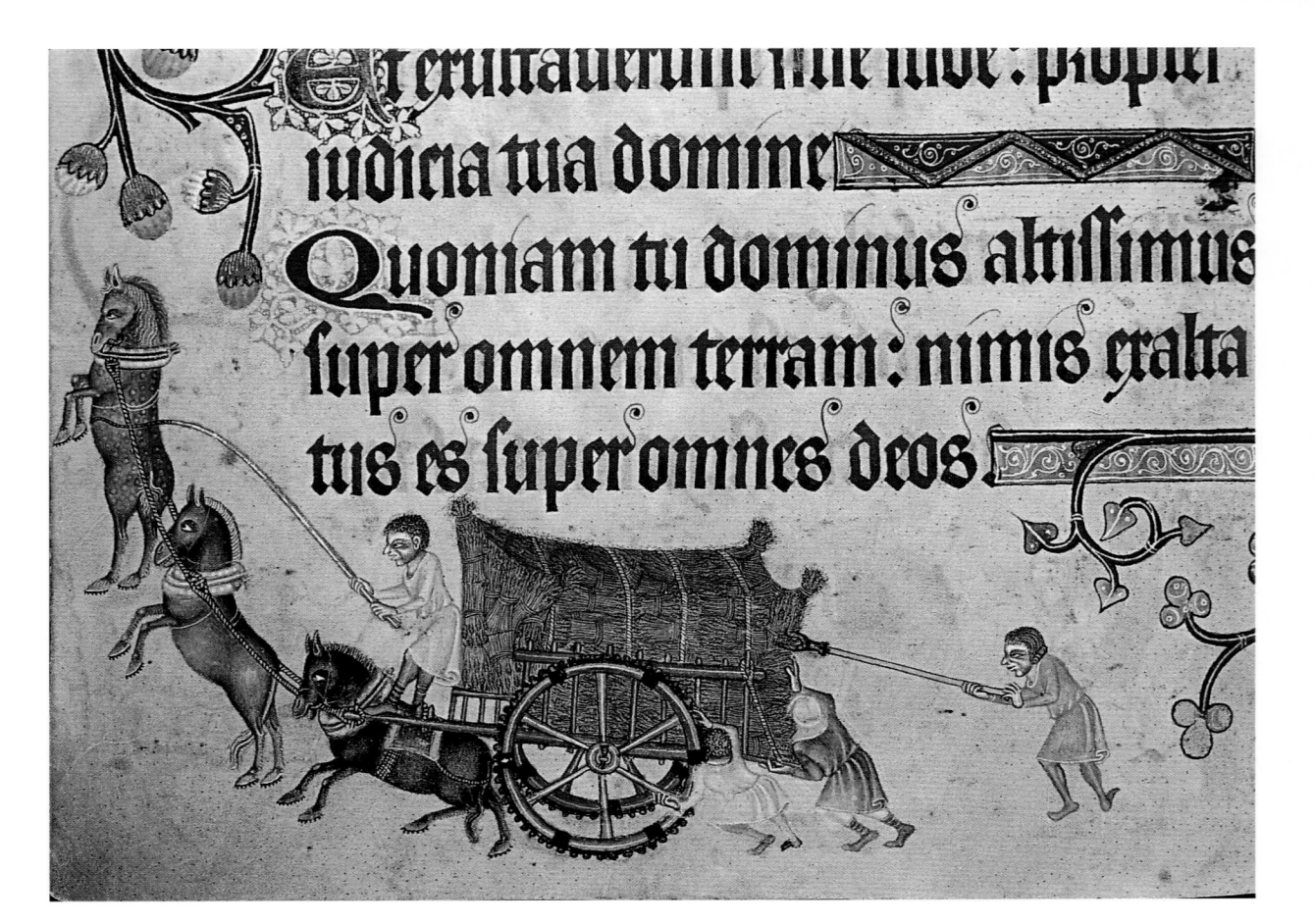

even today the power of an internal combustion engine is expressed in horsepower. The Romans yoked the horse with the same system they used for oxen,[19] though the horse has a different anatomy; when forced to push with its neck against a belt of soft leather, it was unable to pull a heavy load, because the weight would cause the harness to choke it. In the Middle Ages the animal's anatomy was examined more closely, and this led to the introduction of the horse collar (called a *collare di spalla* or shoulder collar in Italian), which radically altered the horse's driving power, multiplying it dramatically (perhaps threefold, by one calculation). The new collar, introduced around the year 1000 and still in use today, is stiff and padded; it rings the animal's chest and shoulders rather than its neck, so that the horse, thrusting against it, can easily pull a plow or a heavy load. A further discovery of the Middle Ages was that horses could be harnessed in a row, one behind the other, so that each contributed to the effort of pulling the wagon (figure 97).[20]

FIGURE 97
A Wagon Loaded with Harvested Grain Is Pulled up a Hill by a Team of Horses.
Miniature, beginning of the fourteenth century.
London, British Library, the Luttrell Psalter, ms. Add. 42130, f. 173v

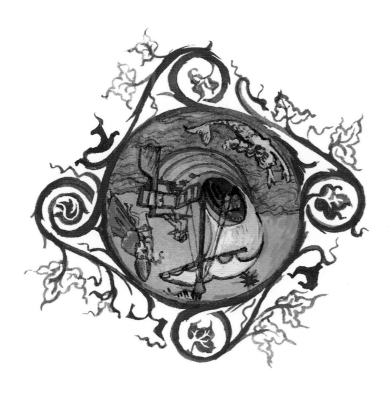

SIX *By Land and Sea*

The Wheelbarrow, the Cart's Kid Sister

For moving small quantities of material over short distances with reduced cost in human fatigue, workers in the Middle Ages invented a simple device, a sort of kid sister of the familiar cart or barrow: the wheelbarrow. The ancient Romans perhaps cared too little about the human effort exerted by their enslaved work force to think of such a thing. Visual documentation of the wheelbarrow is found in the thirteenth century in a miniature from a beautiful manuscript of the Bible. The first letter of the Latin text of Ezra 1:1 ("In diebus Cyri regis Persarum"[1]) is enlarged to frame the miniature, which portrays the reconstruction of the temple of Jerusalem ordered by King Cyrus. At the base of the edifice under construction, a young workman leans against the handles of a wheelbarrow piled with bricks, tilting it to balance the load; he seems to hold a pose for a moment, as though proud of his new instrument, which is actually an evolutionary precursor of the modern handtruck (figure 98).

In the fresco at the Castle of Manta, one small scene depicts a moment of pause, and features a wheelbarrow; the handles rest on vertical supports and the box has a sort of backrest attached so that it can support a greater load (figure 99). The woman pushing it has stopped to take a drink, ignoring the threats of the paralyzed man resting against a cushion and waving a cane, perhaps her husband, who is impatient to get to the fountain of youth. The

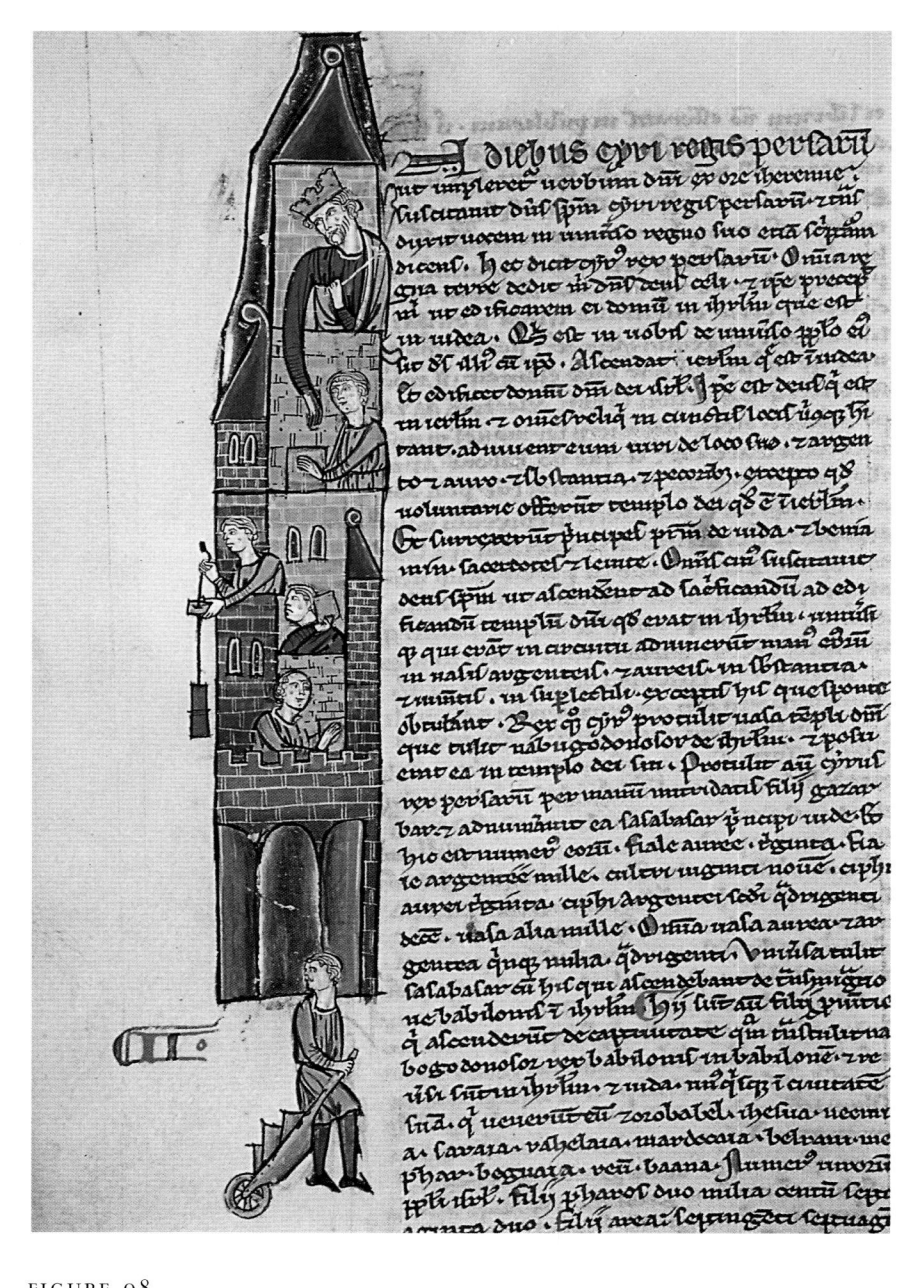

FIGURE 98

The Rebuilding of the Temple of Jerusalem Ordered by Cyrus.

Miniature, thirteenth century.

Paris, Bibliothèque Sainte-Geneviève, ms. 1185, f. 127v

FIGURE 99

An Elderly Couple en Route to the Fountain of Youth;
the Husband Rides in a Wheelbarrow.

Fresco, middle of the fifteenth century.

Cuneo, Castello della Manta

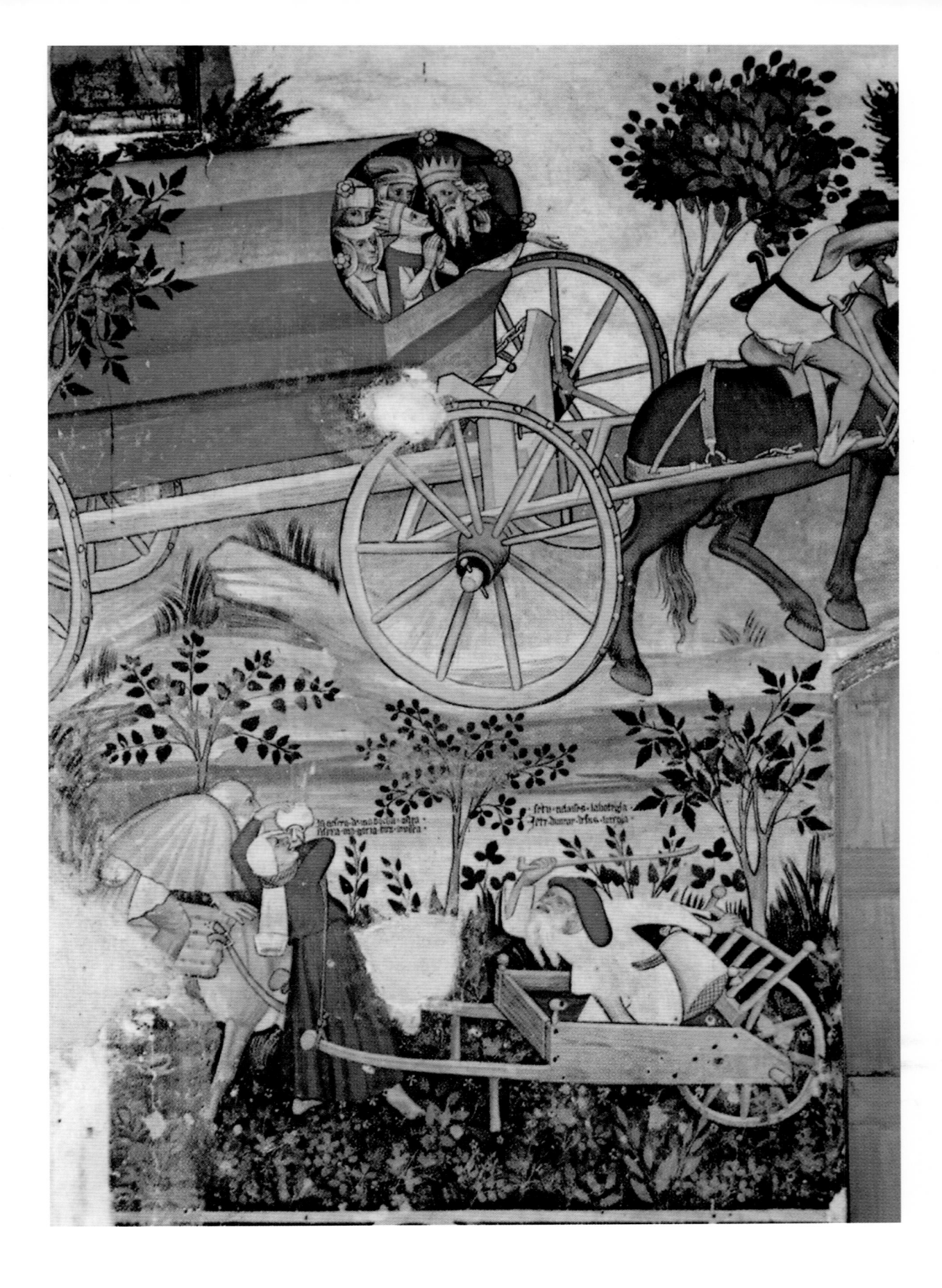

painter has added a few lines of dialogue, with the old man shrieking, "Se tu ne laises la botegla je te dunray desus l'oregla" ("If you don't leave the bottle I will thrash you around the ears")—to which the woman replies sarcastically, "Ia ne sera de ma bocha ostea si sera ma goria bien arossea" ("I won't remove the bottle from my mouth until my throat is well watered").[2]

Flavio Gioia, the Inventor of the Compass Who Never Existed

In the Middle Ages overland transportation, whether on foot or on horseback, was very slow, and whenever possible people preferred to travel by water. Navigators oriented themselves using the compass, something about which Giordano da Pisa was very well informed, as he was about everything else:

> I say first that your faith guides you as the North Star does, that guides navigators, because they watch the sign of the needle and steer by that; by the magnet, that is. The magnet appears to be a common stone, but it is very dear, and it would be better to lose an emerald than to lose it, so useful and necessary is it. We could not do without the magnet. It guides us and shows us the right sign to follow.[3]

The needle of the compass that turns to the North Star comes to the mind of Dante too:

> Then, from the heart of one of those new lights
> there came a voice that drew me to itself
> (I was the needle pointing to the star)

(*Paradiso* 12, 28–30; translated by Mark Musa)

Giovanni da Buti, commenting on these lines in around 1390, explains:

> Navigators have a small box, with a small wheel of light paper that rotates in the center. This wheel has many points, and on one of them that has a star painted on it, the point of a needle is inserted. When navigators want to find where north is, they make the needle giddy with a magnet.[4]

Bossolo (box) and *bussola* (compass) derive from the Latin *buxus* (box tree) and *buxula* (little box): the compass was originally a little box of wood from the boxwood tree. Sailors from the city of Amalfi spread it throughout the Mediterranean between 1100 and 1200, in the course of their voyages to Syria and Egypt during the Crusades.

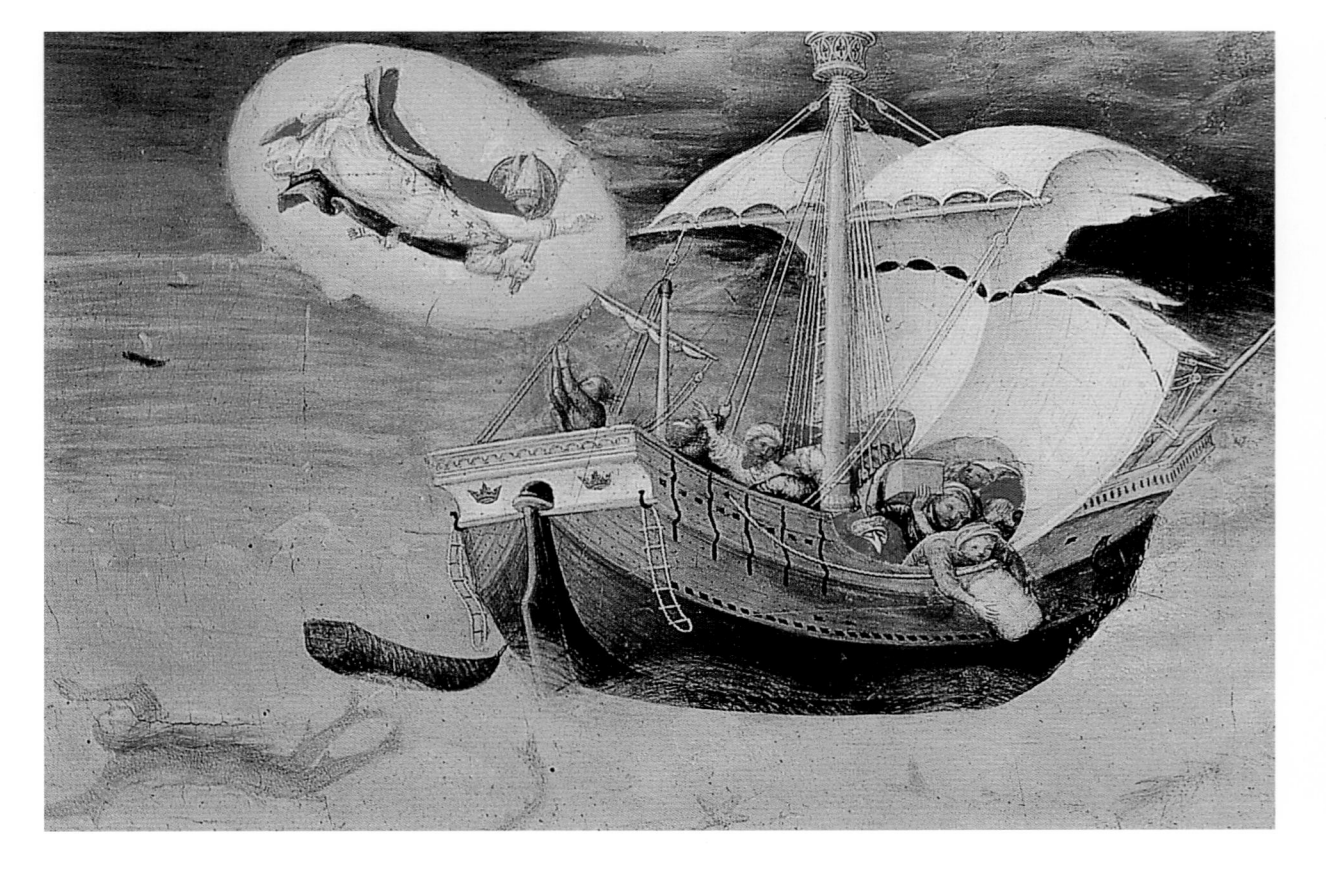

Toward the middle of the fifteenth century, the historian Flavio Biondo wrote that the compass had been invented and perfected by the inhabitants of Amalfi.[5] In 1511 the Bolognese humanist Giambattista Pio relayed that information this way: "At Amalfi, in old Campania, the use of the magnet was invented, it is said by Flavio" ("Amalphi in Campania veteri magnetis usus inventus a Flavio traditur"). The intended meaning of the last three words in the Latin was "according to Flavio," and Pio probably inserted a comma after the word *inventus* to make that clear. But as the phrase was quoted and reproduced, the comma got shifted, changing the meaning radically, so that Flavio Biondo became the inventor of the compass: "At Amalfi, in old Campania, the use of the magnet was invented by Flavio, it is said" ("inventus a Flavio, traditur"). A reckless Neapolitan historian, Scipione Mazzella, claimed that "Flavio" had been born at Gioia in Puglia, but had invented the compass at Amalfi, in Campania. And in Amalfi, until a few years ago, there was still a monument to Flavio Gioia, "inventor of the compass," who in reality had never existed and was conjured up by a misplaced comma!

FIGURE 100
Gentile da Fabriano,
Miracle of Saint Nicholas.
Panel, 1425.
Rome, Pinacoteca Vaticana

The Invention of the Rudder, Santa Claus, and the Mermaid

In the thirteenth century the swiveling rudder was invented. Before that the rudder consisted of a simple oar, and was quite incapable of handling

the waves of a really rough sea. The new rudder was a vertical blade attached to the stern of the ship with a solid iron hinge, its topmost part firmly clamped to the horizontal bar or tiller used to steer it. We can observe one in a painting of Gentile da Fabriano from 1425 (figure 100). The sea is storm-tossed, and shipwreck imminent. The helmsman, unlike his companions who are still trying to cope with the disaster by throwing part of the precious cargo overboard, has abandoned the tiller and, with hands clasped, is invoking Saint Nicholas, who is swooping down from the sky with a flaming torch, like a reassuring beacon. Amid the waves a mermaid with long blond hair regards the saint with amazement. In the Romance languages the word for mermaid is *siren* (*sirena* in Italian and Spanish, *sirène* in French), and sirens in classical antiquity were dangerously attractive bird-women. The mermaid or fish-woman keeps the name and the same dangerous attractiveness, but she is a creature of the Middle Ages.

Saint Nicholas lived in the fourth century, according to tradition, and was the first Bishop of Myra, though his bones were later "translated" to Bari. He was held to be the divine protector of children, whom he aided in various circumstances, resuscitating three lads whom an evil innkeeper had actually pickled in brine, and preventing three young girls from being turned out as streetwalkers with the gift of three golden balls. The feast day of Saint Nicholas was December 6, and on that day in Lorraine, Flanders, and the northern Netherlands during the Middle Ages, a child dressed as the bishop ("Sinter Klaas" in Dutch) and wearing a white beard would go about bringing gifts to good children, while "Father Lash" stood ready, rod in hand, to punish the disobedient ones. Dutch settlers in America brought Sinter Klaas with them, and there his name was anglicized to Santa Claus.

So Santa Claus is all that remains of Saint Nicholas, or all that remained before his final transformation at the hands of Coca-Cola's advertising department, who gave him a red suit and pants in exchange for the long habit of a bishop, and made him fat and jolly, like a certain type of jovial American.[6] In that guise he has even migrated back to Europe under the names Father Christmas, Père Noel, and Babbo Natale.

And here, after reviewing so many concrete inventions of the Middle Ages, it gives me pleasure to end, with the mermaid/siren and Santa Claus/Saint Nicholas, both of them offspring of the world of medieval fantasy. Once they gave form to the emotions and desires of children, and the emotions and fears of adults. Today they make little ones dream, and the adults smile as they listen.

NOTES

1. Reading and Keeping the Books

1. "Forma non glorior excellenti, sed que placere viridioribus annis esset: colore vivido inter candidum et subnigrum, vivacibus oculis et visu per longum tempus acerrimo, qui preter spem supra sexagesimum etatis annum me destituit, ut indignanti michi ad ocularium confugiendum esset auxilium." Francesco Petrarca, *Prose*, ed. Guido Martellotti, Pier Giorgio Ricci, Enrico Carrara, Enrico Bianchi (Milan-Naples: Ricciardi editore, 1955), *Posteritati*, 2–3. [Trans.: the English translation is from *Letters from Petrarch Selected and Translated by Morris Bishop* (Bloomington and London: Indiana University Press, 1966), 5.]

2. I imagine that the *Magister Florentinus*, to whom we owe the "Second León Bible," completed in 960, would have thought Petrarch truly ungrateful for the relief brought by eyeglasses, when we read his description of the strain of copying: "If you want to know the details, I will tell you how much writing weighs one down. It brings dimness to your eyes, curves your spine, twists your ribs and your stomach, sends pain shooting through your kidneys, and fills your whole body with fatigue." Note that harm to eyesight comes first on his list of these detrimental effects. On the *Magister Florentinus*, see Walter Cahn, *La bible romane* (Fribourg: Office du Livre, 1982), 66; and Christiane Klapisch-Zuber, *L'ombre des ancêtres, essai sur l'imaginaire médiéval de la parenté* (Paris: Fayard, 2000), 82, where she gives the Latin original: "Nam si velis scire singulatim, nuntio tibi quam grave est scribere pondus. Oculis caliginem facit, dorsum incorbat, costas et ventrem frangit, renibus dolorem immittit et omne corpus fascidium nutrit."

3. "Non è ancora venti anni che si trovò l'arte di fare gli occhiali, che fanno vedere bene, ch'è una de le migliori arti e de le più necessarie che 'l mondo abbia, e è così poco che ssi trovò: arte novella, che mmai non fu. E disse il lettore: io vidi colui che prima la trovò e fece, e favellaigli." Giordano da Pisa, *Quaresimale fiorentino 1305–1306*, critical edition, ed. Carlo Delcorno (Florence: Sansoni, 1974), sermon 15 (February 23, 1305), 75.

4. "E disse fra Giordano: 'Uno di questi che si battezzaro [i.e., a Jewish convert] fu mio compagno frate, e più volte andai con lui, ed era litterata persona ed era lettore di Napoli.' " [Giordano da Pisa], *Prediche del beato Giordano da Rivalto*, ed. Domenico Moreni (Florence: Magheri, 1831), 2:231, sermon 60 (November 9, 1304, at Florence). The question of the identity of the *lector* in the passage about eyeglasses arises for me, because I do not recall ever having read a sermon of Giordano in which he himself is identified by the term *lector*. Edward Rosen on the other hand is quite certain that the *lector* is Giordano, but provides not a single example to back this up: E. Rosen, "The Invention of Eyeglasses," *Journal of the History of Medicine and Allied Sciences* 11 (1) (1956): 13–47 and 11 (2) (1956): 183–218; see 31–34.

5. "Frater Alexander de Spina, vir modestus et bonus, quae vidit oculis facta, scivit et facere. Ocularia ab aliquo primo facta, communicare nolente, ipse fecit, et omnibus communicavit corde hilari et volente." *Chronica antiqua conventus Sanctae Catharinae de Pisis*, ed. Francesco Bonaini, in *Archivio Storico Italiano*, 6 (2), section 3 (1845): 399–593, at 476. The eulogy continues: "Cantare, scribere, miniare, et omnia scivit quae manus mechanicae valent. Ingeniosus in chorporalibus [Bonaini erroneously transcribes *choralibus*] in domo Regis aeterni fecit suo ingenio mansionem." The corrected reading comes from Rosen, "The Invention of Eyeglasses," 210. The *Chronica* was begun by the Dominican Bartolomeo da San Concordio, who died in 1347, and continued by his confrères; Rosen, "The Invention of Eyeglasses," 20.

6. M. Gilson, "Histoire des lunettes," in *Bulletin de la Societé Belge d'Ophtalmologie* 264 (1) (1997): 7–13, at 7.

7. Unfortunately Rosen, writing for an English-language readership, never gives the passages cited in the original Latin or Italian.

8. "Invenzione degli occhiali, se sia antica o no; e quando, dove, e da chi fossero inventati? Veglia, dedicata all'illustrissimo Francesco Redi," cited from Giovanni Targioni Tozzetti, *Notizie degli aggrandimenti delle scienze fisiche accadute in Toscana nel corso di anni LX del secolo XVII* (Florence: G. Bouchard, 1780), 2:49–62, publication no. 11, 59.

9. Francesco Redi, *Opere* (Milan: Società Tipografica de' Classici italiani, 1809–1811; Classici italiani, vols. 169–177), 7:254.

10. For a surprising list of the falsifications of Redi, see Rosen, "The Invention of Eyeglasses," 16.

11. These were compiled around the middle of the sixteenth century by an anonymous friar who expanded upon the *Chronica antiqua conventus Sanctae Catharinae*; Rosen, "The Invention of Eyeglasses," 20.

12. "Frater Alexander Spina manibus suis quidquid voluisset operabatur, ac charitate victus aliis communicabat. Unde, cum tempore illo quidam vitrea specilla, quae ocularia vulgus vocat, primus adinvenisset, pulchro sane, utili ac novo invento, neminique vellet artem ipsam conficiendi comunicare, hic bonus vir artifex, *illis visis*, statim nullo docente didicit, et alios qui scire voluerunt docuit. Canebat modulate, scribebat eleganter, et descriptos libros picturis, quas minia appellant, ornabat. Nullam prorsus manualium artium ignoravit." *Chronica antiqua conventus Sanctae Catharinae*, ed. Bonaini, 477 and Redi, *Opere*, 5:82–83.

13. As Edward Rosen rightly conjectures in "The Invention of Eyeglasses," 24–25.

14. Targioni Tozzetti, *Notizie*, 51.

15. Rosen, "The Invention of Eyeglasses," 25; Redi, *Opere*, 2:260.

16. The same Pandolfini whom Dati in the *Veglia* introduced to announce the discovery of the sermon of the Dominican.

17. Rosen, "The Invention of Eyeglasses," 194.

18. ". . . vi era un'altra memoria ch'andò male nella restaurazione di quella chiesa, registrata però fedelmente nel nostro Sepoltuario antico, tanto più cara quanto per mezzo di essa veniamo consapevoli del primo inventor degli occhiali, essere stato un gentiluomo di questa patria, così altamente illustrata d'ingegno in ogni materia che ne richieda acutezza. . . . Questo fu messer Salvino degli Armati figliuolo d'Armato, di nobile stirpe. . . . Vedeasi la figura di quest'uomo, distesa su un lastrone, in abito civile, e con lettere attorno che dicevano così: +QUI DIACE SALVINO D'ARMATO DEGL'ARMATI DI FIR. INVENTOR DEGL'OCCHIALI. DIO GLI PERDONI LA PECCATA. ANNO D. MCCCXVII. Questi è quel tale non nominato né espresso dalla *Cronaca* antica manoscritta nel convento de' Padri Domenicani di Pisa, citata da Francesco Redi . . . , leggendovisi come frate Alessandro della Spina, che visse in quei medesimi tempi e che forse fu fiorentino e non pisano, cercasse d'imparar la invenzione di fare gli occhiali da uno che, sapendola, non la voleva insegnare, e che da sè stesso trovasse maniera di lavorargli." Isidoro Del Lungo, "Le vicende d'un'impostura erudita (Salvino degli Armati)," in *Archivio Storico Italiano* 78 (1920): 5–53, at 14 (where the passage is given).

19. Del Lungo, "Le vicende," 17ff.

20. Rosen, "The Invention of Eyeglasses," 187ff., reconstructs the family genealogy.

21. Del Lungo, "Le vicende," 20; Rosen, "The Invention of Eyeglasses," 192.

22. Giuseppe Albertotti, "Note critiche e bibliografiche riguardanti la storia degli occhiali," in *Annali di Ottalmologia e clinica oculistica* 43 (1914): 328–356, at 341ff.

23. Del Lungo, "Le vicende," 43–50. At 46, an etching showing the state of the monument in the church of Santa Maria Maggiore. Today the portrait and the epigraph have disappeared, but the sarcophagus can still be seen.

24. Rosen, "The Invention of Eyeglasses," 196.

25. "MCCC, indicione XIII, die secundo aprilis, nos Raphael Natalis et Johannes De Fontana iusticiarii veteres ordinamus quod aliquis de dicta arte cristalarie non audeat emere nec emi facere, nec vendere nec vendi facere aliquid laborerium de vitreo blancho quod contrafaciat ad cristallum scilicet botoni, manici, roidi de

botacelis et da ogli, tabule de anconis et de crucibus, et lapides ad legendum, sub pena librarum X et perdat laborerium et frangatur." *I capitolari delle Arti Veneziane*, ed. Giovanni Monticolo and Enrico Besta (Rome: Istituto Storico Italiano per il Medio Evo, 1914; Fonti della Storia d'Italia), 3:133.

26. G. Albertotti, "Lettera intorno alla invenzione degli occhiali all'onorevole senatore Isidoro Del Lungo," in *Annali di Ottalmologia e clinica oculistica* 50 (1922): fasc. 1–2, 85–104, at 92. I have mentioned only the use of lenses to correct presbyopia, because the ones for the correction of myopia did not appear until the sixteenth century, and the ones for the correction of astigmatism not until the nineteenth: Gilson, "Histoire des lunettes," 8.

27. Albertotti, "Lettera," 88.

28. *Libro di M. Giovambattista Palatino, cittadino Romano, nel qual s'insegna a scriver ogni sorte di lettere antica et moderna.* In Roma, Campo di Fiore, per Antonio Blodo asolano MDXLV.

29. Albertotti, "Lettera," 88, fig. 1; 89, fig. 2. The mirror for writing also appears in an illustration of Tagliente (*Lo presente libro insegna la vera arte del Excellente scrivere de diverse varie sorti di litere . . . Opera del Tagliente . . .* Stampata in Vinegia per Pietro di Nicolini de Sabbio . . . MDXXXVII), reproduced by Albertotti at 91, fig. 4; a better reproduction in Victor Massena Essling, *Livres à figures venitiens* (Paris: Olschki-H. Leclerc, 1909), 2:455. In the seventeenth century the invention of eyeglasses was attributed to the English philosopher Roger Bacon (1214–1292). What Bacon actually says, following the Arab Alhazen, is that the old and the weak can make use of ground glasses, but he did not make the leap of realizing that they could be placed on the eyes: Rosen, "The Invention of Eyeglasses," 197–199; Jean Gimpel, *La révolution industrielle du Moyen Age* (Paris: Seuil, 1975), 176.

30. In a fresco painted by Tomaso da Modena at Treviso in the convent of San Nicolò, the Dominican Isnardo da Vicenza is shown before a writing desk littered with volumes. In a niche can be seen a sort of ostensory that contains not the consecrated host but a mirror, beside an ink pot with the pen already dipped into the ink. According to Franz Daxecker, "Three Reading Aids Painted by Tomaso da Modena in the Chapter House of San Nicolò Monastery in Treviso, Italy," in *Documenta Opthalmologica* 99 (1999; published in 2000): 219–223, at 220 and fig. 3, this object must rather be a magnifying glass, since a mirror would be inconceivable in the cell of a friar. I am deeply grateful to Franz Daxecker for having freely made available to me offprints and photographs otherwise difficult to find.

31. A list in *Enciclopedia Dantesca* (Rome: Treccani-Enciclopedia Italiana, 1984), s.v. *speccchio*.

32. ". . . firmaverunt inter se ad invicem societatem ad faciendum, construendum et archimiandum dicta occhialia." The observation is Michele Luzzati's; for the transcription of the entire document and a penetrating and detailed analysis, see M. Luzzati, "Una società per la fabbricazione di occhiali alla metà del Quattrocento," in *Antichità Pisane* 1 (1974): 40–45.

33. Gilson, "Histoire des lunettes," 7. The first scholar to publish this miniature (which was signaled by the librarian at that time, Monsieur Gazier), dating it correctly to the middle of the fourteenth century, was R. Bidault, "Deux miniatures du Moyen-Age intéressant l'ophtalmologie," in *Aesculape* 4 (1937): 117–119. A brief notice, without—in this respect—adding anything new, in David Park, *The Fire Within the Eye: An Historical Essay on the Nature and Meaning of Light* (Princeton: Princeton University Press, 1997), 124–125.

34. MS 140 of the Bibliothèque Municipale of Besançon is a composite. The first part (foll. 1–189) is a psalter for use in the diocese of Angoulême, from the end of the thirteenth century. The second part (foll. 190–229) is a fragment of a book of hours, perhaps from Picardy, from the middle of the fourteenth century: it includes an office for the dead (foll. 190–207), the penitential psalms (foll. 208–212), the litanies (foll. 212v–217), and various prayers in French. Finally, the third part (foll. 230–238), from the beginning of the fifteenth century, contains various prayers in Latin. It is not known when the manuscript was assembled; at the beginning of the sixteenth century it belonged to the family of the counts of Leugney, lords of Chalezeule, near Besançon, then in the eighteenth century it passed to the Capuchin convent of Besançon; confiscated at the time of the Revolution, it was finally deposited in the municipal library of the city. For this information, and for a bibliographic update, I am grateful to Madame Marie-Claire Waille of the library of Besançon.

35. *Tomaso da Modena*, catalogue ed. Luigi Menegazzi (Treviso: Editrice Canova, 1979), 115, fig. 120 and table IV.

36. Daxecker, "Three Reading Aids," 219, cites a similar lens with a handle, held by Hippocrates in a sculpture "in the Mauritius rotunda of Konstanz Minster that dates back to 1270." Daxecker cites G. Mühn and W. Roos, "Jahrhunderte Brille," in *Deutsches Museum. Abhandlungen und Berichte, München* 36 (1968): 8; and W. Münchow, "Geschichte der Brille," in *Der Augenarzt* (Berlin: Karl Velhagen, 1966), 7:475–540, at 481.

37. According to Rosen, "The Invention of Eyeglasses," 205, the personage represented is rather Hugues de Saint-Cher. Hugues was a famous exegete who died in 1263, but since eyeglasses were not discovered until several decades later, his evident familiarity with them in this painting would have to be an anachronism by the painter.

38. *Scripta Leonis, Rufini et Angeli Sociorum s. Francisci*, ed. and English trans. by R. B. Brooke (Oxford: Clarendon Press, 1970), nr. 72, 214–215.

39. *Sancti Patris Francisci Assisiensis Opuscula*, ed. Kasper Esser (Grottaferrata: Coll. S. Bonaventurae, 1978), "Epistola toti ordini missa," 146–147.

40. Leonardo Farinelli, "Dalla biblioteca conventuale alla biblioteca pubblica," in *La città e la parola scritta*, ed. Giovanni Pugliese Carratelli (Milan: Libri Scheiwiller-Credito Italiano, 1997), 289–374.

41. Franz Daxecker, "Representations of Eyeglasses on Gothic Winged Altars in Austria," in *Documenta Ophthalmologica* 93 (1997): 169–188, at 171–172, and fig. 5.

42. Vera Trost, *Skriptorium, Die Buchherstellung im Mittelalter* (Stuttgart: Belser Verlag, 1991), 7.

43. Iacopo da Varazze, *Legenda aurea*, introduction by Franco Cardini and Mario Martelli; text of the fourteenth century translation into the *volgare* and notes by Arrigo Levasti (Florence: Le Lettere, 2000), 2:121 and fig. at 118.

44. In this connection a Danish half-ducat of 1647, which depicts a pair of eyeglasses with the motto "Vide mira Domini" ("Behold the marvels of the Lord"), offers an interesting comparison; for a reproduction, see Gilson, "Histoire des lunettes," 13, fig. 20. Those who are not, like Augustine, saints, may need the help of a good pair of eyeglasses, the better to observe the marvels of creation; unless, perhaps, the meaning is that the invention of eyeglasses itself is counted among the marvels of this world.

45. On the various "phases" of the iconography of Saint Jerome: Daniel Russo, *Saint Jérôme en Italie. Étude d'iconographie et de spiritualité (XIIIe–XVe siècle)* (Paris-Rome: La Découverte-École Française de Rome, 1987).

46. Christ holds in his hand the globe of the Earth and sits between two altars; the chalice covered with a corporal that sits on the one on his right has just been taken from the open hatch of the one on his left. Note the extreme realism with which the fringed curtains hung from rings on two iron rods with upturned ends have been painted. The chalice recalls the purpose of the codex, a missal, and at the same time the continual renewal of the sacrifice of Christ that the evangelists long ago narrated. The surface of the globe held by Christ is represented in the form of a T; see C. Frugoni, "La figurazione bassomedioevale dell'Imago mundi," in *"Imago mundi": la conoscenza scientifica nel pensiero bassomedioevale*, Convegni del centro di Studi sulla spiritualità medioevale, 22, 1981 (Accademia Tudertina: Todi, 1983), 225–269.

47. Daxecker, "Representations of Eyeglasses," 170–172, and figs. 1–3.

48. Ibid., 173 and fig. 4. Catherine of Alexandria, in legend, was a highly cultivated princess who lived at the time of the persecutions against the Christians. She declared her faith in public before the emperor, who was unable to rebut her arguments and forced her to enter a dispute against fifty philosophers who were expected to reduce her to silence. But she bested them, and the furious emperor condemned them to burn at the stake; but Catherine succeeded in converting all of them before their martyrdom. Catherine herself, after emerging unscathed from torture between toothed wheels, was decapitated.

49. They might also have a frame of gilded silver, as we see for example in a 1322 inventory of the goods of a Florentine bishop: "unum par occalium foltorum de argento deaurato." Eyeglasses were always an object of value; in 1329 a merchant listed "unum par ochialium" among the things of which he had been robbed, recalling that he had bought them at Florence: Rosen, "The Invention of Eyeglasses," 204.

50. Daxecker, "Representations of Eyeglasses," 172, fig. 6.

51. On the iconography of anti-Semitism, see Bernhard Blumenkranz, *Le juif médiéval au miroir de l'art chrétien* (Paris: Études Augustiniennes, 1966), with a comment on this miniature at 106.

52. "Artefici son, parme, / divenuti/ saputi / ed astuti / tra' sensali: / su' libri co gli ochiali / fanno specchi, / e con penne agli orecchi, / con cambi secchi, / ciascun compera e vende. / Chi presta e chi rende, / chi arappa e chi prende, / e chi acende / usura; / chi ruba e chi fura / sanza cura e vedova e pupillo." Franco Sacchetti, *Il Libro delle rime*, ed. Franca Brambilla Ageno (Florence: Olschki, 1990), frottola CCXLVIII, "O mondo immondo," 394.

53. Daxecker, "Representations of Eyeglasses," 176–177, figs. 10 and 11. The author, in a recent article in collaboration with A. Broucek, "Eine Darstellung der hl. Ottilie mit Lesensteinen," *Gesnerus* 52 (1995): 319–322, maintains that the lenses placed on the book are not to be interpreted as eyeglasses but as magnifying glasses, since they are apparently not attached to each other. Yet I fail to see how *two* magnifying glasses could be used at the same time, and so I hold to the view that the painter did intend to represent actual eyeglasses.

54. Gilson, "Histoire des lunettes," 7–13, figs. 12–14.

55. Del Lungo, "Le vicende," 9. The eyeglasses of San Filippo Neri also became a relic.

56. Gilson, "Histoire des lunettes," 9.

57. "Vedi che questa arca si era tutta chiusa; però era detta arca, non nave, ché la nave si è aperta di sopra, ma quella avea tetto e si era chiusa. Le porte di sotto erano chiuse, e la finestra di sopra era anche chiusa, ma avea la finestra di cristallo, ch'era utile a l'acqua, a ritenerla, e alla luce, a riceverla." Giordano da Pisa, *Quaresimale fiorentino*, sermon 92 (April 10, 1306), 431.

58. "Aecclesiae nostrae fenestrae veteribus pannis usque nunc fuerunt clausae. Vestris felicibus temporibus auricomus sol primum infulsit basilicae nostrae pavimenta per discoloria picturarum vitra cunctorumque inspicientium corda pertemptant multiplicia gaudia, qui inter se mirantur insoliti operis varietates. Quocirca quousque locus iste cernitur tali decoratus ornatu, vestrum nomen die noctuque celebrationibus orationum ascribitur." *Monumenta Germaniae Historica, Epistolae Selectae* III, *Die Tegernseer Briefsammlung*, ed. K. Strecker (Berlin, 1925), 25n24. For commentary: Enrico Castelnuovo, *Vetrate medioevali. Officine, tecniche, maestri* (Turin: Einaudi, 1994), 163ff.

59. "Annus millenus et centenus quadragenus quartus erat Verbi, quando sacrata fuit. Quibus etiam epitaphii versibus hos adjungi delegimus: 'Pars nova posterior dum jungitur anteriori, aula micat medio clarificata suo. Claret enim claris quod dare concopulatur, et quod perfundit lux nova, claret opus.' " *Sugerii De administratione*, in Erwin Panofsky, *Abbot Suger* (Princeton: Princeton University Press, 1979), 50.

60. "Provisum est . . . ut . . . tota [ecclesia] clarissimarum vitrearum luce mirabili et continua interiorem perlustrante pulchritudinem eniteret." *Sugerii Libellus alter de consecratione ecclesiae Sancti Dionysii* in Panofsky, *Abbot Suger*, 101. For commentary: Castelnuovo, *Vetrate medioevali*, 30.

61. On this theme: Klapisch-Zuber, *L'ombre des ancêtres*, 53–55.

62. I refer, obviously, to Christiane Klapisch-Zuber's *L'ombre des ancêtres*.

63. From a document of 1385, describing the use of technology in the countryside around 's-Hertogenbosch, then in the duchy of Brabant, now in the Netherlands;

cited by Lewis Mumford in *Technics and Civilization* (London: Routledge and Kegan Paul, 1934), 125.

64. In a miniature from a manuscript that he himself copied around 1450 for the duke's library.

65. "D'uscio in uscio mettendo il capo, e salendo le scale, si mise andare cercando l'altrui case, e fare dell'impronto per asciugarsi, se fuoco vi trovasse. Andando d'una in altra, per fortuna capitò ad una porta, là dove intrato e andando su, trovò in cucina uno grandissimo fuoco con due pentole piene, e con uno schidone di capponi e di starne, e con una fante assai leggiadra e giovene, la quale volgea il detto arrosto." Franco Sacchetti, *Il Trecentonovelle*, ed. Emilio Faccioli (Turin: Einaudi, 1970), novella 34, 91.

66. G. Boccaccio, *Decameron* 5:10, ed. V. Branca (Turin: Einaudi, 1993), 2:696–698.

67. *Musio* because *murilegus*, a mousecatcher, from the Latin *mus*, mouse. The word is attested in Isidore of Seville, who neglects the classical Latin word for cat, *felis*: "Musio appellatus, quod muribus infestus sit." Isidori Hispalensis episcopi, *Etymologiarum sive originum libri XX*, 12.2.38; ed. W. M. Lindsay (Oxford: Clarendon Press, 1911).

68. Laurence Bobis, *Le chat: histoire et légendes* (Paris: Fayard, 2000).

69. Michel Rouche, in describing life in early medieval Gaul, observes: "The only major innovation [with respect to the Roman period] was in eating utensils: plates supplanted cups and other vessels that could be held in one hand. The goblet and truncated conical vessel became increasingly common, as early as the fifth century in the case of early Christian ceramics. This proves that the Gallic habit of taking meals seated around a table had won out, even in the south, over the Roman custom of banqueting while lying supported on one elbow. The Germans had long eaten sitting up." M. Rouche, "The Early Middle Ages in the West," in *A History of Private Life*, vol. 1, *From Pagan Rome to Byzantium*, ed. Paul Veyne, trans. [from the French original, first published in 1985] by Arthur Goldhammer (Cambridge, Mass.: Belknap Press of Harvard University Press, 1987), 411–549, here at 443–444. On modes of dining in antiquity, see the numerous interesting contributions to *Dining in a Classical Context*, ed. William J. Slater (Ann Arbor: University of Michigan Press, 1991), in particular Katherine D. Dunbabin, "Triclinium and Stibadium," 121–148. The author observes that eating while reclining on a *stibadium* (a semicircular couch for a number of diners) was a custom of late antiquity; a Carthaginian mosaic (fig. 36) from the end of the fourth century, however, shows the diners seated on long benches with high backs, before rectangular tables. This mosaic is preserved at the Musée du Bardo at Tunis. In antiquity those who ate in taverns did so while seated, as did those of low social status generally (Dunbabin, 136). On the traditions surrounding the preparations for the Last Supper in the synoptic gospels, see Silvio Accame, *L'istituzione dell'Eucarestia: Ricerca storica* (Naples: Libreria Scientifica Editrice, 1968). My thanks to Umberto Laffi for bibliographical help.

70. On this subject the bibliography is extensive. I will mention *Libri e lettori nel Medioevo. Guida Storica e critica*, ed. Guglielmo Cavallo (Rome-Bari: Laterza,

1989); Armando Petrucci, "Storia e geografia delle culture scritte," *Letteratura italiana*, ed. Alberto Asor Rosa (Turin: Einaudi, 1982–1989), 7.2.1195–1292; Bernhard Bischoff, *Paleografia latina. Antichità e Medioevo* (Padua: Antenore, 1992); Armando Petrucci, *Medioevo da leggere. Guida allo studio delle testimonianze scritte del Medioevo italiano* (Turin: Einaudi, 1992); *Storia della lettura nel mondo occidentale*, ed. Guglielmo Cavallo and Roger Chartier (Rome-Bari: Laterza, 1995).

71. On this subject, see *Les tablettes à écrire de l'Antiquité à l'époque moderne*, ed. Elisabeth Lalou (Actes du Colloque international du Centre National de la Recherche Scientifique, Paris, Institut de France, 10–11 octobre 1990) (Turnhout: Brepols, 1992), especially E. Lalou, "Inventaire des tablettes médiévales et présentation générale," 231–280, and figs. 1–12.

72. "Temptabat et scribere tabulasque et codicellos ad hoc in lecto sub cervicalibus circumferre solebat . . . , sed parum successit labor praeposterus ac sero inchoatus." Eginardo, *Vita di Carlo Magno*, ed. Giovanni Bianchi (Rome: Salerno Editrice, 1980), ch. 25, 70 (for the Italian translation) and 101 (for the Latin text).

73. " . . . quand a l'escole venoient / le tables d'yvoire prenoient. / Adonc lor veissez escrire / lettres et vers d'amors en cire." See Elisabeth Lalou, "Les tablettes de cire médiévales," in *Bibliothèque de l'Ecole des Chartes* 147 (1989): 123–140, at 131.

74. This was the composition "Quando eu stava in le tu' cathene," edited by Alfredo Stussi, "Versi d'amore in volgare tra la fine del secolo XII e l'inizio del XIII," with a "Nota paleografica" by Antonio Ciaralli and Armando Petrucci and a "Nota musicologica" by Claudio Gallico, *Cultura neolatina* 59 (1999): 1–69.

75. On this, see Lester K. Little, *Religious Poverty and the Profit Economy in Medieval Europe* (London: Elek, 1978), especially 178ff.

76. To indicate this type of argument in the Middle Ages, one grasped the index finger of one's left hand between thumb and index finger of the right hand.

77. "Ed oggi sono cotanti i maestri, tutte le cittadi piene: tanti predicatori, e così buoni e veragi: le scuole in ogne convento, che sono cotante milia, ove cotidianamente si cerca e si dichiara e s'ammaestra la sapienza"; "le Religioni, i frati tutto dì fanno libri: ed a Parigi tutto giorno si fanno libri." Giordano da Pisa, *Prediche del 1304 dell'Avvento e della Quaresima*, ed. D. M. Manni (Florence: Viviani, 1739), 152–53 and 189.

78. *Le livre au Moyen Age*, ed. Jean Glenisson (Paris: Presses du CNRS, 1988), 102 and fig. 20 at 100.

79. Attributed to the shop of Agostino di Giovanni and Agnolo di Volterra: Renzo Grandi, *I monumenti dei dottori e la scultura a Bologna (1267–1348)* (Bologna: Istituto per la Storia di Bologna, 1982), 151–152.

80. Chiara Frugoni, " 'E vedrà ogni carne la salvezza di Dio' (Lc 3,6): le sculture all'interno del battistero," in *Benedetto Antelami e il battistero di Parma*, ed. C. Frugoni (Turin: Einaudi, 1995), 109–144.

81. Another, very similar statue must once have been located inside the Palazzo della Ragione (the Hall of Justice), and is now preserved at the gallery and museum of the ducal palace in Mantua. See Wolfgang Liebenwein, "Princeps Poetarum. Die mittelalterlichen Vergil-Bilder in Mantua," in *2000 Jahre Vergil. Eine Sympo-*

sium, ed. Viktor Pöschl (Wolfenbütteler Forschungen) (Wiesbaden: O. Harrassowitz, 1983), 109–151, and figs. 1–16.

82. *Le origini dell'università*, ed. Girolamo Arnaldi (Bologna: Il Mulino, 1974); Jacques Le Goff, *Gli intellettuali nel Medioevo* (1957; reprint, Milan: Mondadori, 1979); Jacques Verger, *Le università nel Medioevo* (1973; reprint, Bologna: Il Mulino, 1991).

83. Consisting of the trivium (grammar, rhetoric, and dialectic), and the quadrivium (arithmetic, geometry, music, and astronomy).

84. That is, of Arthur, Duke of Brittany (1187–1203). For more on his assassination, see *Jacobi de Vitriaco Historia occidentalis*, critical edition, ed. John Frederick Hinnenbusch (Fribourg: The University Press, 1972), 259. (Jacobus de Vitriaco = Jacques de Vitry.)

85. Ibid., 92.

86. This passage is from a model letter in the *volgare* composed by Pietro de' Boattieri, a master of the *ars dictandi* (the art of composing formal letters) at the end of the thirteenth century. It is cited by Antonio Ivan Pini, " 'Discere turba volens.' Studenti e vita studentesca a Bologna dalle origini dello Studio alla metà del Trecento," in *Studenti e Università degli studenti dal XII al XIX secolo*, ed. Gian Paolo Brizzi and Antonio Ivan Pini (Bologna: Istituto per la Storia dell'Università, 1988), 47–136, at 113; see this work for previous bibliography.

87. This too is a model letter; the author is Boncompagno da Signa, a master of rhetoric and author of numerous didactic works (1165–c. 1250). The passage is cited in Pini, " 'Discere turba volens'," 97. On university life, see Leo Moulin, *La vita degli studenti nel Medioevo* (Milan: Jaca Book, 1992).

88. Here I have obviously adapted the celebrated words of Hamlet from act 3, scene 1: "To die, to sleep; To sleep, perchance to dream."

89. G. Keil, "Spongia somnifera," in *Der Anaesthesist* 38 (1989): 643–648. The sponge was impregnated with the anesthetic mixture, then allowed to dry in the air. At the commencement of the operation the surgeon immersed the sponge in hot water and placed it over the mouth and nose of the patient, who inhaled the vapor but also swallowed a portion of the liquid.

90. "Praeter haec etiamnum a lateribus duo valentes obiciantur, qui circumstantes labare vel unum vel duos qui puerum continent non sinunt." *Celsi De medicina*, 7.26, 2A-O, ed. W. G. Spencer (London: Loeb, 1961), 3:426. See 426–437 for the description of the entire procedure.

91. Boccaccio, *Decameron*, 4:10, 573 (ed. Branca); the translation is taken from Boccaccio, *Decameron*, trans. Mark Musa and Peter Bondanella (New York and London: Norton, 1982), 302–303.

92. See Chiara Frugoni, "The Imagined Woman," chapter 11 of *Silences of the Middle Ages*, ed. Christiane Klapisch-Zuber (*A History of Women in the West*, ed. G. Duby and M. Perrot, vol. 2; Cambridge, Mass.: Belknap Press of Harvard University Press, 1992), 336–422, especially "The Family Scriptorium," 400–407.

93. Attributed to Bettino da Bologna: Grandi, *I monumenti*, 150–151 and figs. 104–109.

94. For a study of this problem in Italian society: Attilio Bartoli-Langeli, *La scrittura dell'italiano* (Bologna: Il Mulino, 2000), especially 77ff.

95. *Le più antiche carte dell'abbazia di S. Maria di Valdiponte (Montelabbate)*, ed. Vittorio De Donato: vol. 1, anni 969–1170 (Rome: Istituto Storico Italiano per il Medio Evo, 1962); vol. 2, anni 1171–1200 (Rome: Istituto Storico Italiano per il Medio Evo, 1988). See in particular the remarks of the editor at 2:xxi–xxii, with references to the unpublished theses of Donatella Nebbiai and Giulia Silvestrini (University of Perugia, 1975–1976 and 1985–1986). Attilio Bartoli-Langeli, "I notai e i numeri (con un caso perugino, 1184–1206)," in *Scienze matematiche e insegnamento in epoca medioevale*, Atti del Convegno internazionale di studio, Chieti, 2–4 maggio 1996, ed. Paolo Freguglia, Luigi Pellegrini, e Roberto Paciocco (Naples: Edizioni Scientifiche Italiane, 2000), 227–254, focuses in detail on the case of Raniero di Perugia and a handful of other notaries who were ahead of their time in using Arabic numerals. My thanks to both Vittorio De Donato and Attilio Bartoli-Langeli for their usual helpfulness and courtesy.

96. Madrid, Biblioteca S. Lorenzo del Escorial, codex Virgilianus, ms. lat. D. I. 2, f. 9v. In general, see further Georges Ifrah, *Storia universale dei numeri* (Milan: Mondadori, 1983).

97. To indicate a particular year the Romans referred to the names of the two consuls who held office in that year; an event would be dated by saying "Under the consulate of X and Y it happened that. . . ." Toward the end of the republic they chose the foundation of Rome as their era, an event they determined to have occurred (by our reckoning) on April 21, 753 B.C.

98. Because in this year Mohammed was forced to flee to Medina. Muslims count the years forward from this hejira or "flight."

99. Federigo Melis, *Documenti per la storia economica dei secoli XII-XVI* (Florence: Olschki, 1972); Marco Spallanzani, "A Note on Florentine Banking in the Renaissance: Orders of Payment and Cheques," in *The Journal of European Economic History* 7 (1978): 145–168; Frederic C. Lane, *I mercanti di Venezia* (Turin: Einaudi, 1982); Federigo Melis, *La banca pisana e le origini della banca moderna*, ed. Marco Spallanzani (Florence: Le Monnier, 1987).

100. On the *monti di pietà*, and for the related bibliography, I refer to the essay by Giuseppina Muzzarelli, "Da sentimento a istituzione: l'ideazione dei Monti di pietà," in the catalogue of the exhibition curated by her, *Uomini, denaro istituzioni. L'invenzione del Monte di pietà* (Bologna: Costa editore, 2000), 9–29.

101. "Si das vinum non das panem; si panem non vestitum, si etc., non das denarios ad solvendum debita, medicinas etc. Da Monti et dedisti omnia. Hic imples septem opera pietatis. De illo denario subvenitur a chi compra panem, vinum, vestitum, medicinas et omnia etc." Muzzarelli, "Da sentimento a istituzione," 20. The acts of bodily charity are: to feed the hungry, to give drink to the thirsty, to dress the unclothed, to lodge pilgrims, to visit the sick, to visit prisoners in jail, and to bury the dead (this last was added only in the fourteenth century). On this subject, see Monica Chiellini Nari, "Le opere di misericordia per immagini," in *La conversione alla povertà nell'Italia dei secoli XII-XIV*, Atti del XXVII Convegno

storico internazionale, Todi 1990 (Spoleto: Centro Italiano di Studi sull'Alto Medioevo, 1991), 415–447.

102. On the "mass of Saint Gregory," that is, the apparition, above the altar at which the pope celebrates the eucharist, of Christ on the cross surrounded by the instruments of the passions (the oldest images date from the middle of the fourteenth century), see *Die Messe Gregors des Grosse. Vision, Kunst, Realität*, ed. Uwe Westfehling (Cologne: Schnutgen Museum-Köln, 1982).

103. My reading of the image departs radically from that of Muzzarelli, "Da sentimento a istituzione," 19. In particular, the *monte* here does not appear to me to be a beehive; compare the one to which San Petronio points in fig. 40 of the present work.

104. The letters IHS are the Latin abbreviation of the initial letters of the name of Jesus in Greek.

105. Charles Moise Briquet, *Les Filigranes, dictionnaire historique des marques du papier dès leur apparition vers 1282 jusqu'en 1600* (a facsimile of the 1907 edition with supplementary material contributed by a number of scholars), ed. Allan Stevenson (Amsterdam: The Paper Publication Society, 1968).

106. See the catalogue of the exhibition *Gutenberg e Roma. Le origini della stampa nella città dei papi (1467–1477)*, ed. Massimo Miglio and Orietta Rossini (Naples: Electa, 1997).

2. Time for Pleasure and Time for Duty

1. On this, and in general for a consideration of gaming in the Middle Ages and the vacillation between regulation and prohibition, see Alessandra Rizzi, *Ludus / ludere. Giocare in Italia alla fine del medioevo* (Rome-Treviso: Viella-Fondazione Benetton, 1995).

2. "El messale so' li dadi, che come vedi el dado à ventuno punto, così el messale del cristiano è composto di ventuno lettara dell'a, b, c. Le lettare del messale del diavolo so' nell'osso. Le lettare sono dello sterco del diavolo, però che lo 'ncostro è suo sterco. Breviari del diavolo so' le carte e naibi. E li ricciuoli de la donna sono e naibi piccoli. El prete è chi giuoca. Tu sai ch' e breviari so' miniati; così sono naibi. Le lettere so' maze, cose da pazi; coppe, cosa da ubriachi e tavernieri; denari cosa da avari; spade, cosa da quistione, briga e ucisioni. Le lettere miniate sono: re, re de' ribaldi; reina, reina delle ribalde; sopra sodomitto; sotto è lussuria." San Bernardino da Siena, *Le prediche volgari*, ed. Ciro Cannarozzi O.F.M.; *Predicazione del 1425 in Siena*, vol. 1 (Florence: Rinaldi, 1958), sermon 12 (May 6), 181–183.

3. Claudio Bellinati, *Atlante della Cappella degli Scrovegni* (Ponzano-Treviso: Vianelli Libri, 2000), fig. at 135. The inscription is unfortunately almost completely lost, and only the following can be made out: "Gerens pennas fatuus . . . lignum arens. . . ." ("the fool dresses in feathers . . . dry wood . . .").

4. "*Introibo* quando dice: 'Vogliamo giocare?' Risponde el cherico: 'che si.' *Kyrie eleison*: ognuno truova e suoi denari. *Gloria in excelsis Deo*: e costoro danno gloria al diavolo e Dio bastemiano. *Dominus vobiscum*: sozzo. Et *cum spiritu tuo*: zara. Dis-

pose santo Ieronimo questo zaro essere Lucifero. *Oremus*, l'orazione, so' e sospiri per lo perdare. La *pistola* [*Epistola*]: stanno ebrii che non mangiarebbero per giocare. *Sequentia sancti Evangeli*: perdi. *Gloria tibi Domine*: venco. *Credo in unum Deum*: quando per venciare, e' s'ingegnavano d'avere el capresto dello impicato. L'*offerta* è la patena e la posta che tu metti, e l'*ostia* è il grosso bianco. El *calice* è il bicchiere del vino; la *Segreta* è l'ira che ti rode di stizza; el *prefazio* è quando tu ti lagni che ài perduto dicendo: 'Oimè!' El *consecrare* è che si trasmuta e tuoi denari in suoi . . . *Dominus vobiscum*: fatto male mentre che ài potuto. *Et cum spiritu tuo*: e anco fattone fare a chi à giocato con teco. *Ite missa est*: ora che vedi avere fatto ogni male, e tu vieni in disperazione. *Deo gratias*: e tu metti in esecuzione la disperazione, e talvolta tu uccidi te stesso proprio. El Vangelo si è che conferma, che poi fatto male di qua, arai pena eterna di là." San Bernardino da Siena, *Le prediche volgari*, 181–183. The citation from Saint Jerome ("Ieronimo") is of course an invention.

5. Jean-Michel Mehl, "Les rois de France et les cartes à jouer," in *Ludica* 2 (1996): 211–220.

6. Gabriele Mandel, *I tarocchi dei Visconti* (Bergamo: Monumenta longobardica, 1974).

7. Chiara Frugoni, "Das Schachspiel in der Welt des Jacobus de Cessolis," in *Das Schachbuch des Jacobus de Cessolis, Codex Palatinus Latinus 961* [vol. 1, texts, vol. 2, facsimile edition] (Stuttgart: Belser Verlag, 1988), 35–75.

8. Franco Sacchetti, *Il Trecentonovelle*, ed. Emilio Faccioli (Turin: Einaudi, 1970), novella 174, 534–536.

9. The wife of a duke, rejected by a young knight faithful to his true love (the chatelaine of Vergy), accuses the knight before her husband of attempting to rape her. The story continues with a series of tragic *coups de scène* and ends with the suicide of the two lovers.

10. C. Frugoni, "Le decorazioni murali come testimonianza di uno 'status symbol'," in *Un palazzo, una città: il Palazzo Lanfranchi* (Pisa: Pacini, 1983), 141–145, at 142.

11. William L. Tronzo, "Moral Hieroglyphs: Chess and Dice at San Savino in Piacenza," *Gesta* 16 (1977): 15–26.

12. This bishop is not securely identifiable. For the passage with commentary, see *Petri Damiani Epistolae. Die Briefe des Petrus Damiani*, ed. K. Reindl (Munich: Monumenta Germana Historica, 1988), part 2, nos. 41–90; no. 57 at 187–188.

13. Harold J. R. Murray, *A History of Chess* (Oxford: Clarendon Press, 1913), 408–415.

14. "Aliud scachum esse, aliud aleam. Aleas ergo auctoritas illa prohibuit, scachos vero tacendo concessit. Ad quod ego: scachum, inquam, Scriptura non ponit, sed utriusque ludi genus aleae nomine comprehendit." *Petri Damiani Epistolae*, 188. The text corresponds to *Patrologia Latina*, vol. 145: "Opusculum vicesimum, Apologeticus ob dimissum episcopatum," 20.7, col. 454.

15. According to Murray, *A History of Chess*, 409, the bishop was perhaps playing chess with the aid of dice.

16. Michel Pastoureau, *L'échiquier de Charlemagne* (Paris: A. Biro, 1990).

17. Aldo Settia, " 'Ut melius doceantur ad bellum': i giochi di guerra e l'addestramento delle fanterie comunali," in *La civiltà del torneo (secc. XII-XVII). Atti del VII Convegno di Studio (Narni 14–15–16 ottobre 1988)* (Narni: Centro Studi Storici, 1990), 79–105; Settia, "La 'battaglia': un gioco violento fra permissività e interdizione," in *Gioco e giustizia nell'italia di Comune*, ed. G. Ortalli (Treviso-Roma: Fondazione Benetton Studi Ricerche-Viella, 1994), 121–132.

18. On this subject, see Julio Caro Baroja, *Il carnevale* (Genoa: Il Melangolo, 1989).

19. *La battaglia di Quaresima e Carnevale*, ed. Margherita Lecco (Parma: Pratiche, 1990), 57–58.

20. From late Latin *[festum] candelorum*, the feast of the candles; the correct form of the Latin word would be *candelarum*. During this feast candles are blessed, while the antiphon "Lumen ad revelationem gentium" is sung.

21. For a discussion of the *Roman de Fauvel* and the miniatures that illustrate the manuscript reproduced here, see Jean-Claude Schmitt, *Les revenants. Les vivants et les morts dans la societé médiévale* (Paris: Gallimard, 1994), 191ff. and figs. 11–14.

22. My subtitle comes from the well-known work of Jacques Le Goff, *La Naissance du Purgatoire* (1981); in English, *The Birth of Purgatory*, trans. Arthur Goldhammer (Chicago: University of Chicago Press, 1983).

23. "Con ciò dunque fosse cosa che san Patricio predicasse per Irlanda e poco pro facesse, pregò Domenedio che mostrasse alcuno segnale per lo quale ispaventati gli uomini sì si pentessero. Sì che per comandamento di Dio fece in alcuno luogo uno grande cerchio col bastone là ove la terra s'aperse, e apparivvi uno grandissimo pozzo e profondissimo. Sì che ebbe revelazione il santo che quivi aveva uno purgatorio, nel quale, chiunque volesse scendere, non li sarebbe mestiere di fare altra penitenzia, né non sentirebbe altro purgatorio per li peccati suoi più, e non ritornerebbero più quindi, ma anderebbero a vita, e quegli che ne reddissoro, sì li convenia dimorare quivi da la mattina insino a l'altra mattina vegnente. Sì che molti v'entravano che mai non reddivano." Iacopo da Varazze, *Legenda aurea*, 1:208. The commemoration of the dead was instituted by the monks of Cluny on November 2, sometime between 1024 and 1033.

24. Beginning in the eleventh century, the various texts of the divine offices celebrated by the clergy were combined in a single book, the *Breviary*. The laity (those who could read) possessed "Books of Hours," which were prayer books; if their original owners were people of means, these often contain splendid miniatures.

25. On the mechanical clock, see Jean Gimpel, *La révolution industrielle du Moyen Age* (Paris: Seuil, 1975), 141–160.

26. Since this was a worksite clock, the duties to which Maurizio had to attend were those of sounding the hours of work.

27. A cracked bell does not produce a clear ringing sound. See Lucio Riccetti, "Il cantiere edile negli anni della Peste Nera," in *Il Duomo di Orvieto*, ed. Lucio Riccetti (Bari-Rome: Laterza, 1988), 139–215, especially 191–194, and the transcription at 192. The author informs me that an article entitled "Maurizio e il camerario. La costruzione dell'orologio di cantiere nella fabbrica del Duomo di Orvieto, 1347–48," the imminent publication of which is announced in the ar-

ticle cited, has not yet appeared. My thanks to Claudio Ciociola for expert advice on the interpretation of the inscriptions.

28. I refer to the work of Alexandre Koyré, *Dal mondo del pressappoco all'universo della precisione. Tecniche, strumenti e filosofia dal mondo classico alla rivoluzione scientifica* (Turin: Einaudi, 1967).

29. Jacques Le Goff, "Merchant's Time and Church's Time in the Middle Ages," in Le Goff, *Time, Work, and Culture in the Middle Ages*, trans. Arthur Goldhammer (Chicago: University of Chicago Press, 1980), 29–42.

30. Gimpel, *La révolution industrielle du Moyen Age*, 157.

31. Carlo M. Cipolla, *Le macchine del tempo, l'orologio e la società (1300–1700)* (Bologna: Il Mulino, 1981), 115–118, where he explains the escapement mechanism.

32. Dominique Flechon, *L'orologiaio, mestiere d'arte* (Milan: Il Saggiatore, 1999), 26.

33. Maurice Daumas, "Le faux échappement de Villard de Honnecourt," *Revue d'histoire des sciences* 35 (1) (1982): 43–54.

34. Silvio Bedini and Francis Maddison, "Mechanical Universe: The Astrarium of Giovanni de Dondi," in *Transactions of the American Philosophical Society* 56 (1966): 6–20. It would appear that an astrological clock similar to Dondi's was made by Richard of Wallingford, abbot of Saint Alban's, between 1327 and 1330. A miniature (5–7 and fig. 8) portrays him beside his clock (British Library, ms. Cotton Nero D VII, f. 20r). Fig. 9 reproduces a miniature from a manuscript of the fifteenth century (Paris, Bibliothèque Nationale, ms. 43657, fr. 455, f. 9) of the *Horloge de Sapience*, a French translation of the work of Heinrich Suso (fourteenth century): it shows the author beside his complex clock.

35. Famianus Strada, *De Bello Belgico* (Lugduni Batavorum [i.e. Leiden], 1643), 13. (Umberto Forti, *Storia della tecnica, dal Medioevo al Rinascimento* [Milan: Sansoni, 1957], 270, erroneously gives the title as *De bello Gallico*).

36. Bibliography in Maria Monica Donato, "Un ciclo pittorico ad Asciano (Siena), palazzo pubblico e l'iconografia 'politica' alla fine del Medioevo," in *Annali della Scuola Normale Superiore di Pisa*, Classe di Lettere, third series, 18 (1988): 1105–1272, at 1236ff.

37. Maria Teresa Rosa Barezzani, "Guido musicus et magister," in *Guido Monaco, magister et musicus*, ed. Graziella de Florentis (Milan: Comune di Talla-Nuove Edizioni, 2000), 71–93.

38. *Dizionario Enciclopedico Universale della musica e dei musicisti* (Turin: Utet, 1983), *Il lessico*, vol. 2, s.v. *guidoniana mano*.

39. "Lo mar liguro ingenera corallo / nel fondo suo, a modo d'albuscello, / pallido, di color tra chiaro e giallo. / Spezzasi come vetro il ramicello / quando si pesca e come più è grosso / e con piu' rami, tanto par più bello. / Si come il ciel lo vede, divien rosso, / e non pur si trasforma di colore, / ma fassi forte e duro che par osso. / Conforta a riguardar, la vista e 'l core / averne seco quando folgor cade; / pietra non so più util né migliore." Fazio degli Uberti, *Il Dittamondo e le Rime* (Bari: Laterza, 1952), vol. I, 3.11, 216. This passage is cited, very imprecisely, by Rosita Levi Pisetzky, *Storia del costume in Italia* (Milan: Treccani-Enciclopedia Italiana, 1964), 1:285.

40. Giordano da Pisa [Giordano da Rivalto], *Prediche recitate in Firenze dal 1303 al 1306*, ed. Domenico Moreni (Florence: Magheri, 1831), predica del 1304, 2:263; Sterling Adolph Callisen, "The Evil Eye in Italian Art," *Art Bulletin* 19 (1937): 452–462 (with examples of the baby Jesus with a cross and a branch of coral hanging from his neck at 457); Christel Meier, *Gemma spiritualis* (Munich: Fink, 1977), 414–460; Liselotte Hansmann and Lenz Kriss-Rettenbeck, *Amulett und Talisman* (Munich: D. W. Callwey, 1966), 22ff. and 41ff.

41. At a later period three circlets, each with five tenfold repetitions of the *Ave Maria*, were introduced as an aid to meditation on the "mysteries" (joyous, dolorous, and glorious) of the life of the Virgin Mary; Gilles Gérard Meerssemann, *Ordo fraternitatis. Confraternite e pietà dei laici nel Medioevo* (Rome: Herder, 1977), 1144–1232.

42. G. Boccaccio, *Decameron*, 5.10, ed. V. Branca (Turin: Einaudi, 1993), 2:696.

43. "Sia col buon anno, s'io non conosco il baccello da' paternostri!" Sacchetti, *Il Trecentonovelle*, novella 209, 638.

44. For this interpretation, see Erwin Panofsky, *Early Nederlandish Painting: Its Origin and its Character* (Cambridge: Harvard University Press, 1953), 349. The interpretation is accepted and reinforced with further arguments in *Hans Memling. Bruges Goenigemuseum, 1994, Catalogue*, ed. D. De Vos (Brugge: Ludion-Bruges Musées communaux, 1994), 124–127.

3. Dressing and Undressing

1. Maria Giuseppina Muzzarelli, *Guardaroba medievale. Vesti e società dal XIII al XVI secolo* (Bologna: Il Mulino, 1999), especially 247–286.

2. The *becchetto* is the part of the headgear that is wound about the top of it, or allowed to hang down.

3. "Signori miei, io ho tutto il tempo della vita mia studiato per apparar ragione, e ora, quando io credea sapere qualche cosa, io truovo che io so nulla, però che cercando degli ornamenti divietati alle vostre donne per gli ordini che m'avete dati, si' fatti argomenti non trovai mai in alcuna legge, come sono quelli ch'elle fanno; e fra gli altri ve ne voglio nominare alcuni. E' si truova una donna col becchetto frastagliato avvolto sopra il cappuccio; il notaio mio dice: 'Ditemi il nome vostro; però che avete il becchetto intagliato'; la buona donna piglia questo becchetto che è appiccato al cappuccio con uno spillo, e recaselo in mano, e dice ch'egli è una ghirlanda. Or va più oltre, truova molti bottoni portare dinanzi; dicesi a quella che è trovata: 'Questi bottoni voi non potete portare'; e quella risponde: 'Messer si, posso, ché questi non sono bottoni, ma sono coppelle, e se non mi credete, guardate, e' non hanno picciuolo, e ancora non c'è niuno occhiello.' " Franco Sacchetti, *Il Trecentonovelle*, ed. Emilio Faccioli (Turin: Einaudi, 1970), novella 137, 357.

4. See above, and chapter 1, note 25.

5. G. Boccaccio, *Decameron*, 8.10, ed. V. Branca (Turin: Einaudi, 1993), 2:1013.

6. "La fante, quasi smemorata, il volea lavare con l'acqua fredda; e 'l Riccio comincia a gridare ch'ella accenda il fuoco e ch'ella metta del ranno a scaldare; ed ella

così fece: e 'l Riccio stette tanto a cervelliera scoperta quanto il ranno si penò a scaldare. Come fu caldo, se n'andò in uno corticino, perché per una fogna la lavatura di quello fastidio avesse l'uscita, e quasi per ispazio di quattr'ore si penò a lavare il capo. Quando del capo e' fu lavato, ma non sì che più dì non gliene venisse fraore, disse alla fante che recasse la pianella; la quale era sì fornita d'ogni parte che né elli, né ella ardivano a toccarla. Ed essendo una bigoncetta nella corte, prese partito d'empierla d'acqua; ed empiuta ch'ella fu, vi cacciò entro la pianella dicendo: 'Sta' costì tanto che ben la vaglia'; ed egli si misse in capo il più caldo cappuccio che avea, ma non sì che per non portare la pianella, per arrota non gli venisse il mal de' denti, di che convenne stesse in casa più dì; e la fante, che parea lavasse ventri, scuscendo la farsata e lavandola per ispazio di due dì." Sacchetti, *Il Trecentonovelle*, novella 164, 475.

7. Chrétien de Troyes, *Érec e Énide*, in *Romanzi* (Florence: Sansoni, 1962), 38. [Trans.: The English translation is made from the Italian one quoted by the author, not the Old French original.]

8. Rosita Levi Pisetzky, *Storia del costume in Italia*, 1:276, citing Max von Bohen, *Die Mode. Nach Bildern und Kunstwerken der Zeit ausgewählt und geschildert* (Munich: Bruckmann, 1907), 1:182.

9. Giuseppe Del Giudice, *Una legge suntuaria inedita del 1290 commento storico-critico . . . : memoria letta all'Accademia Pontaniana . . . con note ed appendici di documenti, la maggior parte inediti* (Naples: Tipografia della Regia Università, 1887), 273–274.

10. "Ecce apparuit ipse Dominus sponsae suae in forma iuvenis denudati, et pauperis ac peregrini, qui aetatis triginta duorum vel trium annorum vel circiter apparebat, et petivit ut sibi pro Deo succurreret pro aliquo indumento. At illa iam ad misericordiae opera solito plus accensa, 'Expecta, inquit, carissime, paululum hic, donec de capella illa revertar, et statim tribuam indumentum.' Retrogressaque ad capellam unde descenderat, tunicam quam sine manicis sub exteriori tunica propter frigus interius deferebat, per pedes, socia iuvante, deposuit caute pariter et honeste, ac cum grandi laetitia pauperi tribuit. Qua recepta, repetit plus ille pauper et ait: 'Eia oro, Domina, ex quo mihi de indumento laneo providistis, ut de lineis tegumentis etiam mihi providere velitis.' Quod illa libentissime annuens 'Veni post me, inquit, carissime, quia quod petis integraliter tibi dabo.' Praecedit igitur sponsa et Sponsus ignotus subsequitur. Illaque paternam domum subintrans, accedit ad locum ubi panni linei patris et germanorum erant reconditi; acceptaque camisia una et femoralibus, letanter pauperi tribuit. Sed ille his habitis adhuc non desistit a petendo: 'Sed obsecro, inquit, Domina, quid faciam de tunica ista, quae manicas ad brachia tegenda non habet? Date mihi aliquas manicas, ut recedam a vobis totus indutus.' Quod illa percipiens, in nullo attaediata, sed magis accensa, domum circumvit, et diligenter quaerit si possit aliquas manicas invenire. Casuque reperit tunicam ancillae domus paternae novam, quam necdum induerat, ad perticam pendentem, quam festine deponens, et manicas inde velociter festine dissuendo auferens, gratiose tribuit pauperi praelibato." Raymond of Capua [Raimundus Capuanus], *Vita S. Catharinae Senensis*, in *Acta Sanctorum, Aprilis III* (Antwerp, 1675); *Vita* 2.1, 887.

11. "Verum rememorans, quod omnes de domo praeter patrem aegre ferebant eleemosynas suas, et ea quae habebant claudebant sub clavibus, ne pauperibus daret; insuper discrete considerans quod ancillae satis abstulerat, nec erat ei totum auferendum, quoniam etiam inops erat." Raymond of Capua, *Vita S. Catharinae Senensis*, 887.

12. Paulus Diaconus, *De gestis Langobardorum*, ed. Lidia Capo (Milan: Fondazione Lorenzo Valla-Mondadori, 1992), 5.38, 286–287.

13. Levi Pisetzky, *Storia del costume*, 2:23.

14. ". . . hanno messo il culo in uno calcetto": Sacchetti, *Il Trecentonovelle*, novella 178, 523.

15. In the top register Saint Paul is portrayed disputing with pagan philosophers, in the center one he is bitten by a viper on Malta (Acts 28:1–7), and in the bottom one he cures several cripples.

16. *Sacramentario del vescovo Warmondo di Ivrea*, facsimile edition with transcription of the text by Ferdinando Dell'Oro (Ivrea: Priuli e Verlucca, 1990), f. 114r.

4. And Then Came the Fork

1. Petrus Damiani, *Opera, De institutione monialis*, ch. 11, Migne, *Patrologia Latina*, 145, col. 744: "Cibos quoque suos manibus non tangebat, sed ab eunuchis eius alimenta quaeque minutius concidebantur in frusta. Quae mox illa quibusdam fuscinulis aureis atque bidentibus ori suo, liguriens, adhibebat." Much interesting information on the history of the fork can be found in Pompeo Molmenti, *La storia di Venezia nella vita privata* (Bergamo: Istituto Italiano d'Arti Grafiche, 1906), I:441. In the dialect of the Veneto, the word for fork is *piròn*, from the Greek *peirein*, to transfix or skewer.

2. "Quid vanius quam ornare mensam mantilibus picturatis, cultellis ebore mani-catis, vasis aureis, vasculis argenteis, cuppis et nappis, varalibus et gradalibus, scutellis et coclearibus, fascinulis et salariis, bacilibus et urceolis, capsulis et flabel-lis? . . . Scriptum est enim: 'Non cum morietur accipiet hec omnia, neque simul descendet cum eo gloria sua.' " *Lotharii cardinalis (Innocentii III) De miseria humane condicionis*, 2.40, ed. Michele Maccarrone (Lugano: Thesaurus Mundi, 1955), 71. The passage is cited in Carla Casagrande and Silvana Vecchio, *I sette vizi capitali. Storia dei peccati nel medioevo* (Turin: Einaudi, 2000), 29.

3. "Cives vocati, quod in unum coeuntes vivant, ut vita communis ornatior fiat et tutior." *Hrabani Mauri De Universo*, in Migne, *Patrologia Latina*, 16, ch. 4, col. 451. On the manuscript Casin. 132, see Rabano Mauro, *De rerum naturis, cod. Casin. 132*, Archivio dell'Abbazia di Montecassino: vol. 1, *Commentari*, ed. Guglielmo Cavallo; vol. 2, *Facsimile* of the codex (Ivrea: Priuli e Verlucca, 1995).

4. Herrad of Hohenbourg, *Hortus deliciarum*, ed. Rosalie Green (London-Leiden: Warburg Institute-Brill, 1979), vol. 2, table 99, 295. My thanks to Professor Alessandro Salerno and his students (class 3, section 1 of the Liceo Scientifico Statale "Luigi Einaudi" of Siracusa) for having suggested the correct interpretation of this image to me. A fork is also to be seen placed on a table in the wedding at Cana, in a miniature from a manuscript from the end of the eleventh century, the

Sacramentario di Warmondo, Ivrea, Biblioteca Capitolare, ms. 31 LXXXVI, f. 127r. See the facsimile edition, *Sacramentario del vescovo Warmondo di Ivrea*.

5. Capernaum was the name of a place in Galilee to which a great multitude of people came to hear Christ (Mark 2:2). Metaphorically, it came to mean a place where many things are heaped up indiscriminately; here the facetious expression "go to Capernaum" means "get gobbled up."

6. ". . . pregava pure Dio, quando fosse stato a mangiare con altrui, che la vivanda fosse rovente, acciò che mangiasse la parte del compagno; e quando erano pere guaste ben calde, al compagno rimaneva il tagliere: d'altro non potea far ragione. Avvenne per caso una volta che mangiando Noddo e altri insieme, ed essendo posto Noddo a tagliere con uno piacevole uomo, chiamato Giovanni Cascio; e venendo maccheroni boglientissimi; e 'l detto Giovanni, avendo più volte udito de' costumi di Noddo, veggendosi posto a tagliere con lui, dicea fra sé medesimo: 'Io son pur bene arrivato, che credendo venire a desinare, e io sarò venuto a vedere trangusgiare Noddo, e anco i maccheroni per più acconcio del fatto; purché non manuchi me, io n'andrò bene.' Noddo comincia a raguazzare i maccheroni, avviluppa, e caccia giù; e n'avea già mandati sei bocconi giù, che Giovanni avea ancora il primo boccone su la forchetta, e non ardiva, veggendolo molto fumicare, appressarlosi alla bocca. E considerando che questa vivanda conveniva tutta andarne in Cafarnau, se non tenesse altro modo, disse fra sé stesso: 'Per certo tutta la parte mia non dee costui divorare.'" Franco Sacchetti, *Il Trecentonovelle*, ed. Emilio Faccioli (Turin: Einaudi, 1970), novella 124, 325.

7. G. Boccaccio, *Decameron*, ed. V. Branca (Turin: Einaudi, 1993), 2:908.

8. Silvano Serventi and Françoise Sabban, *La pasta. Storia e cultura di un cibo universale* (Rome-Bari: Laterza, 2000), 19.

9. The Jerusalem Talmud, however, which was redacted in its definitive form at the end of the fifth century, does make reference to a pasta cooked not in the oven but in water; ibid., 23.

10. The Latin contains several obvious difficulties: there is no verb for cooking or boiling in water, either expressed or easily understandable as implied, only the verb for "to fry"; nor is it entirely clear how *panis* (bread) can mean uncooked pasta. Serventi and Sabban in their translation, 23, evade the first difficulty by supplying a verb: "laganum is a flat thin bread, which is cooked in water first, then fried in oil." They refer to Bruno Laurioux, "Des lasagnes romaines aux vermicelles arabes: quelques réflexions sur les pâtes alimentaires au Moyen Age," in *Mélanges Fossier* (Paris: Publications de la Sorbonne, 1955), 204*n*32, who writes: "Quant à Isidore de Séville, il définira plus tard le laganom comme 'un pain large et mince, qui [est cuit] d'abord dans l'eau, puis frit dans l'huile.'" Laurioux in turn refers to *Etymologiae*, 20.2.487, *Patrologia Latina* vol. 84, col. 708. The critical edition of W. M. Lindsay (Oxford: Clarendon Press, 1911) omits the sentence in question entirely from the text. *Laganum* might have been a thin dry bread, of a kind still used today in Sardinia, that is allowed to swell in water and, once softened, is treated like a pancake (a little like the way bread pudding is made by

soaking leftover pieces of dry bread in milk). I wish to thank Silvano Serventi and Françoise Sabban, who responded with prompt courtesy when I raised these points with them. For them the question remains open: *laganum* in texts preceding Isidore seems to refer not to a bread already cooked, but to a flat cake of unleavened bread; we have no examples of bread softened in water and then fried. But since the passage from Isidore is not genuine, it can have little importance, and leaves us no better informed about the origins of boiled pasta.

11. Serventi and Sabban, *La pasta*, 36ff.

12. Ibid., 59.

13. "Fecesi a ogni chiesa, o alle più, fosse infino all'acqua, larghe e cupe, secono lo popolo era grande; e quivi chi non era molto ricco, la notte morto, quegli, a cui toccava, se lo metteva sopra la spalla, o gittavalo in questa fossa, o pagava gran prezzo a chi lo facesse. La mattina se ne trovavano assai nella fossa, toglievasi della terra, e gittavasi laggiuso loro addosso; e poi veniano gli altri sopr'essi, e poi la terra addosso a suolo a suolo, con poca terra, come si minestrasse lasagne a fornire di formaggio." Marchionne di Coppo Stefani, *Cronaca fiorentina*, *Rerum Italicarum Scriptores* 30, 1, rubric 634, 231, line 19.

14. Luisa Cogliati Aragno, *Tacuinum Sanitatis* (Milan: Electa Editrice, 1979), 5–25, analyzes the manuscripts from which our miniatures come.

15. Fifteenth-century recipes for macaroni, vermicelli, and ravioli can be found in the *Libro de Arte coquinaria* of Maestro Martino, ed. A. Faccioli (Milan: Il Polifilo, 1966).

16. Liège, Bibliothèque Universitaire, *Tacuinum Sanitatis*, ms. 1041, f. 7.

17. Massimo Montanari, *L'alimentazione contadina nell'alto Medioevo* (Naples: Liguori, 1979).

18. Sacchetti, *Il Trecentonovelle*, novella 61, 154.

19. "Quando messer Mastino era nel colmo della rota nella città di Verona, facendo una sua festa, tutti li buffoni d'Italia, come sempre interviene, corsono a quella per guadagnare e recare acqua al loro mulino." Sacchetti, *Il Trecentonovelle*, novella 145, 376.

20. "E segue tanto questa idolatria che s'abbandonano li veri per questi tali, che spesse volte, essendo dipinti, è fatto loro maggiore luminaria e posto più immagini di cera che al nostro Signore. E così spesso s'abbandona la via vecchia per la nuova; e' religiosi spesso ne sono cagione, dicendo spesso che alcuno corpo sotterrato alla chiesa loro averà fatto miracolo, e dipingonlo per tirare, non acqua a lor mulino, ma cera e denari; e la fede si rimane dall'uno de' lati." Sacchetti, *Il Trecentonovelle*, novella 157, 441. A propos of the saints, to whom one should pray only for a good reason, Sacchetti uses another proverb still current: "Scherza co' fanti e lascia stare i santi" ("Joke with servants, but leave the saints alone"); Sacchetti, *Il Trecentonovelle*, novella 110, 287–290.

21. "Intromissus vero quantum murus, portarii vice, permisit, primum in molendinum impetum facit, ubi multum sollicitus est, et turbatur erga plurima, tum molarum mole far comminuendo, tum farinam cribro subtili segregando a furfure. Hic iam vicina domo caldariam implet, se igni coquendum committit, ut

fratribus potum paret, si forte sterilis vindemia cultoris industriae non bene res-
ponderit, et defectu sanguinis uvae, de filia fuerit festucae supplendus. Sed nec
sic se absolvit. Eum enim ad se fullones invitant, qui sunt molendino confines,
rationis jure exigentes, ut sicut in molendino sollicitus est, quo fratres vescant-
ur, ita apud eos paret, quo et vestiantur. Ille autem non contradicit nec
quidquam eorum negat quae petuntur: sed graves illos, sive pistillos, sive
malleos dicere mavis, vel certe pedes ligneos (nam hoc nomen saltuoso fullo-
num negotio magis videtur congruere) alternatim elevans quoque deponens,
gravi labore fullones absolvit: et si joculare quidpiam licet interserere seriis, peccati eorum poenas absolvit. . . . Nam quot equorum dorsa frangeret, quot
hominum fatigaret brachia labor, a quo nos sine labore amnis ille gratiosus absolvit, etiam cum sine ipso nec indumentum nobis pararetur, nec alimentum?
Ipse vero nobiscum participatur, nec aliud de labore suo, quo laborat sub sole,
mercedis exspectat, quam ut, cum omnia diligenter perfecerit, liber permittetur
abire. Tot ergo volubiles rotas rotatu rapido circumducens, sic spumeus exit, ut
ipse quasi moli, et mollior fieri videatur. Excipitur dehinc a domo coriaria, ubi
conficiendis his quae ad fratrum calceamenta sunt necessaria, operosam exhibet
sedulitatem. Deinde minutatim se, et per membra multa distribuens, singulas
officinas, officioso discursu perscrutatur, ubique diligenter inquirens quid quo
ipsius ministerio opus habeat; coquendis, cribrandis, vertendis, terendis, rigan-
dis, lavandis, molendis, molliendis, suum sine contradictione praestans obse-
quium. Postremo, ne quid ei desit ad ullam gratiam, et ne ipsius quaquaversum
imperfecta sint opera, asportans immunditias, omnia post se munda relinquit."
Bernardi, *Descriprio monasterii Clarae vallis*, Migne, *Patrologia Latina*, 185, coll.
570–571. [Trans.: The English translation used in the text, which slightly ab-
breviates the Latin, is taken from *A History of Technology*, vol. 2, *The Mediterranean Civilizations and the Middle Ages*, ed. Charles Singer et al. (Oxford:
Clarendon Press, 1956), 650. In the original edition of the present book, C.
Frugoni likewise adapts her translation of the passage from the Italian edition
of the same source, *Storia della tecnologia*, ed. Charles Singer et al. (Turin: Borin-
ghieri, 1962), 2:660.]

22. It has been calculated that two slaves operating a mill turned by hand could produce on the order of seven kilos of flour in an hour, whereas a water-driven mill
could produce 150 kilos in the same time; Jean Gimpel, *La révolution industrielle
du Moyen Age* (Paris: Seuil, 1975), 14; and 9–32 on the various types of mills.

5. Making War

1. "Que sexta pars dicti molendini fuit Ranucci Boniçi mungnarii, de quo debet an-
nuatim prestari sive solvi ipsi abbati et monasterio pro pensione duo ferra equorum" ("And for this sixth part of the said mill, which once belonged to Ranuc-
cio di Bonizo the miller, an annual payment of two iron horseshoes must
annually be made to the abbot and the monastery"). The document is published
in *Testimonianze medioevali per la storia dei comuni del Monte Amiata*, ed. Nello Bar-
bieri and Odile Redon (Rome: Viella, 1989), 48–49.

2. "Tunc visus est ipse ferreus Karolus, ferrea galea cristatus, ferreis manicis armillatus, ferrea torace ferreum pectus humerosque Platonicos tutatus, hasta ferrea in altum subrecta sinistram impletus. Nam dextra ad invictum calibem semper erat extenta; coxarum exteriora, que propter faciliorem ascensum in aliis solent lorica nudari, in eo ferreis ambiebantur bratteolis. De ocreis quid dicam? Quae et cunctoexercitui solebant ferreae semper esse usui. In clipeo nihil apparuit nisi ferrum. Caballus quoque illius animo et colore ferrum renitebat. Quem habitum cuncti praecedentes, universi ex lateribus ambientes omnesque sequentes et totus in commune apparatus iuxta possibilitatem erat imitatus. Ferrum campos et plateas replebat. Solis radii reverberabantur acie ferri. Frigido ferro honor a frigidiori deferebatur populo. . . . 'O ferrum, heu ferrum!' clamor confusus insonuit civium." Notkeri Balbuli, *Gesta Karoli Magni Imperatoris*, in *Monumenta Germaniae Historica*, *Scriptores rerum Germanicarum nova series*, t. 12, ed. F. Haefele (Berlin: 1959), 2.17, 83–84. [Trans.: The English translation used in the text is taken from Einhard and Notker the Stammerer, *Two Lives of Charlemagne*, trans. Lewis Thorpe (Harmondsworth: Penguin, 1969), 163–164.]

3. For an initial bibliographic orientation, see the entry "Cavalry" by Bertrand Schnerb in *Encyclopedia of the Middle Ages*, ed. André Vauchez, Barrie Dobson, and Michael Lapidge, trans. Adrian Walford (Paris-Rome-Cambridge: Città Nuova-Cerf-J. Clarke, 2000), 1:264–265.

4. For an edition of the text with a facing Italian translation, see *Le leggi dei longobardi. Storia, memoria e diritto di un popolo germanico*, ed. Claudio Azzara and Stefano Gasparri (Milan: Editrice La Storia, 1992).

5. Sandrina Bandera, "L'altare di Sant'Ambrogio: indagine storicoartistica," in *L'altare d'oro di Sant'Ambrogio*, ed. Carlo Capponi (Milan: Banca Agricola Milanese, 1996), 73–111.

6. Jean Gimpel, *La révolution industrielle du Moyen Age* (Paris: Seuil, 1975), 38.

7. "Per insegna d'altra gente il nome si sogliono fare nelle bandiere, nell'armi, negli scudi; onde molte armi sono pur di lettere; siccome quella del senato di Roma, che dice: S. P. Q. R., cioè *Senatus Populusque Romanus* ed è conoscente molto quella arma e quel segno." Giordano da Pisa, *Prediche inedite . . . recitate in Firenze dal 1302 al 1305*, ed. Enrico Narducci and Gaetano Romagnoli (Bologna, 1867) (sermon 29 of 1305), 154.

8. Paulus Diaconus, *De gestis Langobardorum* 1.20, ed. Lidia Capo (Milan: Fondazione Lorenzo Valla-Mondadori, 1992), 40–41.

9. The *martinella* was a bell that took its name from Saint Martin, the protector of cavalry. At Florence, when a war was imminent, the *martinella* was first hoisted above the arch of Porta S. Maria and rung continuously, then, as the troops marched out, erected on the *carroccio*.

10. "Cesaris Augusti Friderici Roma secundi dona tene currum perpes in urbe decus. Hic Mediolani captus de strage triumphos Cesaris ut referat inclita preda venit, hostis in opprobrium pendebit. In urbis honorem mictitur: hunc urbis mictere iussit amor." The epigraph is in Rome, in the Sala del Carroccio of the Palazzo Senatorio. The Latin text is printed, with grave errors of transcription and lack-

ing a translation, in the entry on the epigraph in the catalogue of an exhibition at Palazzo Venezia, Rome, in 1995–1996: *Federico II e l'Italia* (Rome: De Luca-Editalia, 1995), 336–337.

11. Giovanni Sercambi, *Croniche*, ed. Salvatore Bongi (Lucca: Tipografia Giusti, 1892), 1:84–86.

12. Giovanni Sercambi, *Le illustrazioni delle croniche nel codice lucchese di Giovanni Sercambi*, ed. Ottavio Banti and Maria-Laura Testi-Cristiani, 2 vols. (Genoa: Silvio Basile Editore, 1978), vol. 2, fig. 22.

13. The various lords of Lucca, with the indication of the corresponding banners, are recounted in chapters 219–234 of the Bongi edition of Sercambi, *Croniche*, 1:191–198. The illuminator included references even to quite fleeting events that temporarily altered the balance of power. This is the reason there are so many banners of Castruccio Castracani and his sons: they reflect the violent struggles among the members of that family. My thanks to Ottavio Banti for this observation.

14. "Non erat satis, de coelo tonantis ira Dei immortalis, homuncio, nisi (o crudelitas iuncta superbiae) de terra etiam tonuisset, non imitabile fulmen, ut Maro ait, humana rabies imitata est, et quod e nubibus mitti solet ligneo quidem, sed tartareo mittitur instrumento, quod ab Archimede inventum quidam putant, eo tempore quo Marcellus Syracusas obsidebat. Verum ille hoc ut suorum civium libertatem tueretur excogitavit, patriae excidium, vel averteret vel differret, quo vos ut liberos populos, vel iugo vel excidio praematis utimini. Erat haec pestis nuper rara, ut cum ingenti miraculo cerneretur, nunc ut rerum pessimarum dociles sunt animi, ita communis est ut unum quodlibet genus armorum." Petrarca, *De remediis utriusque fortunae*, in *Francisci Petrarchae Opus* (Basel, 1554), tome 1, dialogue 99, 102. The passage is cited from Riccardo Luisi, *Scudi di pietra, I castelli e l'arte della guerra tra Medioevo e Rinascimento*, (Rome-Bari: Laterza, 1996), 111. [Trans.: The English translation is taken from *Petrarch's Remedies for Fortune Fair and Foul*, a modern English translation of *De remediis utriusque fortune* with a commentary by Conrad H. Rawski (Bloomington: Indiana University Press, 1991), vol. 1, dialogue 99, "Heavy Weapons," 270–271.]

15. Miguel de Cervantes, *Don Quixote de la Mancha*, trans. Charles Jarvis (Oxford: Oxford University Press, 1999), part 1, ch. 38, 405–406. The author had personal reasons to resent the use of firearms: during the naval battle at Lepanto in 1571 he was wounded in the chest and the left hand by shots fired from a harquebus, and never regained the use of the hand.

16. Luisi, *Scudi di pietra*, 116ff.

17. ". . . facieno sì grande timolto e romore, che pareva che Iddio tonasse, con grande uccisione di gente e sfondamento di cavalli." Giovanni Villani, *Nuova Cronica*, ed. Giuseppe Porta (Parma: Guanda-Fondazione Pietro Bembo, 1990), 13.67, 2:454.

18. Arsenio Frugoni, "I temi della Morte nell'affresco dei Disciplini a Clusone," in *Bullettino Storico Italiano per il Medioevo* 69 (1957): 1–38, republished in A. Frugoni, *Incontri nel Medio Evo* (Bologna: Il Mulino, 1979), 217–250, at 222. This weapon is a concrete reference to contemporary warfare, in which harquebusiers

were employed alongside archers and crossbowmen as an auxiliary element of the heavy infantry armed with pikes. On the inscription on this "Triumph of Death," see Claudio Ciociola, *"Visibile parlare": agenda* (Cassino: Università degli Studi di Cassino, 1992), 102ff.

19. The yoke of the oxen rests on the withers, where the neck meets the spine, and is held in position by a strap under the neck; the effort is transmitted through the withers.

20. On the padded horse collar, see Gimpel, *La révolution industrielle du Moyen Age*, 55.

6. By Land and Sea

1. The Vulgate text is "In anno primo Cyri regis Persarum." For commentary on this miniature, see François Garnier, *L'âne à la lyre. Sottisier d'iconographie médiévale* (Paris: Le Léopard d'or, 1988), 161–162 and fig. at 163.

2. Marco Piccat, "Le scritte in volgare della Fontana di Giovinezza, dei prodi e delle eroine," in *Le Arti della Manta, il Castello e l'Antica Parrocchiale*, ed. Giuseppe Carità and D. Musso (Turin: Galatea, 1992), 175–209. The author interprets the figure drinking from the bottle as a manservant (183), but the dress she is wearing shows that she is certainly a woman. The story makes an exact counterpart to the scene of seduction between a knight and a girl depicted on the same wall; this is an observation of Maria Luisa Meneghetti, who analyzes the inscriptions but remains uncertain whether it is a manservant or a female servant who is pushing the wheelbarrow: Maria Luisa Meneghetti, " 'Sublimus' e 'humilis': due stili di scrittura," in *"Visibile parlare." Le scritture esposte nei volgari italiani dal Medioevo al Rinascimento*, ed. Claudio Ciociola (Naples: Edizioni Scientifiche Italiane, 1997), 397–408, at 405.

3. Giordano da Pisa, *Prediche del 1304 dell'Avvento e della Quaresima*, ed. D. M. Manni (Florence: Viviani, 1739) (sermon of March 26, 1305), 242.

4. "Anno li naviganti uno bussolo che nel mezzo è impernato una rotella di carta leggeri, la quale gira sul detto perno; e la detta rotella ha molte punte, et ad una di quelle che vi è dipinta una stella, è fitta una punta d'ago; la quale punta li naviganti quando vogliono vedere dove sia tramontana, imbriacano colla calamita." Cited from Umberto Forti, *Storia della tecnica, del Medioevo al Rinascimento* (Milan: Sansoni, 1957), 346.

5. "Fama est qua Amalphitanos audivimus gloriari, magnetis usum, cuius adminiculo navigantes ad arcton diriguntur, Amalfi fuisse inventum." Cited in ibid., 340.

6. Claude Lévi-Strauss, *Babbo Natale giustiziato* (1952; reprint, Palermo: Sellerio, 1995).

SELECT BIBLIOGRAPHY

Albertotti, G. "Lettera intorno alla invenzione degli occhiali all'onorevole senatore Isidoro Del Lungo." *Annali di Ottalmologia e clinica oculistica* 50 (1922): fasc. 1–2, pp. 85–104.

Alighieri, Dante. *Dante's Paradise.* Translated with notes and commentary by Mark Musa. Bloomington: Indiana University Press, 1984.

Bernardino da Siena, San. *Le prediche volgari. Predicazione del 1425 in Siena.* Vol. 1. Ed. Ciro Cannarozzi O.F.M. Florence: Rinaldi, 1958.

Boccaccio, Giovanni. *Decameron.* 2 vols. Ed. Vittore Branca. Turin: Einaudi, 1993.

Castelnuovo, Enrico. *Vetrate medioevali. Officine, tecniche, maestri.* Turin: Einaudi, 1994.

Chronica antiqua conventus Sanctae Catharinae de Pisis. Ed. Francesco Bonaini. *Archivio Storico Italiano* 6:2, sec. 3 (1845): 399–593.

Dante. See Alighieri.

Daxecker, Franz. "Representations of Eyeglasses on Gothic Winged Altars in Austria." *Documenta Ophthalmologica* 93 (1997): 169–188.

——. "Three Reading Aids Painted by Tomaso da Modena in the Chapter House of San Nicolò Monastery in Treviso, Italy." *Documenta Ophthalmologica* 99 (1999; published in 2000): 219–223.

Del Lungo, Isidoro. "Le vicende d'un'impostura erudita (Salvino degli Armati)." *Archivio Storico Italiano* 78 (1920): 5–53.

Forti, Umberto. *Storia della tecnica, dal Medioevo al Rinascimento.* Milan: Sansoni, 1957.

Gilson, M. "Histoire des lunettes." *Bulletin de la Societé Belge d'Ophtalmologie* 264 (1) (1997): 7–13.

Gimpel, Jean. *La révolution industrielle du Moyen Age*. Paris: Seuil, 1975.

Giordano da Pisa [Giordano da Rivalto]. *Prediche recitate in Firenze dal 1303 al 1306*. Ed. Domenico Moreni. Florence: Magheri, 1831.

——. *Prediche del 1304 dell'Avvento e della Quaresima*. Ed. D. M. Manni. Florence: Viviani, 1739.

——. *Prediche del beato Giordano da Rivalto*. Ed. Domenico Moreni. Florence: Magheri, 1831.

——. *Prediche inedite . . . recitate in Firenze dal 1302 al 1305*. Ed. Enrico Narducci. Bologna: Gaetano Romagnoli, 1867.

——. *Quaresimale fiorentino 1305–1306*, critical edition. Ed. Carlo Delcorno. Florence: Sansoni, 1974.

Grandi, Renzo. *I monumenti dei dottori e la scultura a Bologna (1267–1348)*. Bologna: Comune di Bologna, Istituto per la Storia di Bologna, 1982.

Iacopo da Varazze. *Legenda aurea*. Introduction by Franco Cardini and Mario Martelli. Text of the fourteenth-century translation into the *volgare* and notes by Arrigo Levasti. Florence: Le Lettere, 2000.

Isidore of Seville. See Isidorus Hispalensis.

Isidorus Hispalensis episcopus [Isidore, Bishop of Seville]. *Etymologiarum sive originum libri XX*, critical edition. Ed. Wallace Martin Lindsay. Oxford: Clarendon Press, 1911.

Klapisch-Zuber, Christiane. *L'ombre des ancêtres, essai sur l'imaginaire médiéval de la parenté*. Paris: Fayard, 2000.

Levi Pisetzky, Rosita. *Storia del costume in Italia*. Vol. 1. Milan: Treccani-Enciclopedia Italiana, 1964.

Luisi, Riccardo. *Scudi di pietra, I castelli e l'arte della guerra tra Medioevo e Rinascimento*. Rome-Bari: Laterza, 1996.

Murray, Harold J. R. *A History of Chess*. Oxford: Clarendon Press, 1913.

Muzzarelli, Giuseppina. "Da sentimento a istituzione: l'ideazione dei Monti di pietà." In *Uomini, denaro istituzioni. L'invenzione del Monte di pietà* (exhibition catalogue), ed. Giuseppina Muzzarelli. Bologna: Costa editore, 2000.

Panofsky, Erwin. *Abbot Suger*. Princeton: Princeton University Press, 1979.

Paulus Diaconus. *De gestis Langobardorum*. Ed. Lidia Capo. Milan: Fondazione Lorenzo Valla-Mondadori, 1992.

Petrus Damiani. *Petri Damiani Epistolae. Die Briefe des Petrus Damiani*. Ed. Kurt Reindel. Munich: Monumenta Germaniae Historica, 1988.

Pini, Antonio Ivan. " 'Discere turba volens.' Studenti e vita studentesca a Bologna dalle origini dello Studio alla metà del Trecento." In *Studenti e Università degli studenti dal XII al XIX secolo*, ed. Gian Paolo Brizzi and Antonio Ivan Pini. Bologna: Istituto per la Storia dell'Università, 1988, pp. 47–136.

Raymond of Capua [Raimundus Capuanus]. *Vita S. Catharinae Senensis*, in *Acta Sanctorum. Aprilis III*. Antwerp, 1675.

Redi, Francesco. *Opere*. Milan: Società Tipografica de' Classici italiani, 1809–1811; Classici italiani, vols. 169–177; vol. 7.

Rosen, Edward. "The Invention of Eyeglasses." *Journal of the History of Medicine and Allied Sciences* 11 (1) (1956): 13–47; 11 (2) (1956): 183–218.

Sacchetti, Franco. *Il Trecentonovelle*. Ed. Emilio Faccioli. Turin: Einaudi, 1970.

Sacramentario del vescovo Warmondo di Ivrea. Facsimile edition with transcription of the text by Ferdinando Dell'Oro. Ivrea: Priuli e Verlucca, 1990.

Sercambi, Giovanni. *Croniche*. Ed. Salvatore Bongi. Lucca: Tipografia Giusti, 1892.

Serventi, Silvano and Françoise Sabban. *La pasta. Storia e cultura di un cibo universale.* Rome-Bari: Laterza, 2000.

Targioni Tozzetti, Giovanni. *Notizie degli aggrandimenti delle scienze fisiche accadute in Toscana nel corso di anni LX del secolo XVII*. Florence: G. Bouchard, 1780.

INDEX OF PERSONS

(excluding the artists and subjects included in the List of Illustrations)